NEW SWAN SHAKESPEARE

GENERAL EDITOR
BERNARD LOTT, M.A., Ph.D

Henry IV Part 1

WILLIAM SHAKESPEARE

Henry IV Part 1

EDITED BY

JOHN COLMER, M.A., Ph.D.

and

DOROTHY COLMER, M.A.

LONGMAN

LONGMAN GROUP LIMITED
Longman House, Burnt Mill, Harlow,
Essex CM20 2JE, England
and Associated Companies throughout the world.

First published 1965
Fourteenth impression 1986

ISBN 0-582-52727-9

Illustrations by Hans Schwarz

We are indebted to the Senate of University of London
and the University of Cambridge Local
Examinations Syndicate for permission to
reproduce questions from past examination papers.

Produced by Longman Singapore Publishers Pte Ltd
Printed in Singapore

INTRODUCTION

The purpose of this book is to give and explain, in the simplest way, the text of one of Shakespeare's plays. The text itself is complete; notes and glossary have been added to help the reader to understand the play; a section giving hints to examination candidates has been included at the end of the book. To get the greatest pleasure from the play, the reader will need to learn something about its background and its age – and perhaps about Shakespeare himself, for example, or about drama as an art – but his first duty is to understand what the characters are saying and doing, and why they say and do these things.

With this end in view, and to ensure that the help given will in fact simplify the difficulties which are now met with in reading Shakespeare, explanations have been given within the range of a specially-chosen list of 3,000 most commonly used English root-words. Every word in the book which falls outside this list is explained. This is done in the following way:

words which are not in everyday modern English as Shakespeare used them, or which are not now used at all, will be found explained in notes on the pages facing the text;

words which are still used in ordinary modern English with their meanings unchanged, but which are not among the 3,000 root-words of the chosen list, will be found explained in the glossary at the back of the book.

References to one or other of these places, and a study of section 3 of this introduction, should be sufficient to remove all difficulty in the understanding of the text. Explanations of longer passages are also given within the range of the word-list.

The rest of the introduction is arranged under the following headings:

An earlier play, Shakespeare's *King Richard II*, tells how Henry Bolingbroke, assisted to some extent by the Percy family, led a successful rebellion against Richard II. Bolingbroke became King Henry IV of England, but had to defend his title against supporters of the former king.

At the beginning of our play, Henry IV hopes that peace has at last come to the troubled country, but there is still unrest on the borders of Wales and Scotland. The Welsh leader, Owen Glendower, has defeated an English force and captured the leader, Mortimer. Another English army led by young Harry Percy, known as Hotspur, has defeated a Scottish attack, but Hotspur proudly refuses to yield his prisoners to the King unless the King will first ransom Mortimer, who is Hotspur's wife's brother. This the King will not do, asserting that Mortimer's marriage to Glendower's daughter proves him a traitor, unworthy of ransom. Hotspur learns from his father, the Duke of Northumberland, and his uncle, the Duke of Worcester, that Mortimer is the proclaimed heir of Richard II. (Two historical characters are blended by Shakespeare into one Mortimer. See note 78 page 36.) Angered by the King's rejection of his terms, Hotspur readily agrees to a scheme of Worcester's. By setting free their Scottish prisoners, they will win the friendship of Douglas, the Scottish leader. Then the Percy family will join forces with Douglas, Owen Glendower, Mortimer, and the Archbishop of York, to raise a great united army against the King.

Meanwhile the King's heir, Prince Hal, grieves his father by showing little interest in wars and affairs of state. Instead, he wastes his time in taverns with such amusing but irresponsible companions as the witty fat knight Sir John Falstaff. Hal's conduct is in direct contrast with that of Hotspur, who has already won great public honour by his brave victories. King Henry does not realise that Hal's present manners hide a strong sense of royal dignity and that he intends to abandon idle habits and low company when he becomes king.

Falstaff tempts the Prince to join in a robbery on a public road but, instead, the Prince and Poins rob Falstaff and his fellow-thieves. When they are all making merry at the Boar's Head tavern afterwards, news of Hotspur's rebellion arrives, and the Prince is summoned to the Court. There he is censured by his father for showing so little princely pride or family loyalty. The Prince vows that he will prove himself a worthy son and win a noble reputation by defeating Hotspur in the coming battle.

Hotspur is impatient to fight at Shrewsbury, even though Northumberland, Owen Glendower, Mortimer and York, with all their followers, have not yet joined him. Although advised by his friends to wait until he has a larger army, Hotspur engages the much stronger forces of the King.

In the battle Prince Hal reveals his true nature by defending his father against Douglas. The Prince then encounters and defeats Hotspur, and the royal army is victorious. After the battle, the Prince shows mercy and political wisdom by giving an order to set free the captured Douglas.

Falstaff's share in the achievement is comic and inglorious. He captains a wretched band of beggars but leaves them in battle. He carries wine instead of a gun. He pretends to be dead in order to avoid fighting, and then claims to have killed Hotspur, whose body he finds and stabs. The Prince does not expose these deceits.

The play ends with the King's plans to defeat the remaining rebels in separate battles.

2 Henry IV, Part 1 in the Theatre

In the public theatre of Shakespeare's day, the back of the stage could be curtained or screened off to seem like an inside room. The main part of the stage stretched out into the roofless yard where many of the audience stood right up against the platform, viewing the action from three sides. The whole theatre was enclosed by a high wall with balconies from which the rest of the audience looked down on to the stage. The balconies above the back of the stage could be used by the actors.

We can imagine all these areas being used in II.iv. When the sheriff comes to arrest him, Falstaff hides and falls asleep behind the curtain at the back. The other thieves meanwhile go "up above" by stairs leading from the stage to the balcony, leaving the Prince below to receive the sheriff. Similarly in III.i.218-38 the musicians play in a high balcony, Worcester goes off as if to prepare the agreement in another room and Glendower's daughter sings to Mortimer near the back of the stage, so that Hotspur and Lady Percy at the front or side are nearer to many of the audience than to actors in the same scene. Thus it is quite natural for them to laugh about the other characters without fear of being heard:

> Lady Percy Lie still, ye thief, and hear the lady sing in Welsh.
> Hotspur I had rather hear Lady my brach howl in Irish.

The closeness of the audience was often used by comic characters, who openly shared jokes with the people near them. Falstaff probably does this on several occasions, as in his description of his ragged soldiers (IV.ii.11–43), his speech about honour (V.i.127), and his last speech in the play (V.iv.156–8). The audience could also be made to feel that they were listening to the private thoughts of a serious character if he spoke when alone on the stage. This happens at I.ii.161–83, when important information about the Prince's true nature is revealed.

It is not easy to give a convincing performance of a whole battle in the theatre, but several rapid actions at the same time and running fights moving on and off the large stage could convey the idea of a corner of the battle-field. Thus Douglas's attack on Falstaff, with its mock-tragic end, takes place at the same time as Hotspur's fatal encounter with Prince Hal. Although only a few of the main characters speak in the battle-scenes, many others would probably be seen fighting.

The play moved rapidly forward without long pauses, for change of scene was quickly accomplished on the Elizabethan stage. This speed was the result of having no fixed scenery. The players used only such easily moved furniture as a throne for the king's court and benches and drinking cups for the tavern. The dress and speeches of the characters would supply other necessary information. The stage which is the rebel camp in IV.i becomes a road in another part of England as soon as Hotspur leaves and Falstaff enters, for his first words tell us where he is:

> Falstaff Bardolph, get thee before to Coventry; fill me a bottle of sack. Our soldiers shall march through (IV.ii.1).

When Falstaff goes and Hotspur re-enters, we know the stage is the rebel camp again. For the fourth scene of this act, a writing table and chair would indicate a room indoors, the actor's robes would show that he was a leader of the Church, and his first speech, by naming his "cousin Scroop" completes the information to the audience that this is Lord Scroop, Archbishop of York, in his own home.

Clothes were important. Kings, servants, soldiers and many other types of character could be recognised at once by their garments. Suitably dressed boys played the female parts, as acting was not considered right for women.

Performances took place in the afternoon by daylight. The theatre was not darkened for night scenes, nor was there strong artificial light to imitate the sun or moon. Yet we do not need such help, for the characters themselves reveal the time and the weather. Often the bare information is enriched by the fine imagination of the poet, and closely related to the plot. When the sun rises to a day of battle and bloodshed at Shrewsbury, a day that no one can be confident of living through, the description of nature conveys also the awed mood of the waiting soldiers and their readiness for action.

> King   How bloodily the sun begins to peer
>   Above yon busky hill! The day looks pale
>   At his distemperature.
>
> Prince   The southern wind
>   Doth play the trumpet to his purposes,
>   And by his hollow whistling in the leaves
>   Foretells a tempest and a blustering day.
>
> King   Then with the losers let it sympathise,
>   For nothing can seem foul to those that win (v.i.1).

3 The Language and Imagery of the Play

Shakespeare's language differs in minor ways from modern English. Some words and grammatical forms which occur very frequently are listed below instead of being explained in the notes every time they occur. (This list should not be learnt by heart.)

an - (sometimes) "if".

anon - "at once".

ay - "yes".

cousin, coz, used for any close relative.

ere - "before".

fie, an exclamation expressing impatience.

forsooth - "in truth".

hence - "from this place"

herein – "in this place".

hither – "to this place".

house – "noble family".

how now, a greeting or exclamation of surprise.

knave – "dishonest man".

mark – "listen to, pay attention to".

mine – (sometimes) "my".

nay – "no".

ne'er – "never".

oft – "often".

out, an exclamation expressing disapproval.

pray – "please".

prithee – "(I) pray thee; please".

quoth – "said".

sirrah, a way of addressing inferiors. When used otherwise it shows disrespect or very informal friendship.

still – (sometimes) "always; continually".

straight – "at once".

't – "it".

thee – "you" (singular).

thence – "from that place".

thine – "yours" (singular).

thither – "to that place".

thou – "you" (singular), used between friends of equal rank and by a master or lord to a servant or inferior.

ye – "you".

yea – "yes".

whence – "from which place".

whither – "to which place".

withal – "with"; "in addition".

would – (sometimes) "wish".

Verbs are not all exactly as in modern English. After *thou* the usual verb ending is *-est*, *-st*, or *-t*, e.g. *thou sayest, thou hast, thou wilt*. After *he, she* or *it*, the verb-ending is often *-eth* or *-th*, e.g. *he deceiveth me* (II.iv.367), *he doth deny* (I.iii.76).

A few past forms are different from those used in modern English, e.g. *I have forgot* ("forgotten") *the map* (III.i.5), *have holp* ("helped", I.iii.13), *brake* ("broke", I.i.48). The various forms of the verb *do* are often used with another verb without adding any separate meaning:

If you knew
How much they do import you would make haste (IV.iv.5).

The verb *do* is not always used where modern English requires it in asking a question or making a negative statement:

What think you, coz? (I.i.90)

I care not for thee, Kate (II.iii.85).

x

The word *me* sometimes follows a verb without adding any separate meaning, e.g. –

> he that kills me some six or seven dozen of Scots at a breakfast (II.iv.92).

Prose

Nearly half the play, all the part that centres on Falstaff, is in prose. The language of these scenes is full of words and phrases chosen for a variety of comic effects. The humour is very largely a matter of words: we are not asked to laugh merely at a thin young prince drinking with a fat old knight, but to listen to a contest of skill in clever playing with language.

Both Hal and Falstaff make great use of the *pun*, taking words that sound alike but have two or more meanings and passing quickly from one sense to another – *son* and *sun* are an example. Unfortunately, for a modern reader of the play most of these jokes have to be carefully explained, and the excitement and speed of the exchanges may be overlooked.

The comic characters share a love of finding new comparisons to make fun of each other's behaviour and appearance, as in II.iv.210–6 and II.iv.386–97. Falstaff's great size never fails as a source of such jokes. There is also a delight in the mocking imitation of other people's manner of speaking. Falstaff uses a pious preaching style in I.ii.126–30, and he copies well-known writers at II.iv.337, and II.iv.345. The Prince mocks Hotspur's habit of pausing before making a reply (II.iv.96) and imitates the speech of the tavern servants (II.iv.13–15). And, of course, both Hal and Falstaff enjoy play-acting.

Exclamations, oaths, and curses are so frequent in these scenes that they have not all been noted on the page. Those most commonly used are:

> *a plague on*; *what a plague*; *what a pox*. The plague and the pox were serious diseases.
>
> *be hanged*. Hanging was the usual punishment for robbery.
>
> *by 'r lady* – "by our Lady (Mother of Christ)".
>
> *by the Lord* – "by God".
>
> *faith or i' faith* – "in truth".

xi

> *I 'll be sworn* – "I solemnly declare this is true".
> *marry* – "by Mary (Mother of Christ)".
> *'sblood* – "by God's blood".
> *zounds* – "by God's wounds".

Another habit of speech, a kind of comic oath, is much used by Falstaff. It takes the form, "If what I say is untrue, or if I fail, then something extraordinary can be said of or done to me." Falstaff delights in varying, for comic effect, the "something extraordinary". Examples are: "If thou dost it half so gravely . . . hang me up by the heels for a rabbit-sucker, or a poulter's hare" (II.iv.375) and "If I fought not with fifty of them, I am a bunch of radish" (II.iv.162).

Blank verse

A little more than half of the play is written in blank verse, i.e. unrhymed verse with five beats in a line:

> If áll the year were playing hólidáys,
> To sport would bé as tédious as to wórk (I.ii.170).

The beats, called stresses, are not all of the same strength, and their positions may vary slightly, so that the sound need never be uninteresting. In the second line marked above there is relatively little stress on *be* and *as*, but strong stress on *sport* and *work*. Blank verse is very suitable for dignified public speeches as in the first scene of Act I, or Vernon's description of the Prince in armour (IV.i.97–110). But the natural phrases of conversation can also be used, the lines often being divided between different speakers:

Hotspur   We 'll fight with him tonight.

Worcester   It may not be.

Douglas   You give him then advantage

Vernon   Not a whit (IV.iii.1).

The use of blank verse does not prevent characters from expressing themselves in their individual fashion. In III.i there is much humour in the contrast between Owen Glendower's prophetic style and Hotspur's common-sense manner.

> *Glendower* I can call spirits from the vasty deep
>
> *Hotspur* Why, so can. I, or so can any man;
> But will they come when you do call for them?
> (III.i.50)

Blank verse is usually spoken by the noble characters in moments of strong feeling or serious political importance. The Prince, for example, uses blank verse when he is alone or talking to men of high rank, but in taverns, among his low companions, he speaks in prose.

Imagery

The language of a poet is always rich in imagery – the words used of a thing or person are related to the image of something else, and through this image, a store of feelings, ideas, beliefs, memories can be brought to mind at the same time. When the King thinks of the effects of civil war, he describes England through the image of a mother's body wounded and bruised by her own children, whose blood she not only drinks but uses to paint *(daub)* her lips:

> No more the thirsty entrance of this soil
> Shall daub her lips with her own children's blood;
> No more shall trenching war channel her fields,
> Nor bruise her flowerets . . . (I.i.5).

Such imagery makes us feel far more strongly the horror and the unnaturalness of civil war than any simple statement could. At the same time it contains a hope for peace: even while we are shocked by the violence, we realise that Englishmen are one family, and the land, in its natural state, is a pleasant country of fields and flowers.

In speaking of England as if it were a human being, Shakespeare is making use of a device in language called *personification*. When a direct comparison, using "as" or "like", is made, the image is a *simile*. *Metaphor* is a form of imagery in which one thing is spoken of as if it actually were another. So Hotspur is described as "Amongst a grove, the very straightest plant" (I.i.81). Here the metaphor suggests that Hotspur is a growing thing, still young; but he is also the best among many, and he is developing in natural surroundings, unlike Hal, who, in another metaphor, is stained by "riot and dis-honour".

Often the imagery forms a pattern or group of ideas continuing through the play. Those already discussed and many others link up to show how the effects of rebellious disorder extend to the limits of the universe, because such uncontrolled behaviour breaks up the design of healthy natural order in which plants grow straight and true in their right places, sons respect parents, subject obeys king, and the sun and stars move in their appointed places. To displace a lawful king is like planting a wild thorn in place of a garden rose (i.iii.173). A strong ruler is *sun-like majesty* but Hal is like a sun darkened by *foul and ugly mists* (i.ii.168) bringing disease; his lawless acts cause *long-grown wounds* in his relations with his father but when he rides to support the King he is *as gorgeous as the sun at midsummer*. A disloyal subject is like a star or planet moving out of its customary path about the sun, its king. Worcester is asked:

> . . . will you . . .
> . . . move in that obedient orb again
> Where you did give a fair and natural light (v.i.15).

and either Hal or Hotspur must die, for

> Two stars keep not their motion in one sphere,
> Nor can one England brook a double reign
> Of Harry Percy and the Prince of Wales (v.iv.64).

Another group of images concerns the idea of redeeming some-thing, or paying a debt. Hal, by becoming a good king, will *pay the debt I never promiséd* (i.ii.175) so *redeeming time*. The Percys must *redeem their banished honours*. Worcester says:

> The King will always think him in our debt,
> And think we think ourselves unsatisfied,
> Till he hath found a time to pay us home (i.iii.280).

Hal will *redeem* all his past foolishness *on Percy's head* and

> will call him to so strict account
> That he shall render every glory up (iii.ii.149).

xiv

Hotspur distrusts the King

> well we know the King
> Knows at what time to promise, when to pay (IV.iii.52).

In the last Act, Hal proclaims

> It is the Prince of Wales that threatens thee,
> Who never promiseth but he means to pay (V.iv.41).

And the King commends him:

> Thou hast redeemed thy lost opinion (V.iv.47).

Some of these separate images clearly draw attention to the love-less calculating relations existing between many of the characters, but the total effect of having so many references is to build up a strong moral sense that all men owe a debt of duty to each other, and must each account for any misuse of time, honour or reputation.

Other groups of imagery contrast daylight and darkness, the former associated with good, the latter with evil; and numerous metaphors of animal movement give a sense of lively activity all through the play. There are many images of masking or in some other way hiding one's true self; these remind us that the play is, among other things, concerned with the contrast between the real natures of men and the characters they choose to reveal in public.

Shakespeare uses other figures of speech. The chief one is *Irony*, in which the speaker's words are not intended to have their ordinary meaning but to be understood in another sense. Thus when Hotspur thinks of meeting Hal in battle he says

> I will embrace him with a soldier's arm,
> That he shall shrink under my courtesy (V.ii.73).

The friendly-seeming words are used ironically to make a kind of joke with the very serious meaning: "I will attack him with all my strength as a soldier, so that he will fall beneath my great skill with the sword".

Dramatic Irony is used when the words gain added meaning from circumstances which the audience may know about, though some of the characters on the stage do not. Some of the dramatic irony is fully apparent only when the play is seen or read a second time.

Hotspur confidently counts up the number of his "friends true and constant" who have promised to join the rebellion –

> Is there not my father, my uncle, and myself? Lord Edmund Mortimer, my Lord of York, and Owen Glendower? Is there not, besides, the Douglas? (II.iii.19)

These words are remembered as an example of dramatic irony when we know that few of these friends, only his uncle and the Douglas, join Hotspur in battle, and even his uncle is not "true" but deceitful. Perhaps the most striking example of dramatic irony is during the play-acting at the Boar's Head; when Hal says that he will reject Falstaff,

> *Falstaff* Banish not him thy Harry's company, banish plump Jack, and banish all the world.

> *Prince* I do, I will. (II.iv.414)

the audience, remembering Hal's vow to reform (I.ii.161-83) knows that these words can be taken seriously, but for Falstaff, they are part of the pretence.

4 *The Characters*

Henry IV is a guilt-burdened king who rules a rebellious country. Having taken the throne by force, he cannot expect the trust and obedience which would be given to a lawful ruler. Moreover he fears that God will punish him for causing Richard II's death. He hopes to redeem this sin and at the same time unite the warring parties in the country by leading an army to fight a Holy War in Palestine, but cannot go without leaving loyal supporters to defend the English boundaries. In the west, however, Mortimer has been captured by the Welsh and is perhaps friendly with them, while in the north Hotspur refuses to obey the King's command. News of Hotspur's victory against the Scots makes the King speak sadly of the contrast between this ambitious young soldier and his own son Hal, who shows no interest in war or government. Henry fears that the Prince will lose the royal power he himself has taken such risks to win; he may even join the rebels (III.ii.122-8). A traitor himself,

Henry is suspicious of others' loyalty: he will not ransom Mortimer, and distrusts the Percy family who helped him to win the crown.

In state affairs, Henry has many of the characteristics of a good king: he has self-control and a commanding manner in dealing with the Percys; he will not weaken his position by sharing power with former friends; he is quick and decisive in organising the army (v.v.34-40) and in dealing with the defeated Worcester and Vernon (v.v.14-15); he cannot be taken by surprise, for his news service is excellent.

In the dramatically important meeting with his son (III.ii), Henry reveals the scheming, calculating side of his nature. He warns the Prince against lowering his royal dignity by appearing in public too often, speaks scornfully of Richard's mistakes, and is proud of his own skill in hiding his secret motives behind a pleasing outward appearance. Although, before the battle of Shrewsbury, he offers to forgive the rebels and speaks of loving all his people (v.i.104-8), he does not really think his offer will be accepted. Henry IV is almost totally lacking in warmth of feeling and generous human motives; he represents the type of man whose individual character is swallowed up in the public official. Even so, he has succeeded in winning the services of many honest and brave supporters who look upon him as their true king.

While the King's character is fixed and determined by his own past actions, that of his son, *Prince Hal*, seems still unformed at the beginning of the play, though apparently inclining to folly and vice. He seems to be influenced by his low companions: tempted to become a thief he first yields, then refuses, and at last agrees to be present at the robbery at Gad's Hill though not to rob the innocent. The Prince has the warm generous human qualities that his father lacks. He delights in humorous situations, acting a part to fit the occasion and add to the fun not, like his father, merely for political gain. He joins in Poins's plot to trick Falstaff at Gad's Hill, mixes with the tavern-servants as one of them, enjoys fooling Francis, leads Falstaff on in his lying account of the robbery, and takes part in the comic play-acting scene (II.iv). He is high-spirited, witty, and good-humoured, and is quite at ease in the company of Falstaff and his friends, though they speak to him with some respect. This respect, the Prince's unwillingness to join in dishonesty, and his speech at the end of Act I Scene ii help to make his reformation convincing. The rebellion recalls him to royal duty and the pursuit of honour in battle. In a moving scene with his father he confesses his faults and promises to redeem them by overcoming Hotspur. Vernon's speech (iv.i.98–110) prepares us for the complete change in character from the visitor of taverns to the brave knight. The form of his challenge and his praise of Hotspur (v.ii.50–67) and his noble speech over his dead rival (v.iv.87–100) reveal his generous knightly spirit and his lack of boastful pride. After winning glory in battle he treats Falstaff with his old generosity and understanding but shows new political wisdom in pardoning Douglas.

In strong contrast to Hal is *Hotspur*. He too is young, but is married and commands his own army in battle, where he has already won credit against the Scots. Unlike Hal, he does not need to be recalled to the service of honour; everything is sacrificed to it; affection for his wife, loyalty to his king, the safety of the country. He is impatient, rash, and hot-tempered. This can be seen in his refusal to hand over his prisoners (i.iii), his complaints about his share in the division of the kingdom (iii.i) and his unwise eagerness to fight against the King at Shrewsbury even though his promised support has not arrived. Nevertheless he remains an attractive character because of his energy, courage and sense of humour. The latter is revealed in his account of the foolish lord who demanded the prisoners (i.iii) and his mocking treatment of Glendower. Himself too honest and direct to be a good schemer, he is easily deceived by his cunning uncle Worcester. He likes to think of himself as a man of action, scorning poetry (iii.i.123–9) and public speaking (v.ii.91), but in fact he can be both imaginative (i.iii.199–205) and witty (iii.i.64). His wife, *Kate*, is courageous and affectionate, but is unable to influence his actions (ii.iii) or restrain his high spirits (iii.i.224–54).

The most lively character in the play is *Falstaff*. He is there to be enjoyed, a figure of fun. When he is absent, his friends must think up some plan "to drive away the time till Falstaff come" (ii.iv.25), but when Falstaff is on the scene, his quick mind changes everything to laughter. He delights in playing on the meaning of words and making witty references to different things: to the Bible, to plays, to everyday sights and sounds, to his own gross fatness and the

Prince's thin body. If an idea is serious he turns it into fun, and much of the fun comes from his half-seriousness, the use of religious words and phrases to refer to his proposed reformation, which we know he can never achieve. Although he steals, tells lies, and eats and drinks excessively, we are not intended to judge him all the time by ordinary moral standards. He is, like the character of Vice or the Devil in older plays, the comic tempter of a young man; but the Prince is not in grave moral danger with Falstaff, from whose company he gains a better understanding of other people than from his father, the distrustful king. When Hal is recalled to his princely duties, Falstaff's way of life begins to seem meaningless. Falstaff accepts bribes, carries a bottle of wine into battle instead of a gun, dismisses honour as a mere word and takes personal advantage of Hotspur's death. But we, like Hal, can forgive his deceits in the enjoyment of his company.

Of Hal's other drinking companions *Poins* seems most at ease with the Prince, and is probably a young man of higher social rank than the rest.

Among the King's enemies, the *Archbishop of York* thinks only of his own safety, and the Scot, *Douglas*, simply enjoys fighting. *Mortimer* has a claim to be king as Richard II's heir, but takes little part in planning the rebellion and does not fight. *Glendower* enriches the play with his imaginative accounts of strange happenings and his Welsh love of music and poetry. Hotspur, who despises these characteristics, treats Glendower as a foolish boaster when he claims magical power (III.i.51-2). The conflict between the two men is amusing. Hotspur seems to get the better of the exchange, but, in fact, this is largely because Glendower understands the need to be on good terms with his fellow-commander. Like Hotspur, Glendower is naturally high-spirited and quick-tempered, but even when angry he resists being drawn into an open quarrel. Glendower has also a practical side to his nature: he is an able fighter who has won three victories over English forces, and it is he, not Hotspur, who remembers the map (III.i.5) and speeds up the preparation of the rebels' agreement (III.i.137). He does not join Hotspur at the battle of Shrewsbury, either because he had not enough time to collect his army (IV.i.126) or more likely because he had heard prophecies that the battle would be lost (IV.iv.18).

Although the Percys share a great family pride, they do not show mutual affection or trust. *Northumberland*, having encouraged his son's rebellious spirit, neither joins him at Shrewsbury nor sends his army to the battle. His excuse of being ill is probably false: Hotspur shows no sympathy for his father's sickness (IV.i.17). *Worcester* is the chief plotter. He hates the King, for whose sake he abandoned high office under Richard II without gaining anything in return (v.i.30-8). It is Worcester who first turns Hotspur's angry thoughts towards rebellion (I.iii.255-75), and he prevents any chance of a peaceful settlement between the King and the rebels by misreporting Henry's offer of free pardon before the battle (v.ii.34). Worcester's reason for thus deceiving his nephew is fear for his own safety (v.ii.16-25).

In contrast, the King's men unite to face danger: two sons fight at his side; the army is well organised by his loyal cousin, *Westmoreland*; and his honest messenger, *Sir Walter Blunt*, dies for his sake (v.iii.1-13).

5 The Construction of the Play

Henry IV, Part 1 was probably written in 1596. The character we know as Falstaff was first called Oldcastle, but the family of the historical Oldcastle protested at the humorous treatment of their famous ancestor, and the name was changed. Their protest was made in 1597, and this was probably soon after the play was first performed. The play deals with a rebellion which took place nearly two centuries earlier, but the life and manners shown are those of Elizabethan England.

In Shakespeare's day, when England's power and greatness were rapidly increasing, people liked to go to the theatre and see plays about English history. Some of these plays failed to show any connection between the various political events they presented. Shakespeare's history plays are much better constructed than those by other dramatists, for the events are linked by cause and effect and related to the characters concerned.

Many Elizabethans believed that the king was appointed by God as his representative on earth, to attack the king was to attack God. But Henry IV has made himself king by force and has caused the death of the former king, Richard II. Our play is constructed to show the consequences of this act on the lives of the individuals and on the state. Henry's peace of mind is destroyed, the political order is threatened by rebellion, and the king fears that Hal, his son, will be as weak a king as Richard.

In *Henry IV*, state affairs are not just the business of nobles and princes; they affect the lives of all the people in the country. The humorous scenes with Falstaff make us laugh, but they are also connected with serious subjects: the responsibilities of a ruler, the disorganisation of trade and land values in a country threatened by war and full of thieves and beggars, the need for a balanced opinion of honour, and the true nature of justice. The thieves' most frequent joke is about hanging, the death they will suffer when they are caught. The play gives a wonderful picture of the richness and variety of life at the time. In addition to the action of the stage there are lively descriptions of the events we do not see – of Falstaff seeking out all the wealthiest, least warlike men to be soldiers so that they will pay him to release them, of Hal in full armour springing lightly on his horse, of the horses themselves, of the life and activity at inns and of travellers on the road.

Linking together the many parts of the play is the story of how Hal leaves his disorderly ways and becomes a brave and honourable prince. Shakespeare's presentation of Hal's character was influenced by an older type of play, the Morality, which showed the struggle of good and evil for a man's soul. Falstaff is a merry fat knight, but we are also meant to see that he plays a part rather like Vice or the Devil who appeared in some of those older plays to tempt an undecided young man towards evil. Hal, however, informs us very early in the play (1.ii.161-83) that he intends to become a wise and good king, so we know that the temptation is not very strong. The effect of yielding to a quite different kind of temptation is seen in Hotspur; the desire for military glory has taken control of his whole nature. Hal and Hotspur are contrasted all through the play, at first to Hotspur's advantage, but later to Hal's. Falstaff, Hal, and Hotspur present in their speech and actions three different ideas of "honour". For Falstaff it is an empty word, for Hotspur it is the only thing of value, for Hal it becomes a practical virtue.

By the end of the play the evil effects of Henry's crime in taking the throne seem to be under control, and his fears and doubts about his son are shown to be without cause. From mixing with his many companions, Hal has learnt to understand his people, and so when the time comes he will be a more liberal, balanced and wise ruler than his guilt-burdened father can ever be.

The last scene of the play is satisfactory but not as conclusive as we expect. It looks forward to new events instead of bringing the action to a firm end. This is because the adventures of Hal and Falstaff are continued in another play, *Henry IV, Part 2.*

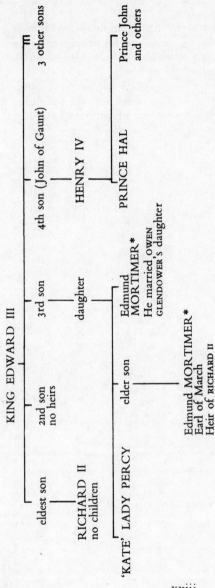

KING EDWARD III

| eldest son | 2nd son no heirs | 3rd son | 4th son (John of Gaunt) | 3 other sons |

RICHARD II
no children

daughter

HENRY IV

'KATE' LADY PERCY — elder son — Edmund MORTIMER*
He married OWEN GLENDOWER's daughter

PRINCE HAL

Prince John and others

Edmund MORTIMER*
Earl of March
Heir of RICHARD II

---

* *Shakespeare confuses these two Mortimers*

The eldest son and his heirs inherit a king's title. If the eldest son leaves no heirs, the second son inherits the crown, and so on through all the sons and their children. When there are no sons, daughters can inherit. Richard II rightly became King, for his dead father had been Edward III's eldest son. When Richard died childless, the heir to the kingdom was Edmund Mortimer, Earl of March, who was the heir of Edward III's third son; but before Richard II's death, Henry Bolingbroke, son of Edward III's fourth son had already seized the throne and was ruling as King Henry IV.

DRAMATIS PERSONAE

KING HENRY *the Fourth*

HENRY, PRINCE OF WALES, *called* HAL *or* HARRY, *the King's eldest son*

JOHN, DUKE OF LANCASTER, *the King's second son*

EARL OF WESTMORELAND, *the King's cousin and friend*

SIR WALTER BLUNT, *a knight in the King's service*

HENRY PERCY, EARL OF NORTHUMBERLAND

HENRY PERCY, *called* HOTSPUR *or* HARRY, *Northumberland's son*

EARL OF WORCESTER, *Northumberland's brother*

EDMUND MORTIMER, EARL OF MARCH

EARL OF DOUGLAS, *sometimes called* THE DOUGLAS

OWEN GLENDOWER

SIR RICHARD VERNON

RICHARD SCROOP, ARCHBISHOP OF YORK

SIR MICHAEL, *a friend of the Archbishop*

SIR JOHN FALSTAFF ⎫
POINS   ⎪
                                    ⎬ *drinking companions of Prince Hal*
PETO   ⎪
BARDOLPH   ⎭

GADSHILL, *a robber*

LADY PERCY, *Hotspur's wife and Mortimer's sister*

LADY MORTIMER, *Mortimer's wife and Glendower's daughter*

MISTRESS QUICKLY, *hostess of the Boar's Head tavern in Eastcheap*

Lords, Officers, Sheriff, Vintner, Chamberlain, Drawers, two Carriers, Ostler, Messengers, Travellers, and Attendants

The action takes place in England and Wales.

(I.i) The English king, Henry IV, has just won a battle against rebels at home and hopes that the country will suffer no more civil war. He begins to talk about leading an army over the sea to win Jerusalem for the Christians. His plans are interrupted by bad news: an English army under Mortimer has been defeated by the Welsh under Glendower, and the Scots are attacking in the north. But good news follows fast: the Scots have been defeated by young Harry Percy (often called Hotspur). King Henry regrets that his own eldest son, Harry (Prince Hal), lives a wild life instead of winning noble victories. There is another cause for anxiety: the Earl of Worcester, Hotspur's uncle, hates the king, and because of this, Hotspur refuses to send Henry IV more than one of the many Scottish nobles he has captured in the battle.

1 *So shaken . . . broils* (line 3) – "Even though we are so shaken and pale *(wan)* with worry, let us find a time for our disturbed *(frighted)* peace to pause for breath *(pant)*, and speak breathlessly *(breathe short-winded accents)* of new battles *(broils)*". Peace is *personified* – see Introduction, p. xiii. The meaning is that although there has already been so much fighting, there is peace for the moment, and this is the time, not to rest, but to begin a war of a different kind.

2 *stronds* – "shores". The King refers to the shores of Palestine, the Holy Land; there the holy places where Christ had lived and died were in the hands of the Muslims, the followers of the Prophet Muhammad.

3 *No more . . . children's blood* – "never again shall the soil (of England) drink up the blood of her own children (i.e. of Englishmen) fighting in their own country".

4 *arméd hoofs . . . paces* – "the heavy hoofs of war-horses going into battle".

5 *opposéd eyes* – "men facing each other as enemies".

6 *meteors . . . heaven*. Meteors and other strange sights in the sky were believed to be signs of trouble and danger.

7 *one nature, of one substance bred* – "of one kind, of one race". The King reminds his hearers of the natural unity that has been unnaturally destroyed by civil war.

8 *intestine shock* – "shock felt right inside (the country)".

9 *close* – "meeting in battle".

10 *civil butchery* – "civil war". The word *butchery*, "cutting up of meat", suggests the horrible nature of war.

11 *in mutual . . . ranks* – "joined together in the same ranks, a manner that suits (fellow-countrymen) well".

12 *The edge . . . master*. War shall no longer damage the soldiers' own country like a carelessly carried knife that wounds its owner.

13 *As far . . . levy* (line 22). The King has vowed to collect *(levy)* an army *(power)* and take it right to the tomb *(sepulchre)* of Christ, *whose soldier now* he is. The tomb was at Jerusalem. Kings use *we*, plural pronoun, instead of *I* when making royal statements.

14 *holy fields*, places in Palestine made holy by Christ's presence.

15 *bitter* – "cruel", associated with great pain and sorrow. Christ was put to death by being nailed to a wooden cross, taking the punishment for men's wrongdoing (and so, *for our advantage*).

ACT ONE

Scene I. London. The Palace

Enter the KING, LORD JOHN OF LANCASTER, EARL OF
WESTMORELAND, SIR WALTER BLUNT, *with others.*

KING

So shaken[1] as we are, so wan with care,
Find we a time for frighted peace to pant,
And breathe short-winded accents of new broils
To be commenced in stronds[2] afar remote:
No[3] more the thirsty entrance of this soil   5
Shall daub her lips with her own children's blood;
No more shall trenching war channel her fields,
Nor bruise her flowerets with the arméd hoofs[4]
Of hostile paces: those opposéd eyes[5],
Which, like the meteors[6] of a troubled heaven,   10
All of one nature,[7] of one substance bred,
Did lately meet in the intestine shock[8]
And furious close[9] of civil butchery,[10]
Shall now, in mutual well-beseeming ranks,[11]
March all one way, and be no more opposed   15
Against acquaintance, kindred, and allies.
The edge[12] of war, like an ill-sheathéd knife,
No more shall cut his master. Therefore, friends,
As far[13] as to the sepulchre of Christ –
Whose soldier now, under whose blessed cross   20
We are impresséd and engaged to fight –
Forthwith a power of English shall we levy,
Whose arms were moulded in their mothers' womb
To chase these pagans in those holy fields[14]
Over whose acres walked those blessed feet   25
Which, fourteen hundred years ago, were nailed
For our advantage on the bitter[15] cross.
But this our purpose now is twelve month old,

1

16 *bootless . . . go* – "It is unnecessary (*bootless*) for us to tell you that we will go", (since you already know this).

17 *Therefor . . . now* – "that is not the purpose of our present meeting (but to discuss the practical arrangements)".

18 *Of* – "from".

19 *cousin.* This word was used in Shakespeare's time for almost any relation. Westmóreland had married Henry's half-sister.

20 *yesternight* – "last night".

21 *dear expedience* – "desired expedition", i.e. to the Holy Land.

22 *hot in question* – "being eagerly discussed".

23 *limits of the charge* – "rules for the men responsible for managing the expedition".

24 *athwart* – "across" (cutting across their purpose and so causing them to stop).

25 *post . . . worst was* – "messenger from Wales, bearing serious news, the worst of which was".

26 *irregular.* Glendower did not fight *regular* open battles but led small groups of men making surprise attacks.

27 *corpse* – "bodies". In modern English the plural is "corpses". Mortimer was taken alive; the bodies referred to here are those of his men.

28 *misuse* – "dishonourable treatment".

29 *Brake off* – "interrupted"

30 *other* – "other news".

31 *uneven* – "unpleasing".

32 *thus . . . import* – "this is what it had to say".

33 *Holy-rood Day*, Holy Cross Day, a festival in the Christian Church in honour of the recovery of the Cross after it had been captured. It is held on 11th September.

34 *approvéd* – "of proved bravery".

35 *Holmedon*, a place in the extreme north-east of England near the Scottish border.

36 *sad* – "grave".

37 *shape of likelihood* – "the way the situation would probably develop".

And bootless[16] 't is to tell you we will go;
Therefor[17] we meet not now. Then let me hear   30
Of[18] you, my gentle cousin[19] Westmoreland,
What yesternight[20] our Council did decree
In forwarding this dear[21] expedience.

WESTMORELAND

My liege, this haste was hot[22] in question,
And many limits[23] of the charge set down   35
But yesternight when, all athwart,[24] there came
A post[25] from Wales, loaden with heavy news,
Whose worst was that the noble Mortimer,
Leading the men of Herefordshire to fight
Against the irregular[26] and wild Glendower,   40
Was by the rude hands of that Welshman taken,
A thousand of his people butcheréd,
Upon whose dead corpse[27] there was such misuse,[28]
Such beastly shameless transformation,
By those Welshwomen done, as may not be   45
Without much shame retold or spoken of.

KING

It seems then that the tidings of this broil
Brake[29] off our business for the Holy Land.

WESTMORELAND

This matched with other[30] did, my gracious lord,
For more uneven[31] and unwelcome news   50
Came from the north, and thus it did import:[32]
On Holy-rood[33] Day, the gallant Hotspur there,
Young Harry Percy, and brave Archibald,
That ever valiant and approvéd[34] Scot,
At Holmedon[35] met, where they did spend   55
A sad[36] and bloody hour –
As by discharge of their artillery,
And shape[37] of likelihood, the news was told –

3

38 *them* – "the news".

39 *pride of their contention* – "at the height of their struggle".

40 *any way* – "either way", i.e. which side was winning. Since the messenger left before the battle was over he could not give a report of how it ended.

41 *industrious* – "always anxious to serve".

42 *new lighted* – "having just got down from".

43 *Stained . . . soil* – "stained with all the different colours of mud that he has ridden through between *(betwixt)* Holmedon and this palace *(seat)* of mine *(ours* – Henry's)".

44 *smooth* – "pleasing".

45 *Balked . . . blood* – "lying defeated in ridges thick with their own blood".

46 *who is . . . tongue* – "whose fine reputation is always the subject when men are talking about honour". The King's strong words of praise build up a striking picture of Hotspur and excite our eager interest in him before he appears. The speech also expresses the King's disappointment in his son and points to a contrast between Hotspur and Hal, a contrast that is later fully developed in the action of the play.

47 *Fortune's minion,* someone specially favoured by fortune.

48 *O that . . . and he mine* (line 89). It was said that fairies played tricks on humans by night. One such trick was to steal a strong healthy baby and leave a weak one in its place. The King remembers this story when he thinks that Harry Percy (Hotspur) behaves more like a prince than his own son, Harry Plantagenet (Prince Hal).

For he that brought them,[38] in the very heat
And pride[39] of their contention did take horse,   60
Uncertain of the issue any[40] way.

KING

Here is a dear, a true industrious[41] friend,
Sir Walter Blunt, new lighted[42] from his horse,
Stained[43] with the variation of each soil
Betwixt that Holmedon and this seat of ours;   65
And he hath brought us smooth[44] and welcome news.
The Earl of Douglas is discomfited;
Ten thousand bold Scots, two and twenty knights,
Balked[45] in their own blood, did Sir Walter see
On Holmedon's plains; of prisoners Hotspur took   70
Mordake, Earl of Fife and eldest son
To beaten Douglas, and the Earls of Athol,
Of Murray, Angus, and Menteith.
And is not this an honourable spoil?
A gallant prize? ha, cousin, is it not?

WESTMORELAND

                    In faith,   75
It is a conquest for a prince to boast of.

KING

Yea, there thou mak'st me sad, and mak'st me sin
In envy that my Lord Northumberland
Should be the father to so blest a son,
A son who[46] is the theme of honour's tongue,   80
Amongst a grove the very straightest plant,
Who is sweet Fortune's[47] minion and her pride;
Whilst I, by looking on the praise of him,
See riot and dishonour stain the brow
Of my young Harry. O[48] that it could be proved   85
That some night-tripping fairy had exchanged
In cradle-clothes our children where they lay,

49 *let him from my thoughts* - "let him (Hal) leave my thoughts".

50 *surprised* - "captured by sudden attack".

51 *To his own use* - "for his own advantage". A prisoner taken in battle might be set free in exchange for a promise not to fight again and the payment of money, a ransom.

52 *Malevolent to you in all aspects* - "who desires to harm you in all circumstances". Men who believed that the stars could influence people used the word *aspect* for the positions of the planets in relation to each other and believed that some of these aspects brought danger (were *malevolent*). Westmoreland uses these words to describe how the Earl of Worcester hates the King.

53 *Which makes him* - "who (Worcester) makes him (Hotspur)". *Which* for "who" was common in Shakespeare's time.

54 *prune . . . dignity* - "behave proudly *(prune)* and raise up his youthful strength to defy your dignity". *Prune* (preen - "arrange the feathers"), *bristle, crest* develop the picture of Hotspur acting like a bird proudly displaying its feathers.

55 *so inform the lords* - "tell that to the lords (the members of The Council)".

56 *to us* - "back to us".

57 *more is to be said . . . utteréd* - "more must be said and done than I can say or do in public in my present state of anger".

And called mine Percy, his Plantagenet!
Then would I have his Harry, and he mine.
But let[49] him from my thoughts. What think you, coz,   90
Of this young Percy's pride? The prisoners
Which he in this adventure hath surprised[50]
To his own use[51] he keeps, and sends me word
I shall have none but Mordake, Earl of Fife.

WESTMORELAND

This is his uncle's teaching; this is Worcester,   95
Malevolent[52] to you in all aspects,
Which[53] makes him prune[54] himself and bristle up
The crest of youth against your dignity.

KING

But I have sent for him to answer this;
And for this cause awhile we must neglect   100
Our holy purpose to Jerusalem.
Cousin, on Wednesday next our Council we
Will hold at Windsor, so[55] inform the lords:
But come yourself with speed to us[56] again,
For more[57] is to be said and to be done   105
Than out of anger can be utteréd.

WESTMORELAND

I will, my liege.

                                           [Exeunt

(I ii) In this scene we see Prince Hal enjoying the conversation of the fat knight Sir John Falstaff, who is a drinker and law-breaker but very merry company. Their speeches play with the various meanings of words. They discuss a plan to rob some rich travellers the next day at Gad's Hill. The Prince hesitates and in the end refuses to join in, but, though he will not rob honest men, he later agrees to assist Ned Poins in playing a trick on Falstaff. Hal and Poins, in disguise, will hide until the robbery is completed and will then attack Falstaff and his friends and rob them of their stolen goods.

When he is left alone, the Prince reveals that his character is not so wild as it appears. He intends one day to behave very differently and show himself a truly kingly man.

1 *Hal*, short friendly form of the name "Henry".

2 *lad* - "boy". This informal way of addressing the Prince shows that the two are on familiar terms.

3 *fat-witted* - "stupid"

4 *sack*, a white wine.

5 *unbuttoning*, loosening his clothes because he has eaten so much at supper.

6 *to demand . . . know* - "to ask correctly for what you really want to know".

7 *a devil*, an oath, that is, a word or words of little or no meaning added either to make a speech stronger or coarser or to swear that it is true.

8 *leaping-houses* - "houses of vice where men pay to be received by women".

9 *hot wench* - "passionate girl".

10 *be so superfluous* - "go so far beyond what is necessary". The Prince thinks that for Falstaff's interests - sleep, wine, and sex - it is not necessary to know the time of the day.

11 *near me* - "near to understanding me". Falstaff jumps from the Prince's use of *day* - "24 hours" - to *day* as opposed to night.

12 *we that take purses* - "we thieves".

13 *seven stars*, probably the group of stars called the Pleiades.

14 *Phoebus* - "the sun". Phoebus Apollo was the name of the Greek sun-god. Falstaff here sings a line from a song.

15 *prithee* - "pray thee".

16 *sweet*, often used where we now say "fine" or "pleasant".

17 *thy Grace*. *Grace* is used in three senses in lines 17-20: *thy Grace* an address to a man of high rank; *grace* - "virtue"; *grace* - words of thanks to God spoken before eating (as a *prologue* is spoken before a play).

18 *by my troth* - "by my honour" (a mild oath).

19 *an egg and butter*, a small meal which would deserve, according to Falstaff, saying only a little grace.

20 *roundly* - "plainly".

Scene II. London.

Enter PRINCE OF WALES *and* SIR JOHN FALSTAFF.

FALSTAFF

Now, Hal,[1] what time of day is it, lad?[2]

PRINCE

Thou art so fat-witted[3] with drinking of old sack,[4] and unbuttoning[5] thee after supper, and sleeping upon benches after
noon, that thou hast forgotten to demand[6] that truly which
thou wouldst truly know. What a devil[7] hast thou to do with   5
the time of the day? Unless hours were cups of sack, and
minutes capons, and clocks the tongues of bawds, and dials
the signs of leaping-houses,[8] and the blessed sun himself a fair
hot wench[9] in flame-coloured taffeta, I see no reason why thou
shouldst be so superfluous[10] to demand the time of the day.   10

FALSTAFF

Indeed, you come near[11] me now, Hal, for we that take[12]
purses go by the moon and the seven[13] stars, and not "by
Phoebus,[14] he, that wandering knight so fair": and I prithee[15]
sweet[16] wag, when thou art king, as God save thy Grace[17] –
Majesty I should say, for grace thou wilt have none –   15

PRINCE

What, none?

FALSTAFF

No, by my troth,[18] not so much as will serve to be prologue to
an egg and butter.[19]

PRINCE

Well, how then? Come, roundly,[20] roundly.

21 *let not us . . . day's beauty* – "do not let us who work at night be called thieves by day". There is a play on the meanings of *night* and *knight* (squires of the body were the attendants of knights; by *squires of the night's body*, Falstaff means thieves). There is also a play of meaning on *beauty* and *booty* (stolen property). Falstaff is asking for them to be called by nobler titles than thieves.

22 *Diana's foresters* – "followers of Diana", who was goddess of the Moon and of hunting, and, according to Falstaff, of robbers too, because they work by moonlight.

23 *gentlemen of the shade*. The phrase is intended by Falstaff to suggest a noble title; compare Gentlemen of the Chamber, that is, members of the royal court.

24 *minions of the moon* – "favourites of the moon", a title instead of "robbers".

25 *of good government,* used in two senses: (i) "well-behaved", and (ii) "subjects of a good ruler".

26 *countenance,* used in two senses: (i) "face", and (ii) "permission".

27 *steal,* used in two senses: (i) "creep softly", and (ii) "rob".

28 *it holds well* – "the comparison is a good one".

29 *doth ebb . . . by the moon* – (our fortune) "flows away *(doth ebb)* then flows back again, like the tide of the sea, for we are governed by the moon just as the tide is".

30 *Lay by* – "Lay down your weapons".

31 *Bring in* – "Bring in more food and wine".

32 *the ladder,* the ladder up which a condemned man would climb to the gallows before he was hanged. Hanging was formerly the punishment for thieves.

33 *flow*. The Prince is still likening fortune to the movement of a tide.

34 *Hybla,* a town in Sicily, famous for its honey.

35 *old lad of the castle* – "wild fellow". These words could be used to describe any man who behaved wildly. They may also refer to an early form of the play when the character we now know as Falstaff was called Oldcastle. The descendants of Sir John Oldcastle, who was put to death for his religious opinions in 1418, objected to having a character called "Oldcastle".

36 *is not . . . durance* – "does not a leather garment wear well?" There is also a second meaning, "remember the risk of prison", for a buff jerkin was the leather garment worn by the officer who arrested people, and *durance* could mean either "prison" or "strong enough to wear for a long time".

37 *quiddities,* plays on words using fine shades of meaning.

38 *a plague,* the name of a disease, used here as a mild oath, "what the devil".

39 *a pox,* another disease used as an oath.

40 *called her . . . reckoning,* in two senses: (i) "called her to give an account of herself"; (ii) "asked for the bill".

41 *oft* – "often".

10

FALSTAFF

Marry then sweet wag, when thou art king, let[21] not us that 20
are squires of the night's body be called thieves of the day's
beauty: let us be Diana's[22] foresters, gentlemen[23] of the shade,
minions[24] of the moon; and let men say we be men of good[25]
government, being governed as the sea is, by our noble and
chaste mistress the moon, under whose countenance[26] we steal.[27] 25

PRINCE

Thou sayest well, and it holds[28] well too, for the fortune of us
that are the moon's men doth ebb[29] and flow like the sea, being
governed as the sea is, by the moon – as for proof now, a purse
of gold most resolutely snatched on Monday night, and most
dissolutely spent on Tuesday morning, got with swearing 30
"Lay[30] by!", and spent with crying "Bring[31] in!", now in as
low an ebb as the foot of the ladder,[32] and by and by in as high
a flow[33] as the ridge of the gallows.

FALSTAFF

By the Lord thou sayest true, lad; and is not my hostess of the
tavern a most sweet wench? 35

PRINCE

As the honey of Hybla,[34] my old[35] lad of the castle; and is[36]
not a buff jerkin a most sweet robe of durance?

FALSTAFF

How now, how now, mad wag? What, in thy quips and thy
quiddities?[37] What a plague[38] have I to do with a buff jerkin?

PRINCE

Why, what a pox[39] have I to do with my hostess of the tavern? 40

FALSTAFF

Well, thou hast called[40] her to a reckoning many a time and
oft.[41]

11

42 *I'll give thee thy due* – "I'll give you the praise you deserve". The words can also mean "I'll pay you my debt", but this is not Falstaff's intention.

43 *so far . . . credit* – "(I have paid for) as much as I had enough money for, and when my money was gone, I have used my reputation as a pledge to obtain goods with a promise to pay later".

44 *heir apparent* – "prince who will become king when the present king dies". Falstaff plays on the similarity of sound to *here apparent*, but does not finish the sentence.

45 *and resolution . . . the law* – "and will boldness *(resolution)* be hindered *(fubbed)* as it is with the out-of-date restraint *(curb)* of old father Fool *(Antic)*, the law". Falstaff shows his lack of respect for the law by likening it to the figure of the Fool in earlier (morality) plays. He is not asking Hal for information but making suggestions.

46 *O rare!* – "O splendid!"

47 *brave* – "excellent".

48 *in some sort . . . humour* – "to some extent it suits my character".

the ridge of the gallows

PRINCE

Did I ever call for thee to pay thy part?

FALSTAFF

No, I 'll[42] give thee thy due, thou hast paid all there.

PRINCE

Yea, and elsewhere, so far[43] as my coin would stretch; and 45
where it would not I have used my credit.

FALSTAFF

Yea, and so used it that were it not here apparent that thou art
heir[44] apparent – But I prithee sweet wag, shall there be gallows
standing in England when thou art king? and resolution[45] thus
fubbed as it is with the rusty curb of old father Antic the law? 50
Do not thou when thou art king hang a thief.

PRINCE

No, thou shalt.

FALSTAFF

Shall I? O rare![46] By the Lord, I 'll be a brave[47] judge!

PRINCE

Thou judgest false already: I mean thou shalt have the hanging
of the thieves, and so become a rare hangman. 55

FALSTAFF

Well, Hal, well; and in some sort[48] it jumps with my humour,
as well as waiting in the court, I can tell you.

PRINCE

For obtaining of suits?

13

49 *suits*, used in two senses: (i) "requests"; (ii) "clothes".

50 *lean* – "poorly supplied". The hangman would have a good supply of suits, for he was given the clothes of his victims.

51 *gib cat* – "male cat". Falstaff is probably thinking of the melancholy wailing sound made by cats at night.

52 *lugged* – "dragged by the ear". ·Bears were used in a cruel sport, "bear-baiting". The bear had to defend itself against fierce dogs which were set to attack it.

53 *Lincolnshire,* this eastern English county was famous for its bagpipes, a musical instrument.

54 *What sayest . . . Moor-ditch,* the hare, a solitary animal, was considered melancholy and so was Moorditch, a foul evil-smelling ditch in London.

55 *comparative* – "fond of comparing one thing with another".

56 *I would to God* – "I wish". In the rest of this speech and in several others, Falstaff imitates the style of speaking used by the Puritans, a religious group who spent much time praying and preaching against luxury and wickedness and who used in ordinary speech an earnest, balanced, religious style more suitable for public prayer.

57 *commodity* – "supply".

58 *marked him not* – "paid no attention to him".

59 *wisdom cries out in the streets,* a reference to the Bible, *Proverbs* I v.20; 8 v.1.

60 *thou hast damnable iteration* – "you have a damnable habit of repeating things (to your own advantage)". The humour of this whole speech depends on the contrast between the religious style and Falstaff's actual character.

61 *if a man should speak truly* – "to tell the truth".

62 *give over* – "cease to practise (this evil life)".

63 *I 'll be damned . . . Christendom* – "I will not be sent to hell for any king's son in all the Christian world".

14

FALSTAFF

Yea, for obtaining of suits,[49] whereof the hangman hath no lean[50] wardrobe. 'Sblood, I am as melancholy as a gib[51] cat, 60 or a lugged[52] bear.

PRINCE

Or an old lion, or a lover's lute.

FALSTAFF

Yea, or the drone of a Lincolnshire[53] bagpipe.

PRINCE

What[54] sayest thou to a hare, or the melancholy of Moor-ditch?

FALSTAFF

Thou hast the most unsavoury similes, and art indeed the most 65 comparative[55] rascalliest sweet young prince. But Hal, I prithee trouble me no more with vanity. I[56] would to God thou and I knew where a commodity[57] of good names were to be bought: an old lord of the Council rated me the other day in the street about you, sir, but I marked[58] him not; and yet he talked very 70 wisely, but I regarded him not; and yet he talked wisely, and in the street too.

PRINCE

Thou didst well, for wisdom[59] cries out in the streets and no man regards it.

FALSTAFF

O, thou hast damnable iteration,[60] and art indeed able to cor- 75 rupt a saint. Thou hast done much harm upon me, Hal; God forgive thee for it. Before I knew thee, Hal, I knew nothing; and now am I, if[61] a man should speak truly, little better than one of the wicked. I must give[62] over this life, and I will give it over. By the Lord, and I do not I am a villain. I 'll be 80 damned[63] for never a king's son in Christendom.

15

64 *take* – "steal". Hal takes no notice
of Falstaff's pretended religious
seriousness. He changes the subject
without ceremony, turning the
conversation to the matter which
he knows Falstaff is really interested
in.

65 *Jack,* familiar form of the name
"John".

66 *make one* – "be one of the company".

67 *baffle.* To *baffle* was to punish a
traitor knight by either hanging
him by the heels, head down, or
hanging his picture or his shield the
wrong way up.

68 *amendment* – "improvement"; but
the Prince speaks ironically. He is
laughing at Falstaff's sudden change
from religion to an agreement to
steal. Falstaff, always ready with an
excuse, replies that stealing is the
work God calls him to *(my vocation)*
and is therefore not wrong.

69 *Gadshill,* a thief who is called "Gadshill" because Gad's Hill is the name
of the place where he often robs
travellers. Gadshill (the man) has
planned a robbery *(set a match)* for
early the next morning at Gad's
Hill (the place).

70 *O, if men . . . for him?* Falstaff, knowing the Christian doctrine that men
are saved for eternal joy by the
mercy and grace of God, says that
if, instead, each man were judged
by his merit alone, no punishment
in hell would be severe enough for
Gadshill.

71 *omnipotent* – "complete".

72 *Stand,* the thief's call to the man he
is going to rob.

73 *true* – "honest".

74 *Good morrow, Ned* – "Good morning, Ned (a familiar form for the
name *Edward*)".

75 *What says . . . Sugar.* Poins greets
Falstaff with playful names based on
the regret *(remorse)* he regularly
feels after drinking too much
sugared wine. In the earlier morality
plays virtues, vices and spiritual
states were represented by dramatic
characters. The French title, *Monsieur* ("Mr.") suggests that remorse
is foreign to Falstaff's nature.

76 *agrees* – "agree".

77 *Good Friday,* a day when Christians
were not permitted by their religion
to take anything but the smallest
amounts of very plain food and
drink. Falstaff is accused, as a joke,
of having agreed to let the devil
have his soul in return for rich wine
and food on Good Friday.

78 *his due* – "what is owed to him".
The proverb usually has the sense
"Give the devil (or the bad man)
such praise as he deserves"

PRINCE

Where shall we take[64] a purse tomorrow, Jack?[65]

FALSTAFF

'Zounds, where thou wilt, lad, I 'll make[66] one; an I do not, call me villain and baffle[67] me.

PRINCE

I see a good amendment[68] of life in thee, from praying to purse-taking.   85

FALSTAFF

Why, Hal, 't is my vocation, Hal; 't is no sin for a man to labour in his vocation.

Enter POINS

Poins! – Now shall we know if Gadshill[69] have set a match. O, if men[70] were to be saved by merit, what hole in hell were hot   90
enough for him? This is the most omnipotent[71] villain that ever cried "Stand!"[72] to a true[73] man.

PRINCE

Good morrow, Ned.[74]

POINS

Good morrow, sweet Hal. What[75] says Monsieur Remorse? What says Sir John Sack – and Sugar? Jack! how agrees[76] the   95
devil and thee about thy soul, that thou soldest him on Good Friday[77] last for a cup of Madeira and a cold capon's leg?

PRINCE

Sir John stands to his word: the devil shall have his bargain, for he was never yet a breaker of proverbs: he will give the devil his due.[78]   100

79 *Then art . . . the devil.* By keeping to his word, Falstaff has sold his soul to the devil; and he will therefore be damned for keeping his word.

80 *Else . . . the devil* – "Otherwise (if he did not keep his promise) he would have been *(had been)* damned for cheating *(cozening)* the devil". Hal points out that Falstaff loses either way.

81 *pilgrims . . . to Canterbury.* Pilgrims went to visit the shrine of St Thomas à Becket.

82 *vizards* – "masks".

83 *lies* – "stays at the inn". Rochester is 30 miles from London, a day's journey in Shakespeare's time. Gad's Hill is a short way out of Rochester, on the London road.

84 *secure* – "safely".

85 *crowns,* coins worth five shillings.

86 *and be hanged,* an impatient oath.

87 *Yedward,* familiar form of the name Edward.

88 *chops* – "fat cheeks", used as an insulting name.

89 *make one* – "be one of us (thieves)".

90 *Who, I rob?* This appears to be the first time the Prince has been asked to join in a robbery, though he has made jokes about stealing.

91 *thou camest not . . . shillings,* used in two senses: (i) "you are not a true member of the king's family *(blood royal)* if you dare not stand as a thief with us for ten shillings"; (ii) "you are a false coin *(royal* – a coin worth ten shillings) if you do not equal ten shillings".

there are pilgrims[81] *going to Canterbury*

18

POINS

Then[79] art thou damned for keeping thy word with the devil.

PRINCE

Else[80] he had been damned for cozening the devil.

POINS

But my lads, my lads, tomorrow morning, by four o'clock early at Gad's Hill, there are pilgrims[81] going to Canterbury with rich offerings, and traders riding to London with fat 105 purses. I have vizards[82] for you all; you have horses for yourselves. Gadshill lies[83] tonight in Rochester; I have bespoke supper tomorrow night in Eastcheap. We may do it as a secure[84] as sleep. If you will go, I will stuff your purses full of crowns:[85] if you will not, tarry at home and be hanged.[86]   110

FALSTAFF

Hear ye, Yedward,[87] if I tarry at home and go not, I'll hang you for going.

POINS

You will, chops?[88]

FALSTAFF

Hal, wilt thou make[89] one?

PRINCE

Who,[90] I rob? I a thief? Not I, by my faith.   115

FALSTAFF

There 's neither honesty, manhood, nor good fellowship in thee, nor thou camest[91] not of the blood royal, if thou darest not stand for ten shillings.

PRINCE

Well then, once in my days I 'll be a madcap.

92 *come what will* – "let the consequences be what they will". The Prince considers the consequences of his not becoming a thief: he may lose his friends by not joining them; yet he decides to stay at home. He has more respect for the law and for his own responsible position than Falstaff realises.

93 *I'll be a traitor then.* Falstaff threatens to be a traitor to Hal when he becomes king (if Hal does not keep his word and join in the robbery).

94 *lay him down . . . shall go* – "I will put before him *(lay him down)* such reasons for taking part in this adventure that he will certainly *(shall)* go".

95 *Well, God . . . profiting* – "May God give you (Poins) heavenly power to persuade, and him (Prince Hal) the power to improve himself by listening". The whole of this speech is in the style of a Puritan. (See note 56, line 67).

96 *move* – "persuade".

97 *for recreation sake* – "for the fun of it".

98 *prove* – "become".

99 *abuses* – "crimes".

100 *want countenance* – "are in need of favour and protection from a great man" (such as the Prince).

101 *the latter spring* – "autumn"; *Allhallown summer*, a season of fine weather about All Saints *(All Hallows)* Day, 1 November, in late autumn. Both phrases refer to Falstaff's continued enjoyment of youthful follies when he is growing old.

102 *if you and I . . . shoulders* – "then you and I will rob them, or if we do not, you may cut off my head". The second half of the sentence is not seriously intended.

FALSTAFF

Why, that 's well said.   120

PRINCE

Well, come[92] what will, I 'll tarry at home.

FALSTAFF

By the Lord, I 'll[93] be a traitor then, when thou art king.

PRINCE

I care not.

POINS

Sir John, I prithee leave the Prince and me alone. I will lay[94] him down such reasons for this adventure that he shall go.   125

FALSTAFF

Well, God[95] give thee the spirit of persuasion and him the ears of profiting; that what thou speakest may move,[96] and what he hears may be believed; that the true prince may (for recreation[97] sake) prove[98] a false thief; for the poor abuses[99] of the time want[100] countenance. Farewell, you shall find me in Eastcheap. 130

PRINCE

Farewell, the latter [101] spring! Farewell, All–hallow summer!
                                                [*Exit* FALSTAFF

POINS

Now, my good sweet honey lord, ride with us tomorrow. I have a jest to execute that I cannot manage alone. Falstaff, Bardolph, Peto, and Gadshill shall rob those men that we have already waylaid – yourself and I will not be there: and when 135 they have the booty, if[102] you and I do not rob them, cut this head off from my shoulders.

103 *wherein . . . to fail* – "we can please ourselves by failing to appear at the meeting place".

104 *which they shall . . . upon them* – "as soon as they have accomplished this (robbery) we will attack them".

105 *'t is like that* – "it is likely that".

106 *know us . . . to be ourselves* – "recognise us by our horses, by our clothes *(habits)*, and by all the articles we wear or use *(every other appointment)*".

107 *I have . . . garments,* "I have covers *(cases)* made of coarse cloth *(buckram)* for the occasion *(the nonce),* to mask our well-known *(noted)* outer garments".

108 *doubt* – "fear".

109 *too hard for us* – "too difficult for us to defeat".

110 *turned back,* turned their backs towards the danger and so "ran away".

111 *if he fight . . . arms* – "if he continues to fight when he sees that nothing is to be gained, I'll cease to carry weapons". The right to wear a sword was limited to men of rank.

112 *virtue* – "value".

113 *fat rogue* – "fat wrong-doer (i.e. Falstaff)".

114 *wards,* defensive movements in sword-fighting.

115 *in the reproof . . . jest* – "proving that what Falstaff says is false will be the best part of the joke"

116 *tomorrow night,* perhaps a mistake for "tonight", as the robbery was arranged for early the next morning. But perhaps the Prince is thinking of the supper to follow the robbery.

22

PRINCE

How shall we part with them in setting forth?

POINS

Why, we will set forth before or after them, and appoint them
a place of meeting, wherein[103] it is at our pleasure to fail; and   140
then will they adventure upon the exploit themselves, which[104]
they shall have no sooner achieved but we 'll set upon them.

PRINCE

Yea, but 't is[105] like that they will know[106] us by our horses, by
our habits, and by every other appointment to be ourselves.

POINS

Tut, our horses they shall not see; I 'll tie them in the wood;   145
our vizards we will change after we leave them; and sirrah,
I[107] have cases of buckram for the nonce, to immask our noted
outward garments.

PRINCE

Yea, but I doubt[108] they will be too hard[109] for us.

POINS

Well, for two of them, I know them to be as true-bred cowards   150
as ever turned[110] back; and for the third, if he fight[111] longer
than he sees reason, I 'll forswear arms. The virtue[112] of this jest
will be the incomprehensible lies that this same fat rogue[113]
will tell us when we meet at supper: how thirty at least he
fought with, what wards,[114] what blows, what extremities he   155
endured; and in the reproof[115] of this lives the jest.

PRINCE

Well, I'll go with thee. Provide us all things necessary, and
meet me tomorrow[116] night in Eastcheap; there I 'll sup. Farewell.

117 *unyoked humour* – "lazy nature".

118 *contagious clouds.* It was believed that clouds could bring diseases (were *contagious*).

119 *when he please . . . wondered at* – "when he *(the sun)* decides to reveal himself again, because he has been absent *(wanted)* he may be the more admired".

120 *they* – "holidays".

121 *rare accidents* – "events which occur seldom".

122 *this loose . . . throw off* – "cease to practise this undisciplined way of life".

123 *pay the debt I never promiséd* – "perform duties that I am not expected to perform (because my present conduct shows no sign of my good intentions)".

124 *By how much . . . men's hopes* – "by a great improvement over my present behaviour I shall show how wrong men are who expect ill of me". *falsify* – "prove wrong", *hopes* – "what men expect", either good or bad. The Prince continues to think of his present behaviour as if it were a promise of what he intends in the future, and so speaks of it as *my word*.

125 *sullen ground* – "dull background". The background is the part of a design or picture which is seen around and behind the principal object. The Prince's reformed character will seem even better in contrast with his former manner, just as a bright metal gains in brilliance when seen against a dull background. The series *bright, sullen, glittering, foil*, build up the contrast through images of light and dark.

126 *I'll so . . . skill* – "I will do wrong *(offend)* in such a way that it produces a good result"; *skill* – "good policy".

127 *Redeeming time* – "gaining a profit from this time which I appear to be wasting".

128 *think least* – "least expect".

POINS

Farewell, my lord.   160

[*Exit*

PRINCE

I know you all, and will awhile uphold
The unyoked[117] humour of your idleness.
Yet herein will I imitate the sun,
Who doth permit the base contagious[118] clouds
To smother up his beauty from the world,   165
That, when[119] he please again to be himself,
Being wanted, he may be more wondered at
By breaking through the foul and ugly mists
Of vapours that did seem to strangle him.
If all the year were playing holidays,   170
To sport would be as tedious as to work;
But when they[120] seldom come, they wished-for come,
And nothing pleaseth but rare[121] accidents:
So when this loose[122] behaviour I throw off,
And pay[123] the debt I never promiséd,   175
By[124] how much better than my word I am,
By so much shall I falsify men's hopes;
And like bright metal on a sullen[125] ground,
My reformation, glittering o'er my fault,
Shall show more goodly, and attract more eyes   180
Than that which hath no foil to set it off.
I 'll[126] so offend, to make offence a skill,
Redeeming[127] time when men think[128] least I will.

[*Exit*

(I.iii) The King demands the Scottish prisoners recently captured by Hotspur, but the latter will not yield them unless his wife's brother, Mortimer, captured by Owen Glendower, is redeemed by the King. The King refuses angrily and leaves. Northumberland and Worcester reveal their discontent with this King whom they have helped to the throne, and tell Hotspur that the former King, Richard II, had proclaimed Mortimer his heir. Worcester advises Hotspur to return the captured Scots to their own country, thus winning their friendship. Worcester, Northumberland, and Hotspur plan to gain the support of all the King's enemies and persuade them to rebel against him.

1 *My blood . . . indignities* – "My nature has been too passionless *(cold)* and calm, not inclined to show anger *(to stir)* at these disrespectful acts *(indignities)*".

2 *found me* – "seen that I am so", but also "found me out".

3 *tread upon my patience* – "take advantage of my patience".

4 *I will . . . young down* (line 7) – "I will from this time onward be the king that I am, mighty and to be feared, rather than follow my natural character *(condition)* which has been as smooth as oil and soft as the small feathers on a bird *(down)*".

5 *title of respect* – "claim to be respected".

6 *Our house* – "Our noble family", that is the Percy family to which Worcester, Northumberland and Hotspur belong.

7 *scourge of greatness,* the King's threat to use his authority *(greatness)* as if it were a whip *(scourge)* to enforce respect.

8 *holp to make so portly* – "helped to make so stately". When Henry Bolingbroke returned to England from exile, the Percy family helped him to become Henry IV.

9 *get thee gone* – "go immediately".

10 *presence is . . . peremptory* – "appearance and behaviour *(presence)* is too bold and shows you are unwilling to accept rule *(peremptory)*".

11 *majesty* – "the King", but also "the greatness and dignity of a king".

12 *moody frontier . . . brow* – "angry defiance *(frontier)* of a subject's frown".

13 *good leave* – "permission".

Scene III. Windsor. The Council Room.

Enter the KING, NORTHUMBERLAND, WORCESTER, HOTSPUR, SIR WALTER BLUNT, *with others.*

KING

My blood[1] hath been too cold and temperate,
Unapt to stir at these indignities,
And you have found[2] me – for accordingly
You tread[3] upon my patience: but be sure
I[4] will from henceforth rather be myself,   5
Mighty and to be feared, than my condition,
Which hath been smooth as oil, soft as young down,
And therefore lost that title[5] of respect
Which the proud soul ne'er pays but to the proud.

WORCESTER

Our[6] house, my sovereign liege, little deserves   10
The scourge[7] of greatness to be used on it,
And that same greatness too which our own hands
Have holp[8] to make so portly.

NORTHUMBERLAND
My lord, –

KING

Worcester, get[9] thee gone, for I do see
Danger and disobedience in thine eye.   15
O sir, your presence[10] is too bold and peremptory;
And majesty[11] might never yet endure
The moody[12] frontier of a servant brow.
You have good[13] leave to leave us. When we need
Your use and counsel we shall send for you.   20
                                        [*Exit* WORCESTER

[*To* NORTHUMBERLAND] You were about to speak.

14 *not with . . . denied* – "kept back (instead of being sent to the King) but not with such a strong refusal".

15 *delivered* – "reported".

16 *envy* – "hatred".

17 *misprision* – "misunderstanding".

18 *dry* – "thirsty".

19 *chin new reaped* – "beard closely clipped", worn thus by men of fashion in Shakespeare's day.

20 *like a stubble-land at harvest-home* – "like a field from which corn has been newly cut at harvest time".

21 *perfuméd like a milliner*. The *milliner* sold goods perfumed to attract buyers. Hotspur's anger at the messenger's lady-like disdain for the battle-weary soldiers is put forward as a first excuse for his refusal to hand over the prisoners.

22 *he held . . . snuff* (line 40) – "he held a box of perfume *(pouncet-box)* which, from time to time *(ever and anon)* he smelled (gave *his nose*), and took away again. His nose *(who)*, angry at this treatment, next time it came showed its annoyance by sneezing; *snuff* is used in two senses: (i) "anger"; (ii) "powder used to cause sneezing".

23 *still* – "all the time".

24 *holiday and lady terms*, words *(terms)* fit for special occasions *(holiday)* not ordinary use, and fit only for use by women.

25 *questioned me*, in two senses: (i) "asked me questions"; (ii) "talked away to me".

26 *amongst the rest* – "as part of his endless chatter".

27 *in* – "on".

28 *To be . . . popinjay*. The loose grammar reflects Hotspur's anger. *popinjay* – "parrot", a brightly coloured bird that imitates the human voice.

29 *grief* – "pain".

30 *neglectingly* – "without much thought".

31 *brisk* – "smartly dressed"

like a stubble-land[20] *at harvest-home*

28

NORTHUMBERLAND

Yea, my good lord.
Those prisoners in your Highness' name demanded,
Which Harry Percy here at Holmedon took,
Were, as he says, not[14] with such strength denied
As is delivered[15] to your Majesty.   25
Either envy[16] therefore, or misprision,[17]
Is guilty of this fault, and not my son.

HOTSPUR

My liege, I did deny no prisoners;
But I remember, when the fight was done,
When I was dry[18] with rage and extreme toil,   30
Breathless and faint, leaning upon my sword,
Came there a certain lord, neat and trimly dressed,
Fresh as a bridegroom, and his chin[19] new reaped
Showed like a stubble-land[20] at harvest-home.
He was perfumèd[21] like a milliner,   35
And 'twixt his finger and his thumb he held[22]
A pouncet-box, which ever and anon
He gave his nose, and took 't away again –
Who therewith angry, when it next came there,
Took it in snuff – and still[23] he smiled and talked;   40
And as the soldiers bore dead bodies by,
He called them untaught knaves, unmannerly,
To bring a slovenly unhandsome corse
Betwixt the wind and his nobility.
With many holiday[24] and lady terms   45
He questioned[25] me; amongst[26] the rest, demanded
My prisoners in[27] your Majesty's behalf.
I then, all smarting with my wounds being cold,
To be[28] so pestered with a popinjay,
Out of my grief[29] and my impatience   50
Answered neglectingly,[30] I know not what,
He should, or he should not, for he made me mad
To see him shine so brisk[31] and smell so sweet,

29

32 *waiting-gentlewoman,* a female of good family serving a lady of rank.

33 *God save the mark,* an oath, here expressing scorn.

34 *sovereignest* – "the very best".

35 *parmacety,* a form of medicine.

36 *And that . . . a soldier* (line 63). Hotspur imitates the messenger's delicate, unsoldierly style of speech.

37 *Which many . . . so cowardly* – "which had destroyed many a good brave soldier in cowardly fashion".

38 *bald, unjointed* – "empty, disconnected".

39 *indirectly* – "without attending carefully".

40 *Come current* – "be accepted as true".

41 *May reasonably . . . now* (line 75) – "may with reason be forgotten *(die)* and not be used to harm *(wrong)* him or to accuse him of disloyalty *(impeach)* as long as *(so)* he now withdraws it".

42 *yet* – "still".

43 *But* – "except".

44 *brother-in-law . . . Mortimer.* Hotspur married a sister of Edmund Mortimer, who was Glendower's prisoner.

45 *on my soul,* an oath.

46 *magician,* Glendower believed that he had magic powers (see III.i.50). The King here uses the word *magician* scornfully.

47 *Earl of March.* Edmund Mortimer is meant, but he was not Earl of March. This title belonged to his nephew.

And talk so like a waiting-gentlewoman[32]
Of guns, and drums, and wounds, God[33] save the mark!   55
And telling me the sovereignest[34] thing on earth
Was parmacety[35] for an inward bruise,
And[36] that it was great pity, so it was,
This villainous saltpetre should be digged
Out of the bowels of the harmless earth,   60
Which[37] many a good tall fellow had destroyed
So cowardly; and but for these vile guns
He would himself have been a soldier.
This bald,[38] unjointed chat of his, my lord,
I answered indirectly,[39] as I said;   65
And I beseech you, let not his report
Come[40] current for an accusation
Betwixt my love and your high Majesty.

SIR WALTER BLUNT

The circumstance considered, good my lord,
Whate'er Lord Harry Percy then had said   70
To such a person, and in such a place,
At such a time, with all the rest retold,
May[41] reasonably die, and never rise
To do him wrong, or any way impeach
What then he said, so he unsay it now.   75

KING

Why, yet[42] he doth deny his prisoners,
But[43] with proviso and exception:
That we at our own charge shall ransom straight
His brother-in-law,[44] the foolish Mortimer,
Who, on my soul,[45] hath wilfully betrayed   80
The lives of those that he did lead to fight
Against that great magician,[46] damned Glendower,
Whose daughter, as we hear, the Earl[47] of March
Hath lately married. Shall our coffers then
Be emptied to redeem a traitor home?   85

31

48 *and indent . . . forfeited themselves –* "shall we come to terms with cowards *(fears)* when they have given themselves up?"

49 *starve –* "die".

50 *fall off –* "revolt".

51 *Needs no more but –* "needs only".

52 *mouthéd wounds.* Mortimer's open wounds were like mouths, which if they had been able to speak, would have proclaimed his loyalty.

53 *confound the . . . hardiment –* "spend almost an hour in matching courage".

54 *Three times . . . Severn's flood –* "They paused three times for breath and, agreeing to a temporary peace, drank three times from the quickly flowing water of the River Severn" (a river which flows through Wales).

55 *affrighted with –* "frightened by".

56 *crisp head.* Used with a human head, crisp is "curled", but with surface *(head)* of water, it means "made uneven by very small waves".

57 *Never did bare . . . wounds –* "wretched *(bare)* and rotten cunning *(policy)* never used such deadly wounds to disguise *(colour)* its action *(her working)*".

58 *Nor never . . . willingly –* "nor is it possible that the noble Mortimer could have intended to receive so many wounds (in order to deceive you into thinking him loyal)".

59 *slandered with revolt –* "falsely accused of treason".

60 *Thou dost belie him –* "Your opinion of him is not the true one".

61 *encounter –* "fight".

62 *durst –* "dared".

32

Shall we buy treason, and indent[48] with fears
When they have lost and forfeited themselves?
No, on the barren mountains let him starve;[49]
For I shall never hold that man my friend
Whose tongue shall ask me for one penny cost   90
To ransom home revolted Mortimer.

HOTSPUR

Revolted Mortimer!
He never did fall[50] off, my sovereign liege,
But by the chance of war. To prove that true
Needs[51] no more but one tongue for all those wounds,   95
Those mouthéd[52] wounds, which valiantly he took,
When on the gentle Severn's sedgy bank,
In single opposition, hand to hand,
He did confound[53] the best part of an hour
In changing hardiment with great Glendower.   100
Three[54] times they breathed, and three times did they drink,
Upon agreement, of swift Severn's flood,
Who then, affrighted[55] with their bloody looks,
Ran fearfully among the trembling reeds,
And hid his crisp[56] head in the hollow bank,   105
Bloodstainéd with these valiant combatants.
Never[57] did bare and rotten policy
Colour her working with such deadly wounds;
Nor[58] never could the noble Mortimer
Receive so many, and all willingly.   110
Then let not him be slandered[59] with revolt.

KING

Thou dost belie[60] him, Percy, thou dost belie him:
He never did encounter[61] with Glendower.
I tell thee, he durst[62] as well have met the devil alone
As Owen Glendower for an enemy.   115
Art thou not ashamed? But sirrah, henceforth
Let me not hear you speak of Mortimer:

33

63 *with the speediest means* – "as quickly as you can".

64 *such a kind* – "such a manner", a threat of punishment.

65 *license* – "permit".

66 *hear of it* – "hear more from me about it", another threat.

67 *An if* – "Even if".

68 *I will . . . straight* – "I will follow (him) immediately".

69 *ease my heart* – "relieve my angry feelings".

70 *Albeit . . . head* – "although I risk having my head cut off".'

71 *and let . . . mercy* – "and may my soul be condemned to hell".

72 *down-trod* – "not allowed to live according to his high rank".

73 *ingrate and cankered* – "ungrateful and rotten at heart".

74 *struck this heat up* – "stirred up this angry passion".

Send me your prisoners with the speediest[63] means,
Or you shall hear in such[64] a kind from me
As will displease you. My Lord Northumberland,   120
We license[65] your departure with your son.
Send us your prisoners, or you will hear[66] of it.

[*Exit* KING, *with* BLUNT *and attendants*

HOTSPUR

An[67] if the devil come and roar for them
I will not send them. I will[68] after straight
And tell him so, for I will ease[69] my heart,   125
Albeit[70] I make a hazard of my head.

NORTHUMBERLAND

What, drunk with choler? Stay, and pause awhile;
Here comes your uncle.

Re-enter WORCESTER

HOTSPUR
                Speak of Mortimer?
'Zounds, I will speak of him, and let[71] my soul
Want mercy if I do not join with him,   130
Yea, on his part I 'll empty all these veins,
And shed my dear blood, drop by drop in the dust,
But I will lift the down-trod[72] Mortimer
As high in the air as this unthankful King,
As this ingrate[73] and cankered Bolingbroke.   135

NORTHUMBERLAND
Brother, the King hath made your nephew mad.

WORCESTER
Who struck[74] this heat up after I was gone?

75 *forsooth* – "in truth" Here it suggests scorn in the speaker.

76 *eye of death.* This may mean either "a look which threatened death" or "a look which showed his fear of death"

77 *Trembling,* either with anger or with fear.

78 *proclaimed . . . next of blood.* Shakespeare confuses (as at lines 79 and 83) the uncle Edmund Mortimer with his nephew Edmund, Earl of March. It was the nephew who was proclaimed Richard II's heir.

79 *unhappy* – "unfortunate".

80 *Whose wrongs . . . pardon* – "may God forgive us the wrongs we did him".

81 *intercepted* – "interrupted".

82 *deposed, and shortly murderéd.* Shakespeare's play *Richard II* tells how Richard was removed from the position of king *(deposed)*, and soon after *(shortly)* murdered.

83 *And for . . . scandalised* – "And on account of whose death we are generally and publicly *(in the world's wide mouth)* blamed *(scandalised)*".

84 *But soft, I pray you* – "But please stop, and tell me". Hotspur interrupts. He wants to bring them back to the subject of Richard's heir.

HOTSPUR

He will forsooth[75] have all my prisoners;
And when I urged the ransom once again
Of my wife's brother, then his cheek looked pale,   140
And on my face he turned an eye[76] of death,
Trembling[77] even at the name of Mortimer.

WORCESTER

I cannot blame him. Was not he proclaimed,[78]
By Richard that dead is, the next of blood?

NORTHUMBERLAND

He was, I heard the proclamation:
And then it was, when the unhappy[79] King   145
(Whose[80] wrongs in us God pardon!) did set forth
Upon his Irish expedition,
From whence he, intercepted,[81] did return
To be deposed[82] and shortly murderéd.   150

WORCESTER

And[83] for whose death we in the world's wide mouth
Live scandalised and foully spoken of.

HOTSPUR

But[84] soft, I pray you, did King Richard then
Proclaim my brother Edmund Mortimer
Heir to the crown?

NORTHUMBERLAND

He did. Myself did hear it.   155

HOTSPUR

Nay, then I cannot blame his cousin King
That wished him on the barren mountains starve.
But shall it be that you that set the crown

85 *forgetful man.* Hotspur accuses the King of having forgotten the help he received from the Percy family in seizing the throne.

86 *blot . . . subornation* – "disgrace of helping murder".

87 *a world of curses* – "general condemnation".

88 *base second means* – "mere scorned assistants".

89 *cords, the ladder . . . rather?* – "ropes (used to hang a man), the ladder (up which he mounted to the gallows) or more truly the hangman". Although Richard II was not hanged, Hotspur chooses these words to suggest that Henry used the Percys to perform dishonourable acts.

90 *the line . . . range* – "the degree and class in which you are placed". But *line* also suggests the hangman's *cords*, and *predicament* also suggests the sense "dangerous situation" as well as "class".

91 *subtle* – "scheming".

92 *gage them . . . behalf* – "pledge both nobility and power on behalf of an unjust cause".

93 *rose.* Richard was a member of the house of Lancaster, whose family sign was the red rose.

94 *canker,* used in two senses: (i) "an inferior rose"; (ii) "a spreading sore".

95 *fooled* – "deceived".

96 *these shames . . . underwent* – "you suffered these dishonours".

97 *yet time . . . honours* – "there is still time in which to win back the good reputations that you have lost".

98 *thoughts* – "opinions".

99 *disdained* – "full of disdain".

100 *answer* – "repay".

101 *Peace* – "Be silent".

102 *unclasp a secret book* – "reveal secret information".

103 *quick–conceiving discontents, quick* in two senses: (i) "rapid"; (ii) "alive"; *conceiving* in two senses also: (i) "understanding"; (ii) "bringing forth"; *discontents* – "thoughts and feelings of ill-will".

104 *I'll read . . . and dangerous* – "I will tell you of secret *(deep)* dangerous plans". The verb *read* continued the idea of unclasping a book.

105 *o'erwalk* – "walk across".

106 *On the unsteadfast . . . spear* – "on the unsteady *(unsteadfast)* foothold of a spear (a long staff with a metal point, used as a weapon)". Heroes in stories of the Middle Ages made a bridge by laying a spear across a river or stream.

Upon the head of this forgetful[85] man,
And for his sake wear the detested blot[86]   160
Of murderous subornation – shall it be
That you a world[87] of curses undergo,
Being the agents, or base[88] second means,
The cords,[89] the ladder, or the hangman rather?
– O, pardon me, that I descend so low,   165
To show the line[90] and the predicament
Wherein you range under this subtle[91] King!
Shall it for shame be spoken in these days,
Or fill up chronicles in time to come,
That men of your nobility and power   170
Did gage[92] them both in an unjust behalf
(As both of you, God pardon it, have done)
To put down Richard, that sweet lovely rose,[93]
And plant this thorn, this canker[94] Bolingbroke?
And shall it in more shame be further spoken,   175
That you are fooled,[95] discarded, and shook off
By him for whom these shames[96] ye underwent?
No, yet[97] time serves wherein you may redeem
Your banished honours, and restore yourselves
Into the good thoughts[98] of the world again: 180
Revenge the jeering and disdained[99] contempt
Of this proud King, who studies day and night
To answer[100] all the debt he owes to you,
Even with the bloody payment of your deaths.
Therefore, I say –

WORCESTER

Peace,[101] cousin, say no more.   185
And now I will unclasp[102] a secret book,
And to your quick-conceiving[103] discontents
I 'll read[104] you matter deep and dangerous,
As full of peril and adventurous spirit
As to o'er-walk[105] a current roaring loud   190
On[106] the unsteadfast footing of a spear.

107 *If he fall . . . swim* – "If he (a man
who enters upon such an adven-
ture) fails, we can say good-bye to
him. He must either fail *(sink)* or
succeed *(swim)*".

108 *Send danger . . . grapple*. The general
sense of these lines is: Provided
that honour can be won in any
place, then I will gladly encounter
danger there at any time.

109 *O the blood . . . hare* – "O it is more
exciting *(blood more stirs)* to begin
a very dangerous adventure than
a minor one". *Rouse* was a word
used of hunting a large animal,
start of a small one.

110 *By heaven . . . fellowship* (line 206).
In this speech Hotspur, who has
not heard Northumberland's remark to Worcester, is so excited
by his visions of honour, personified as a woman, that he does not
attend to the secrets Worcester
has promised to reveal. "I think
(methinks) it would be easy to
jump up to the moon and bring
honour back, or to dive into the
bottom of the sea and lift up
drowned honour by her hair
(locks), on condition that *(so)* the
man who thus wins her may use
(wear) all signs and titles of bravery
(her dignities) without having any
partner *(corrival)* to share them".
A *fathom-line*, a rope or chain with
a heavy weight at one end, is used
to measure the depth of the sea in
units of six feet (a *fathom*)

111 *out upon . . . fellowship* – "I have no
patience with *(out upon)* this sharing (of honour) with another".

112 *He apprehends . . . attend* – "He
seizes on a host of figures of speech
but not the real substance of what
he ought to hear". *Figures* also has
the sense "appearances" compared
with *form* ("substance").

113 *give me audience* – "please listen to
me", speaking to Hotspur.

114 *I cry you mercy* – "I ask your
pardon".

HOTSPUR

If he fall[107] in, good night, or sink, or swim!
Send[108] danger from the east unto the west,
So honour cross it from the north to south,
And let them grapple: O, the blood[109] more stirs   195
To rouse a lion than to start a hare!

NORTHUMBERLAND

Imagination of some great exploit
Drives him beyond the bounds of patience.

HOTSPUR

By heaven,[110] methinks it were an easy leap
To pluck bright honour from the pale-faced moon,   200
Or dive into the bottom of the deep
Where fathom-line could never touch the ground,
And pluck up drownéd honour by the locks,
So he that doth redeem her thence might wear
Without corrival all her dignities: 205
But out[111] upon this half-faced fellowship!

WORCESTER

He apprehends[112] a world of figures here,
But not the form of what he should attend.
Good cousin, give[113] me audience for a while.

HOTSPUR

I cry[114] you mercy.

WORCESTER

                    Those same noble Scots   210
That are your prisoners –

41

115 *if a Scot* – a play on the meaning of *scot* ("a small payment").

116 *by this hand*, an oath which has the sense of "by force".

117 *You start away . . . purposes* – "You follow your own thoughts and do not listen to my plans".

118 *that's flat* – "that's certain (and I shall not argue about it)".

119 *holla* – "call aloud".

120 *starling shall* – "starling which shall". A *starling* is a common bird which may be taught to speak.

121 *still* – "all the time".

122 *All studies . . . defy, Save* – "I here solemnly give up *(defy)* all plans except".

123 *pinch* – "distress".

124 *sword and buckler*, used scornfully to suggest a wild fellow who fought in taverns with these weapons.

125 *But that . . . mischance* – "except that I believe his father dislikes him and would be pleased if he had an accident *(mischance)*".

sword and buckler [124]

HOTSPUR

I 'll keep them all;
By God he shall not have a Scot of them;
No, if a Scot[115] would save his soul he shall not.
I 'll keep them, by this hand![116]

WORCESTER

You start[117] away,
And lend no ear unto my purposes.   215
Those prisoners you shall keep –

HOTSPUR

Nay, I will: that's flat![118]
He said he would not ransom Mortimer,
Forbade my tongue to speak of Mortimer,
But I will find him when he lies asleep,
And in his ear I 'll holla[119] "Mortimer!"   220
Nay, I 'll have a starling[120] shall be taught to speak
Nothing but "Mortimer", and give it him
To keep his anger still[121] in motion.

WORCESTER

Hear you, cousin, a word.

HOTSPUR

All studies[122] here I solemnly defy,   225
Save how to gall and pinch[123] this Bolingbroke;
And that same sword-and-buckler[124] Prince of Wales –
But[125] that I think his father loves him not
And would be glad he met with some mischance –
I would have him poisoned with a pot of ale!   230

WORCESTER

Farewell, kinsman; I'll talk to you
When you are better tempered to attend.

43

126 *wasp-stung* – "bad-tempered", as if stung by a flying insect *(wasp)*.

127 *Tying . . . thine own* – "listening only to yourself".

128 *Nettled* – "stung as if by nettles (wild plants that sting)".

129 *pismires* – "ants".

130 *politician*, not simply someone who knows much about state affairs, but "cunning schemer".

131 *mad-cap Duke*, Edmund Langley, Duke of York, fifth son of Edward III. He was not gay or wild *(mad-cap)*, but did prefer pleasure to politics.

132 *kept* – "lived".

133 *bowed my knee* – "formally acknowledged my loyalty". Shakespeare presents this action in *Richard II* II.iii.41-44.

134 *Ravenspurgh*, a harbour in Yorkshire where Henry Bolinbroke landed on his return from exile.

135 *Berkeley castle*, in Gloucestershire, a county in the west of England.

136 *candy deal* – "sickening amount". Candy, a sugary substance, used here to suggest contempt for Henry's display of friendship.

137 *Look when* – "Whenever".

138 *cozeners* – "cheaters", but also with a play on "cousin".

139 *I have done* – "I have finished (speaking)".

140 *to it again . . . leisure* – "continue with this stream of talk, we will wait until you are ready *(stay your leisure)*".

NORTHUMBERLAND

Why, what a wasp-stung[126] and impatient fool
Art thou to break into this woman's mood,
Tying[127] thine ear to no tongue but thine own!   235

HOTSPUR

Why, look you, I am whipped and scourged with rods,
Nettled,[128] and stung with pismires,[129] when I hear
Of this vile politician[130] Bolingbroke.
In Richard's time – what do you call the place?
A plague upon it, it is in Gloucestershire –   240
'T was where the mad-cap Duke[131] his uncle kept,[132]
His uncle York – where I first bowed[133] my knee
Unto this king of smiles, this Bolingbroke,
'Sblood, when you and he came back from Ravenspurgh.[134]

NORTHUMBERLAND

At Berkeley[135] castle.   245

HOTSPUR

You say true.
Why, what a candy[136] deal of courtesy
This fawning greyhound then did proffer me!
"Look[137] when his infant fortune came to age",
And "gentle Harry Percy", and "kind cousin".   250
O, the devil take such cozeners![138] – God forgive me!
Good uncle, tell your tale; I[139] have done.

WORCESTER

Nay, if you have not, to[140] it again,
We will stay your leisure.

HOTSPUR

I have done, i' faith.

45

141 *Then once . . . deliver them up* – "Then to return to the subject of your Scottish prisoners again. Let them go free".

142 *the Douglas' son. The* is used for the head of Scottish noble families. Douglas's son is mentioned first in I.i.70–71.

143 *your only . . . powers* – "your only means of raising an army *(powers)*".

144 *which, for . . . reasons* – "which (that is, the army) for various *(divers)* reasons".

145 *bosom* – "confidence".

146 *well-belov'd* – "loved well by all".

147 *bears hard* – "feels anger for".

148 *brother's death . . . Scroop.* Lord Scroop, Earl of Wiltshire, had been put to death at Bristol *(Bristow)* for opposing Bolingbroke's claim to the throne.

149 *I speak this not in estimation* – "what I say is not just a guess".

150 *And only stays . . . bring it on* – "and only waits until the right moment for bringing the plans to fulfilment".

151 *I smell it* – "I guess your secret meaning".

152 *Before . . . let'st slip* – "Before the hare *(the game)* is running you always let the hounds loose *(let'st slip)*", that is, Northumberland suggests that Hotspur is foolishly eager.

153 *cannot choose but be* – "cannot be otherwise than".

WORCESTER

Then[141] once more to your Scottish prisoners.   255
Deliver them up without their ransom straight,
And make the Douglas'[142] son your only[143] mean
For powers in Scotland, which,[144] for divers reasons
Which I shall send you written, be assured
Will easily be granted. [*To* NORTHUMBERLAND] You, my
     lord,   260
Your son in Scotland being thus employed,
Shall secretly into the bosom[145] creep
Of that same noble prelate well-belov'd,[146]
The Archbishop.

HOTSPUR

Of York, is it not?

WORCESTER

                    True, who bears[147] hard
His brother's[148] death at Bristow, the Lord Scroop.   265
I speak not this in estimation,[149]
As what I think might be, but what I know
Is ruminated, plotted, and set down,
And only stays[150] but to behold the face
Of that occasion that shall bring it on.   270

HOTSPUR

I smell[151] it. Upon my life it will do well!

NORTHUMBERLAND

Before[152] the game is afoot thou still let'st slip.

HOTSPUR

Why, it cannot[153] choose but be a noble plot;
And then the power of Scotland, and of York,
To join with Mortimer, ha?

154 *well aimed* – "well intended".

155 *And 't is . . . a head* – "And there is a very good reason to make us hasten to save our own lives *(heads)* by collecting together a military force *(head)*".

156 *For, bear . . . as we can* – "for, even if we behave as calmly as we can".

157 *pay us home* – "pay us his debt (by destroying us)".

158 *To make us strangers . . . love* – "to make us unused to kind looks from him", i.e. he no longer gives them the friendly looks they once had from him.

159 *No further . . . direct your course* – "Do not proceed any further in this scheme than I shall indicate in letters".

160 *When time . . . suddenly* – "When the right moment comes, which will be very soon *(suddenly)*".

161 *fashion* – "arrange".

162 *happily* – "with luck".

163 *To bear . . . uncertainty* – "to possess by armed might our fortunes which at the moment we hold uncertainly from the King".

164 *sport* – "public performance". Hotspur longs for the time of secrecy to pass quickly and be replaced by the loud activity of battles *(fields)*.

WORCESTER

And so they shall.   275

HOTSPUR

In faith it is exceedingly well[154] aimed.

WORCESTER

And[155] 't is no little reason bids us speed,
To save our heads by raising of a head;
For, bear[156] ourselves as even as we can,
The King will always think him in our debt,   280
And think we think ourselves unsatisfied,
Till he hath found a time to pay[157] us home.
And see already how he doth begin
To make us strangers[158] to his looks of love.

HOTSPUR

He does, he does; we'll be revenged on him.   285

WORCESTER

Cousin, farewell. No further[159] go in this
Than I by letters shall direct your course.
When[160] time is ripe, which will be suddenly,
I 'll steal to Glendower and Lord Mortimer,
Where you and Douglas and our powers at once,   290
As I will fashion[161] it, shall happily[162] meet
To bear[163] our fortunes in our own strong arms,
Which now we hold at much uncertainty.

NORTHUMBERLAND

Farewell, good brother; we shall thrive, I trust.

HOTSPUR

Uncle, adieu: O, let the hours be short
Till fields, and blows, and groans applaud our sport![164]

[*Exeunt*

(II.i) This scene takes place in the open courtyard of an inn at Rochester. It is early in the morning and still dark, but two carriers are already preparing for their day's journey. They complain to one another of the poor lodging they have had. Gadshill enters and questions them, but they distrust him and will not reveal their plans. They go to call some gentlemen who have a large amount of money with them and want the carriers' company for greater safety. Meanwhile the chamberlain of the inn helps Gadshill to plan his robbery by giving all the information he needs. The scene is one of darkness, secrecy and mistrust, made humorous by the simple suspicions of the carriers and Gadshill's smooth talk full of double meanings.

1 *Carrier*, a man whose trade is to transport goods from one place to another. The blunt unpolished speech of these carriers shows that they are rustics. For example they often omit the definite article "the" – *jade, peas, beans*, and it is not always possible to give an exact meaning to their words, for they sometimes repeat a popular saying or belief without considering its suitability.

2 *Heigh-ho*, an exclamation or perhaps a yawn.

3 *four by the day* – "four o'clock in the morning".

4 *Charles' wain*, a group of stars in the northern sky, now called "the Plough" or "the Great Bear". The carrier can tell the time by the position of the stars; when he sees Charles' wain in the sky above the inn's new chimney, he realises that he is late in setting out.

5 *ostler*, inn-servant who looked after horses.

6 *Anon* – "At once", used by inn-servants in reply to a call for service.

7 *Tom*, the ostler's name.

8 *beat Cut's saddle . . . point* – "beat Cut's saddle so that some of the soft filling *(flocks)* gets into the front part *(point)*". *Cut* is the name of the horse.

9 *jade*, horse of poor quality.

10 *wrung in the withers* – "rubbed sore on the ridge between the shoulders".

11 *out of all cess* – "excessively".

12 *Peas . . . the bots.* The carriers complain that the peas and beans supplied for the horses are very damp *(dank . . . as a dog)* and that to feed them on such mouldy food is the quickest *(next)* way to give them the *bots* (a disease caused by worms breeding inside horses).

13 *this house . . . upside down* – "this inn is completely disorganised".

14 *never joyed . . . oats* – "was never happy after the price of oats rose". Oats being an important part of a horse's diet, a rise in price could mean a lower profit for the ostler, who earned his living by caring for horses.

15 *it was the death of him* – "that (the increased price) killed him".

16 *this be the most villainous . . . fleas* – "this inn must contain more fleas than any other on the road to London".

17 *tench*, a fish marked with spots rather like flea-bites.

18 *ne'er a king christen . . . better bit* – "no Christian king could have been bitten more (by fleas)".

19 *since the first cock* – "since midnight" (when cocks were believed to crow for the beginning of the new day).

ACT TWO

Scene I. Rochester. An Inn Yard
Enter a Carrier[1] with a lantern in his hand.

FIRST CARRIER

Heigh-ho![2] An it be not four[3] by the day, I 'll be hanged;
Charles'[4] wain is over the new chimney, and yet our horse not
packed. What, ostler![5]

OSTLER (*calling from inside*)

Anon,[6] anon.

FIRST CARRIER

I prithee, Tom,[7] beat[8] Cut's saddle, put a few flocks in the   5
point; poor jade[9] is wrung[10] in the withers out[11] of all cess.

Enter another CARRIER

SECOND CARRIER

Peas[12] and beans are as dank here as a dog, and that is the next
way to give poor jades the bots: this[13] house is turned upside
down since Robin Ostler died.

FIRST CARRIER

Poor fellow never joyed[14] since the price of oats rose; it[15] was   10
the death of him.

SECOND CARRIER

I think this be the most villainous[16] house in all London road
for fleas; I am stung like a tench.[17]

FIRST CARRIER

Like a tench! By the mass, there is ne'er a king[18] christen could
be better bit than I have been since[19] the first cock.   15

20 *they will allow . . . chimney* – "the inn-keepers *(they)* will not provide us with a chamber-pot *(jordan)*, and so we urinate *(leak)* in the *(your)* fireplace". "Your" for "the" was common in unpolished speech.

21 *chamber-lye* – "urine".

22 *like a loach* – "excessively". A *loach* is a small fish. It was believed that fleas could breed on fish.

23 *What, ostler! Come away* – "Ostler! Come along".

24 *ràzes* – "roots". Ginger was imported from the East; two roots of ginger would therefore have been a valuable cargo.

25 *Charing Cross*, in the centre of London.

26 *pannier*, large basket carried by a pack-animal or at the back of a cart.

27 *hast thou . . . thy head* – "can't you see?" The carrier accuses the ostler of neglecting the carrier's goods.

28 *An 'twere . . . villain* – "If to break open your head *(pate)* would not be a good thing to do *(as good deed as drink)*, I am an absolute *(very)* villain". *As good deed as drink* was a popular saying.

29 *Hast no faith in thee?* – "Can't you be trusted?"

30 *what 's o'clock?* – "what time is it?"

31 *two o'clock*. Either the Carrier is deceiving Gadshill about the time, or his earlier guess (line 1) has now been corrected.

32 *soft* – "let us be cautious".

33 *I know . . . of that*, a popular saying – "You can't trick me as easily as that". The Carrier suspects that Gadshill is dishonest.

An Inn Yard

SECOND CARRIER

Why, they will allow[20] us ne'er a jordan, and then we leak in
your chimney; and your chamber-lye[21] breeds fleas like a
loach.[22]

FIRST CARRIER

What,[23] ostler! Come away, and be hanged, come away!

SECOND CARRIER

I have a gammon of bacon and two razes[24] of ginger to be   20
delivered as far as Charing[25] Cross.

FIRST CARRIER

God's body! The turkeys in my pannier[26] are quite starved.
What, ostler! A plague on thee, hast[27] thou never an eye in
thy head? canst not hear? An[28] 't were not as good deed as
drink to break the pate on thee, I am a very villain. Come, and 25
be hanged! Hast no faith[29] in thee?

Enter GADSHILL

GADSHILL

Good morrow, carriers; what 's[30] o'clock?

FIRST CARRIER

I think it be two[31] o'clock.

GADSHILL

I prithee lend me thy lantern to see my gelding in the stable.

FIRST CARRIER

Nay, by God, soft![32] I know[33] a trick worth two of that, i' faith. 30

GADSHILL

I pray thee lend me thine.

34 *Ay, when? Canst tell?* These words were commonly used to refuse a request mockingly or scornfully.

35 *I'll see thee hanged first,* a very blunt way of saying "no".

36 *Sirrah* – "Sir", used scornfully.

37 *mean to come* – "intend to arrive".

38 *Time enough* – "In good time".

39 *with a candle* – "by candle-light", i.e. after dark. This answer gives little information. The carriers suspect that Gadshill is a thief and do not want to tell him their plans.

40 *they will . . . company* – "they want travelling-companions". The gentlemen wish the carriers to go with them because a large group of travellers is less likely to be attacked by robbers than a small group.

41 *great charge* – "many valuable things to look after".

42 *Chamberlain,* servant who looked after the guests' rooms at an inn.

43 *At hand quoth pick-purse,* a popular saying. A *pick-purse* was a thief who stole from purses. The saying is a play on two meanings of *at hand*: (i) "here and ready" (the meaning that suits the Chamberlain), and (ii) "almost in my hand" (the meaning that suits a *pick-purse*).

44 *even as fair as* – "just the same as".

45 *thou variest . . . labouring* – "the difference between you and a pick-purse is no more than the difference between the man who gives instructions and the man who does the work", i.e. you too are a thief. Inn servants often helped robbers with information (*direction*) about travellers' wealth and their plans for their journey. They were therefore regarded with suspicion.

46 *thou layest the plot how* – "you make the plan of how (to perform the robbery)".

47 *Good morrow* – "Good morning".

48 *holds current* – "proves true".

49 *yesternight* – "last night".

50 *franklin in the Wild of Kent,* a landowning farmer in the Weald of Kent (a rich fertile district in southeast England).

51 *marks,* money worth thirteen shillings and fourpence in Shakespeare's day. Three hundred marks would be £200, a very large sum of money at that time.

52 *tell* – "count", or simply "say".

53 *abundance of charge* – "much to look after". An auditor being a royal officer, would have public money and goods in his care.

54 *God knows what* – "although I do not know exactly how much".

55 *eggs and butter,* a quickly prepared breakfast.

56 *will away presently* – "want to start their journey very soon". The thirty miles from Rochester to London was a long day's journey. By setting out very early, the travellers hope to avoid the dangers of approaching London after nightfall, but will have to risk going over Gad's Hill, just outside Rochester, in the dark hours before daylight. On Gad's Hill, Falstaff and the other robbers are already waiting, while Gadshill checks that there has been no alteration in the travellers' plans

SECOND CARRIER

Ay,[34] when? Canst tell? Lend me thy lantern, quoth he! Marry,
I 'll[35] see thee hanged first.

GADSHILL

Sirrah[36] carrier, what time do you mean[37] to come to London?

SECOND CARRIER

Time[38] enough to go to bed with a candle,[39] I warrant thee;   35
come, neighbour Mugs, we 'll call up the gentlemen; they[40]
will along with company, for they have great charge.[41]

[Exeunt CARRIERS

GADSHILL

What ho! Chamberlain![42]

Enter CHAMBERLAIN

CHAMBERLAIN

"At[43] hand, quoth pick-purse."

GADSHILL

That 's even[44] as fair as "At hand, quoth the chamberlain": for   40
thou variest[45] no more from picking of purses than giving
direction doth from labouring; thou layest[46] the plot how.

CHAMBERLAIN

Good[47] morrow, master Gadshill. It holds[48] current that I told
you yesternight:[49] there's a franklin[50] in the Wild of Kent hath
brought three hundred marks[51] with him in gold; I heard him   45
tell[52] it to one of his company last night at supper – a kind of
auditor, one that hath abundance[53] of charge too, God[54] knows
what. They are up already, and call for eggs[55] and butter – they
will[56] away presently.

55

57 *Saint Nicholas' clerks,* The spirit of Saint Nicholas was believed to watch over scholars *(clerks)* and travellers, including thieves on the road. So *Saint Nicholas' clerks* was used as a fine-sounding title for "roadside robbers".

58 *I 'll give thee this neck* – "I 'll let you cut my throat".

59 *I 'll none of it* – "I don't want to have anything to do with it"

60 *keep that . . . hangman* – "keep your neck for it will be needed when you are hanged (as a robber)".

61 *thou worshippest Saint Nicholas* – "you are a roadside thief".

62 *as truly . . . falsehood may.* The Chamberlain suggests that as Gadshill is a dishonest man *(a man of falsehood)* he cannot worship *truly,* i.e. "honestly".

63 *What talkest thou* – "Why do you talk".

64 *I 'll make . . . gallows* – "I shall be one of two bodies hanging from the gallows" – the other being fat Falstaff.

65 *old Sir John* – "Falstaff".

66 *no starveling* – "not a thin, starving little man"; in fact, a very large fat one.

67 *Tut,* a sound indicating impatience.

68 *Troyans,* companions in drinking and law-breaking. Gadshill is thinking chiefly of Prince Hal, but is careful not to mention his name or reveal too much of the truth. Very little information is contained in the rush of unusual words and double meanings with which he continues his speech.

69 *the which* – "who".

70 *to do . . . some grace* – "to honour (with their presence) the profession (of robbery)".

71 *for their . . . all whole* – "for the sake of their own reputation arrange that nobody should be punished".

72 *foot-landrakers* – "robbers who roam *(rake)* on foot".

73 *long-staff sixpenny strikers.* Some thieves used a long staff to knock or pull their victim from his horse; they would then steal *(strike)* his money, however little. Gadshill scorns such mere "sixpenny" robbers.

74 *mad mustachio purple-hued malt worms* – "uncontrollable, fierce, red-faced habitual drinkers". A *mustachio* (now spelt "moustache"), a growth of hair on the upper lip, was considered a sign of manly courage or fierceness. The noun *mustachio* is here used as an adjective. *Malt* is a substance used in making strong drink and so *malt worm* was used to mean "habitual heavy drinker".

75 *nobility,* a play on two meanings: (i) "men of high rank"; (ii) "men of good character".

76 *tranquillity* – "peace of mind". As Gadshill used the word in a list of types of people, the Chamberlain would probably suppose that it was a mock-word formed to match *nobility* and meant "people who live at peace with themselves".

77 *burgomasters* – "high officials of a town".

78 *oneyers.* The exact meaning of this word is not known. It may be made up by Gadshill to make "great ones" sound even greater; or it may be a word used by lawyers to mean "officers who have some of the king's money in their possession".

79 *can hold in* – "are self-disciplined". Three possible meanings of *hold in* are blended: (i) "keep secrets"; (ii) "remain with the group"; (iii) "stick to their purpose" (of robbery).

80 *strike,* used in two senses: (i) "steal"; (ii) "hit".

(notes continued on page 58)

56

GADSHILL

Sirrah, if they meet not with Saint[57] Nicholas' clerks, I 'll give 50
thee this neck.[58]

CHAMBERLAIN

No, I 'll none[59] of it. I pray thee keep[60] that for the hangman,
for I know thou worshippest[61] Saint Nicholas, as truly[62] as a
man of falsehood may.

GADSHILL

What[63] talkest thou to me of the hangman? If I hang, I 'll[64]   55
make a fat pair of gallows: for if I hang, old[65] Sir John hangs
with me, and thou knowest he is no starveling.[66] Tut,[67] there
are other Troyans[68] that thou dreamest not of, the which[69] for
sport sake are content to do[70] the profession some grace, that
would (if matters should be looked into) for[71] their own credit   60
sake make all whole. I am joined with no foot-landrakers,[72] no
long-staff[73] sixpenny strikers, none of these mad[74] mustachio
purple-hued maltworms, but with nobility[75] and tranquillity,[76]
burgomasters[77] and great oneyers,[78] such as can hold[79] in, such
as will strike[80] sooner than speak, and speak[81] sooner than   65
drink, and drink sooner than pray – and yet, 'zounds, I lie, for
they pray continually to their saint the commonwealth,[82] or
rather not pray to her, but prey on her, for they ride up and
down on her, and make her their boots.[83]

CHAMBERLAIN

What, the commonwealth their boots? Will[84] she hold out   70
water in foul way?

GADSHILL

She will, she will, justice hath liquored[85] her; we steal as in
a castle,[86] cock-sure; we have the receipt[87] of fern-seed, we
walk invisible.

88 *beholding* – "indebted".

89 *our purchase* – "the goods we steal".

90 *true* – "honest".

91 *Nay, rather . . . thief*. The Chamberlain says he would be more likely to believe Gadshill if he claimed to be speaking not as an honest man but as what he is, namely, a false thief. He could also expect a share of stolen goods from a thief, but not from an honest man.

92 *Go to* – "Never mind that", a phrase of mild protest.

(notes continued from page 56)

81 *speak*, used in two senses: (i) "talk"; (ii) "hit". Thieves used a private language of words and phrases to refer to the details of their robberies so that others could not understand.

82 *commonwealth*, used in two senses: (i) "the state"; (ii) "abundant wealth", which the thieves would like.

83 *boots*, used in two senses: (i) "stolen goods"; (ii) "boots".

84 *Will she . . . foul way*, used in two senses: (i) "Will the boots keep the feet dry on a muddy road?" (ii) "Will the country protect you if you get into trouble?"

93 *homo*, Latin for "man". Gadshill claims to be a true (honest) man. The Chamberlain says he is a thief. Gadshill then tries to prove that he has a right to be called truly a man by referring to a well-known passage in a school grammar book. The passage explains the difference between a "proper" and a "common" noun and gives *homo* as an example of a "common" noun. Gadshill misapplies the example to support his claim.

94 *muddy* – "stupid".

85 *liquored*, used in two senses: (i) "greased (the boots) to keep out water"; (ii) "made her (the *commonwealth*) drunk (and so unable to see the robbers)".

86 *as in a castle, cock-sure* – "in complete and perfect safety".

87 *the receipt of fern-seed* – "information about how to use fern-seed". Fern-seed was believed to become visible once a year on Midsummer Eve (June 23) and if gathered then, with the right magical words, would make those who carried it invisible.

(II.ii) In this scene the Prince and his friends have met in darkness and secrecy on Gad's Hill, ready to attack and rob their victims. While waiting, they mock Falstaff as he stumbles about breathlessly searching for his horse, which has been hidden by Poins. Gadshill arrives with news that the rich travellers are approaching. Leaving Falstaff, Peto, Bardolph and Gadshill to carry out the main robbery, the Prince and Poins quickly disguise themselves. These two then attack Falstaff and the other thieves, who run away, leaving the stolen money behind.

1 *frets . . . velvet* – "worries". *Velvet* was sometimes stiffened with gum but this caused the threads to "become loose", a second meaning of *fret*.

2 *close* – "hidden".

3 *fat-kidneyed*, the kidneys are surrounded by fat; the phrase fits Falstaff's size.

CHAMBERLAIN

Nay, by my faith, I think you are more beholding[88] to the   75
night than to fern-seed for your walking invisible.

GADSHILL

Give me thy hand– thou shalt have a share in our purchase,[89]
as I am a true[90] man.

CHAMBERLAIN

Nay,[91] rather let me have it as you are a false thief.

GADSHILL

Go[92] to, *homo*[93] is a common name to all men. Bid the ostler   80
bring my gelding out of the stable. Farewell, you muddy[94]
knave.

[*Exeunt*

Scene II. Gad's Hill. The Highway
Enter PRINCE, POINS, *and* PETO

POINS

Come, shelter, shelter! I have removed Falstaff's horse, and he
frets[1] like a gummed velvet.

PRINCE

Stand close![2]   [*They hide*

Enter FALSTAFF

FALSTAFF

Poins! Poins, and be hanged! Poins!

PRINCE (*coming forward*)

Peace, ye fat-kidneyed[3] rascal, What a brawling dost thou keep!   5

FALSTAFF

Where 's Poins, Hal?

59

4 *is walked* – "has walked".

5 *I am accursed* – "I am a fool (I have brought a curse upon myself)".

6 *but . . . squier* – "only *(but)* four feet by the measuring rod *(squier)*".

7 *break my wind* – "become breathless".

8 *I doubt . . . that rogue* – "I do not doubt that I shall die a good Christian death, in spite of all this, if I escape *(scape)* hanging for killing Poins", i.e. "if I can restrain myself from murdering him".

9 *this two and twenty year* – "during the last twenty-two years".

10 *medicines* – "drugs with magical power".

11 *It could not be else* – "There is no other explanation for my loving him".

12 *I'll starve ere* – "I'd rather die than".

13 *rob a foot further*, in two senses: (i) "do any more robbing"; (ii) "go any further towards the robbery on foot", i.e. without a horse.

14 *as good . . . true man* – "a very good thing to do, to become an honest man".

15 *veriest varlet* – "most complete villain".

16 *Eight yards . . . with me* – "For me to walk eight yards over uneven ground is (as hard a journey as) seventy miles (to other men)".

17 *Whew,* the sound of a whistle.

18 *list* – "listen".

19 *colt* – "trick".

20 *colted . . . uncolted*, a play on the two meanings of *colt*: (i) "a young horse"; (ii) "to trick". Falstaff is *colted* ("tricked") by being *uncolted* ("having his horse stolen").

PRINCE

He is walked[4] up to the top of the hill; I 'll go seek him.

[*He hides*

FALSTAFF

I am accursed[5] to rob in that thief's company; the rascal hath removed my horse and tied him I know not where. If I travel but[6] four foot by the squier further afoot, I shall break[7] my 10 wind. Well, I doubt[8] not but to die a fair death for all this, if I scape hanging for killing that rogue. I have forsworn his company hourly any time this[9] two and twenty years, and yet I am bewitched with the rogue's company. If the rascal have not given me medicines[10] to make me love him, I 'll be hanged. 15 It[11] could not be else, I have drunk medicines. Poins! Hal! A plague upon you both! Bardolph! Peto! I 'll starve[12] ere I 'll rob[13] a foot further – an 't were not as good[14] a deed as drink to turn true man, and to leave these rogues, I am the veriest[15] varlet that ever chewed with a tooth. Eight[16] yards of uneven 20 ground is threescore and ten miles afoot with me, and the stony-hearted villains know it well enough. A plague upon it when thieves cannot be true one to another! [*They whistle*] Whew![17] A plague upon you all; give me my horse, you rogues, give me my horse and be hanged! 25

PRINCE *(coming forward)*

Peace, ye fat guts; lie down, lay thine ear close to the ground, and list[18] if thou canst hear the tread of travellers.

FALSTAFF

Have you any levers to lift me up again, being down? 'Sblood, I 'll not bear my own flesh so far afoot again for all the coin in thy father's exchequer. What a plague mean ye to colt[19] me 30 thus?

PRINCE

Thou liest, thou art not colted,[20] thou art uncolted.

61

21 *shall I . . . ostler.* The Prince purposely misunderstands Falstaff's *help me to my horse* ("help me to find my horse") and pretends that Falstaff has ordered him like a servant to bring the horse.

22 *heir-apparent,* a play on two meanings: (i) "heir-apparent"; (ii) "here apparent", i.e. now visible here.

23 *ta'en, I'll peach for this* — "arrested, I'll inform on you for this (taking my horse)".

24 *An I . . . poison* (line 38) – "May I be poisoned by a drink of sack if I do not have common songs made up about you all and sung to unpleasant tunes". Falstaff is threatening to shame them publicly. Ballads attacking public figures were common in Shakespeare's time.

25 *so forward* – "so far advanced".

26 *setter,* man who brings information to thieves.

27 *Case ye . . . vizards* – "Cover your clothes, put on your masks".

28 *make us all* – "make us all rich".

29 *To be hanged.* Falstaff takes Gadshill's *make* to mean "cause" and suggests there is enough money to cause them all to be hanged for stealing.

shall[21] *I be your ostler?*

FALSTAFF

I prithee, good Prince Hal, help me to my horse, good king's
son.

PRINCE

Out, ye rogue, shall[21] I be your ostler?   35

FALSTAFF

Hang thyself in thine own heir-apparent[22] garters! If I be
ta'en,[23] I'll peach for this. An[24] I have not ballads made on you
all, and sung to filthy tunes, let a cup of sack be my poison –
when a jest is so forward,[25] and afoot too! I hate it.

Enter GADSHILL *and* BARDOLPH

GADSHILL

Stand!   40

FALSTAFF

So I do, against my will.

POINS

O, 't is our setter,[26] I know his voice. [*Coming forward with*
PETO] Bardolph, what news?

BARDOLPH

Case[27] ye, case ye, on with your vizards; there 's money of the
King's coming down the hill; 't is going to the King's exchequer.   45

FALSTAFF

You lie, ye rogue, 't is going to the King's tavern.

GADSHILL

There 's enough to make[28] us all.

FALSTAFF

To be hanged.[29]

30 *front* – "attack from in front".

31 *if they . . . on us* – "if they escape *(scape)* from the fight with you, then they will meet *(light on)* us". In fact, the Prince uses this plan as an excuse for Poins and himself to leave their companions.

32 *Some* – "About".

33 *What, a coward* – "What, are you a coward?" The light-hearted references to Falstaff's supposed cowardice prepare the audience for the comic scene when Falstaff runs away and for his comic self-defence in Act II, Scene iv.

34 *Paunch,* a playful name referring to Falstaff's fatness. A *paunch* is a fat stomach.

35 *Gaunt.* Hal's grandfather took his name from the town of Gaunt (now spelt Ghent). Falstaff denies that he is *gaunt* in its usual sense of "very thin".

36 *stand fast,* i.e. "do not run away"

37 *hard by* – "close by".

38 *stand close* – "remain hidden".

PRINCE

Sirs, you four shall front[30] them in the narrow lane; Ned Poins
and I will walk lower – if they scape[31] from your encounter,   50
then they light on us.

PETO

How many be there of them?

GADSHILL

Some[32] eight or ten.

FALSTAFF

'Zounds, will they not rob us?

PRINCE

What,[33] a coward, Sir John Paunch?[34]   55

FALSTAFF

Indeed, I am not John of Gaunt[35] your grandfather, but yet no
coward, Hal.

PRINCE

Well, we leave that to the proof.

POINS

Sirrah Jack, thy horse stands behind the hedge; when thou needst
him, there thou shalt find him. Farewell, and stand[36] fast.   60

FALSTAFF

Now cannot I strike him, if I should be hanged.

PRINCE

Ned, where are our disguises?

POINS

Here, hard[37] by, stand[38] close.

[*Exeunt* PRINCE *and* POINS

39 *Now, my masters . . . business* –
"Now, my friends *(masters)* may
we each have a share *(dole)* of good
luck, say I – let every man do his
part".

40 *down with them* – "knock them
down".

41 *whoreson* – "son of an immoral
woman", used as a term of contempt.

42 *caterpillars*. Because *caterpillars* eat
greedily and destroy crops, the
word was often used contemptu-
ously of thieves and others who
grew rich at honest workers' expense. Here and in his next speech,
Falstaff enjoys describing the travellers in terms more suited to himself.

43 *bacon-fed* – "fat".

44 *us youth*. Falstaff numbers himself
among the young people.

45 *undone* – "ruined".

46 *gorbellied* – "fat-stomached".

47 *chuffs*, a term of contempt for un-
generous rich people.

48 *your store* – "the main bulk of your
possessions".

49 *bacons* – "fat men".

50 *young men must live*, an excuse for
the robbery. Falstaff, still calling
himself a young man, claims that
the young need to take money from
their elders in order to keep themselves alive.

51 *grandjurors*, wealthy and respectable
men, chosen to assist the judge of a
high court.

52 *jure*, an invented word taken from
the middle of *grandjurors*. The
general sense of *We 'll jure ye* is
"We 'll make you wish you were
not so important".

53 *argument* – "a subject of talk".

FALSTAFF

Now, my masters,[39] happy man be his dole, say I – every man
to his business.   65

Enter the TRAVELLERS

FIRST TRAVELLER

Come, neighbour, the boy shall lead our horses down the hill;
we 'll walk afoot awhile and ease our legs.

THIEVES

Stand!

SECOND TRAVELLER

Jesus bless us!

FALSTAFF

Strike, down[40] with them, cut the villains' throats! Ah, whore-   70
son[41] caterpillars,[42] bacon-fed[43] knaves, they hate us[44] youth!
Down with them, fleece them!

FIRST TRAVELLER

O, we are undone,[45] both we and ours for ever!

FALSTAFF

Hang ye, gorbellied[46] knaves, are ye undone? No, ye fat
chuffs,[47] I would your store[48] were here! On, bacons,[49] on!   75
What, ye knaves! young[50] men must live. You are grandjurors,[51] are ye? We 'll jure[52] ye, faith.
                                    [*They rob them and bind them. Exeunt*

Re-enter the PRINCE *and* POINS, *disguised*

PRINCE

The thieves have bound the true men; now could thou and I rob
the thieves, and go merrily to London, it would be argument[53]
for a week, laughter for a month, and a good jest for ever.   80

54 *Stand close* – "Remain hidden"
55 *masters* – "friends".
56 *share . . . before day* – "share out (the money) and then ride our horses away before sunrise".
57 *arrant* – "complete".
58 *no equity stirring* – "no justice in the world".
59 *wild duck,* a very timid bird.
60 *possessed with fear* – "very much afraid".

61 *Each takes his fellow for an officer.* Because the frightened thieves are separated in the darkness, each one, hearing another, assumes that the noise is made by an officer of the law.
62 *lards* – "drops grease on", a reference to Falstaff's fatness.
63 *Were 't not for laughing* – "If the thought of him did not make me laugh so much".

POINS

Stand[54] close, I hear them coming.

[*They hide*

Enter the Thieves again

FALSTAFF

Come, my masters,[55] let us share,[56] and then to horse before
day; an the Prince and Poins be not two arrant[57] cowards
there 's no equity[58] stirring; there 's no more valour in that
Poins than in a wild[59] duck.   85

[*As they are sharing the* PRINCE *and* POINS *set upon them*

PRINCE

Your money!

POINS

Villains!

[*They all run away, and* FALSTAFF *after a blow
or two runs away too, leaving the booty behind.*

PRINCE

Got with much ease. Now merrily to horse:
The thieves are all scattered, and possessed[60] with fear
So strongly that they dare not meet each other;   90
Each[61] takes his fellow for an officer!
Away, good Ned – Falstaff sweats to death,
And lards[62] the lean earth as he walks along.
Were 't[63] not for laughing, I should pity him.

POINS

How the fat rogue roared.   95

[*Exeunt*

(II.iii) This scene opens with Hotspur reading a letter from an unnamed writer who tells him that his rebellion is badly planned and ill-timed. Instead of considering the truth of this warning, Hotspur becomes angry, calls the writer a coward and a possible traitor, and impatiently hastens his preparations for war. Lady Percy enters, and asks her husband to explain his recent restlessness, for he has been talking in his sleep about guns and fighting. Hotspur will not give a direct answer but, promising that Lady Percy shall follow him, rides off to join his fellow-rebels.

1 *letter*. This is a reply from an un-named person whom Hotspur has asked to join the rebellion.

2 *there*, with Hotspur and the rebels.

3 *house*, a play on two meanings: (i) "noble family"; (ii) "dwelling place".

4 *lord fool* – "foolish lord".

5 *uncertain . . . too light*. Hotspur fails to recognise the truth of what he reads: that his friends are not to be trusted *(uncertain)*, the time is badly chosen *(unsorted)*, and the whole rebellion is too weak *(light)*.

6 *Say you so* – "Do you say so".

7 *hind*. Hotspur expresses his scorn by calling the writer of the letter a mere "rustic servant" *(hind)*.

8 *What a lack-brain is this* – "What a fool this (letter-writer) is".

9 *laid* – "planned".

10 *frosty-spirited* – "timid"; he seems *frosty* to the "fiery" Hotspur.

11 *my Lord of York*, Richard Scroop, Archbishop of York.

12 *brain* – "knock out his brains".

13 *Is there not*, Hotspur counts up those who have promised to support his rebellion. Of the six only two supported him at the battle of Shrewsbury – Worcester and Douglas.

14 *letters . . . in arms* – "letters (promising) to meet me fully prepared for battle".

15 *pagan* – "lacking faith (in Hotspur's plan)".

16 *an infidel* – "one who does not believe (that he will succeed)".

17 *very sincerity* – "perfect honesty". Hotspur uses scornfully the words with which the letter-writer himself might explain his betrayal of the plot.

18 *cold heart* – "cowardice", the real reason why the cautious letter-writer might reveal Hotspur's plot to the King.

19 *will he to . . . proceedings* – "he will go to the King and reveal *(lay open)* all our plans *(proceedings)*".

20 *I could . . . an action* (line 28) – "I (am so angry with myself that I) would like to divide myself into two people, each beating the other for attempting to persuade *(moving)* such a weak cowardly person". Hotspur compares the writer of the letter to a dish of weak thin milk from which the cream has been removed.

21 *within these two hours* – "in less than two hours".

Scene III. Warkworth. The Castle.
Enter HOTSPUR *alone, reading a letter.*[1]

HOTSPUR

"But, for mine own part, my lord, I could be well contented to be there,[2] in respect of the love I bear your house." He could be contented: why is he not then? In respect of the love he bears our house: he shows in this, he loves his own barn better than he loves our house.[3] Let me see some more. "The purpose you undertake is dangerous" – Why, that 's certain; 't is dangerous to take a cold, to sleep, to drink; but I tell you, my lord[4] fool, out of this nettle, danger, we pluck this flower, safety. "The purpose you undertake is dangerous, the friends you have named uncertain,[5] the time itself unsorted, and your whole plot too light, for the counterpoise of so great an opposition." Say[6] you so, say you so? I say unto you again, you are a shallow cowardly hind,[7] and you lie. What a lack-brain[8] is this! By the Lord, our plot is a good plot, as ever was laid,[9] our friends true and constant: a good plot, good friends, and full of expectation: an excellent plot, very good friends; what a frosty-spirited[10] rogue is this! Why, my Lord[11] of York commends the plot and the general course of the action. 'Zounds, an I were by this rascal, I could brain[12] him with his lady's fan. Is[13] there not my father, my uncle, and myself? Lord Edmund Mortimer, my Lord of York, and Owen Glendower? Is there not, besides, the Douglas? Have I not all their letters[14] to meet me in arms by the ninth of the next month; and are they not some of them set forward already? What a pagan[15] rascal is this, an infidel![16] Ha! You shall see now in very sincerity[17] of fear and cold[18] heart will[19] he to the King, and lay open all our proceedings! O, I could[20] divide myself and go to buffets, for moving such a dish of skim milk with so honourable an action! Hang him, let him tell the King. We are prepared. I will set forward tonight.

Enter LADY PERCY

How now, Kate? I must leave you within[21] these two hours.

22 *stomach* – "appetite".

23 *golden*. Hotspur's sleep had formerly been peaceful and therefore of great value.

24 *bend thine eyes upon* – "look at".

25 *lost . . . thy cheeks* – "become pale".

26 *my treasures . . . of thee* – "the pleasure of your company which I value *(treasure)* and which I (as your wife) have a right to enjoy".

27 *thick-eyed* – "dull-eyed".

28 *curst* – "bad-tempered".

29 *faint* – "light".

30 *And heard . . . heady fight* (line 56). Hotspur's passionate interest in the rebellion is shown clearly in this account of his broken sleep; all the words he uses are military terms.

31 *iron*, "hard, fierce".

32 *terms of manage* – "words of command".

33 *field* – "battle-place".

34 *sallies*, rushings out to attack.

35 *palisadoes*, fences of stakes.

36 *frontiers*, battle positions facing the enemy.

37 *basilisks*, powerful heavy guns.

38 *culverin*, heavy guns, not as large as basilisks.

39 *currents* – "movements".

40 *heady* – "quick-moving".

41 *late-disturbéd* – "recently disturbed".

42 *hest* – "command".

43 *heavy* – "important and serious".

44 *in hand* – "in preparation".

45 *else he loves me not* – "if he does not tell me *(else)*, he does not love me".

46 *packet* – "parcel (of letters)".

the field 33

LADY PERCY

O my good lord, why are you thus alone?
For what offence have I this fortnight been
A banished woman from my Harry's bed?
Tell me, sweet lord, what 'is't that takes from thee
Thy stomach,[22] pleasure, and thy golden[23] sleep?   35
Why dost thou bend[24] thine eyes upon the earth,
And start so often when thou sit'st alone?
Why hast thou lost[25] the fresh blood in thy cheeks,
And given my treasures[26] and my rights of thee
To thick-eyed[27] musing, and curst[28] melancholy?   40
In thy faint[29] slumbers I by thee have watched,
And heard[30] thee murmur tales of iron[31] wars,
Speak terms[32] of manage to thy bounding steed,
Cry "Courage! To the field!"[33] And thou hast talked
Of sallies,[34] and retires, of trenches, tents,   45
Of palisadoes,[35] frontiers,[36] parapets,
Of basilisks,[37] of cannon, culverin,[38]
Of prisoners' ransom, and of soldiers slain,
And all the currents[39] of a heady[40] fight.
Thy spirit within thee hath been so at war,   50
And thus hath so bestirred thee in thy sleep,
That beads of sweat have stood upon thy brow
Like bubbles in a late-disturbéd[41] stream,
And in thy face strange motions have appeared,
Such as we see when men restrain their breath   55
On some great sudden hest.[42] O, what portents are these?
Some heavy[43] business hath my lord in[44] hand,
And I must know it, else[45] he loves me not.

HOTSPUR

What ho!

Enter a Servant

Is Gilliams with the packet[46] gone?

47 *even now* – "only a short time ago".
48 *back* – "jump on the (horse's) back".
49 *Esperance* – "Hope". *Espérance*, a French word, was the war-cry of the Percy family.
50 *What is it carries you away* – "What reason takes you away"; *carries you away* can also mean "excites you". Hotspur pretends to misunderstand the question completely.

51 *such a deal . . . tossed with* – "such an excitable temper *(spleen)* as you are moved by *(tossed with)*".

SERVANT

He is, my lord, an hour ago.   60

HOTSPUR

Hath Butler brought those horses from the sheriff?

SERVANT

One horse, my lord, he brought even[47] now.

HOTSPUR

What horse? A roan, a crop-ear is it not?

SERVANT

It is, my lord.

HOTSPUR

　　　　　That roan shall be my throne.
Well, I will back[48] him straight: O Esperance![49]   65
Bid Butler lead him forth into the park.

　　　　　　　　　　　　　　　　　[*Exit* Servant

LADY PERCY

But hear you, my lord.

HOTSPUR

What sayest thou, my lady?

LADY PERCY

What[50] is it carries you away?

HOTSPUR

Why, my horse, my love, my horse.   70

LADY PERCY

Out, you mad-headed ape!
A weasel hath not such[51] a deal of spleen

75

52 *doth stir about his title*. Again Shakespeare confuses the two Mortimers.
It was not Kate's brother, but her
nephew who was the heir to the
throne (compare I.iii.144).

53 *line* – "strengthen".

54 *afoot* – "on foot". Hotspur is pretending to misunderstand his wife's
meaning; *go* (line 77) could mean
"walk".

55 *paraquito* – "parrot". This brightly
coloured bird can be taught to
speak but not to understand.

56 *An if* – "if".

57 *Love*. Hotspur suddenly returns to
Lady Percy's words at line 65.

58 *play with mammets* – "play with
dolls", but *play* also suggests
"swordplay", "fighting with
swords'.

59 *tilt with lips* – "kiss"; *tilt*, which
usually means "fight", shows that
Hotspur is still thinking of war and
it follows on from *play*.

60 *cracked crowns*, a play on two meanings: (i) "broken heads"; (ii)
"cracked coins".

61 *pass them current*, continues the two
meanings: (i) "cause them (broken
heads) to be common"; (ii) "use
them (cracked coins) as if they were
good ones".

62 *God's me*, an oath.

63 *What wouldst . . . with me?* – "What
do you want?"

64 *a-horseback* – "on my horse's back".

65 *nor reason whereabout* – "nor think
about where I may be".

As you are tossed with. In faith,
I 'll know your business, Harry, that I will.
I fear my brother Mortimer doth[52] stir   75
About his title, and hath sent for you
To line[53] his enterprise. But if you go –

HOTSPUR

So far afoot,[54] I shall be weary, love.

LADY PERCY

Come, come, you paraquito,[55] answer me
Directly unto this question that I ask;   80
In faith, I 'll break thy little finger, Harry,
An[56] if thou wilt not tell me all things true.

HOTSPUR

Away,
Away, you trifler! Love[57] I love thee not,
I care not for thee, Kate; this is no world   85
To play with mammets,[58] and to tilt[59] with lips;
We must have bloody noses, and cracked[60] crowns,
And pass[61] them current too. God's me![62] my horse!
What say'st thou, Kate? What[63] wouldst thou have with me?

LADY PERCY

Do you not love me? Do you not indeed?   90
Well, do not then, for since you love me not
I will not love myself. Do you not love me?
Nay, tell me if you speak in jest or no.

HOTSPUR

Come, wilt thou see me ride?
And when I am a-horseback[64] I will swear   95
I love thee infinitely. But hark you, Kate,
I must not have you henceforth question me
Whither I go, nor[65] reason whereabout:

66 *I know you . . . Percy's wife* – "I
know that you are wise but, as
your husband, I know the limits of
your wisdom".

67 *closer* – "more secret".

68 *so far will I trust thee,* i.e. not at all.
She will not tell Hotspur's secrets
because he is not going to let her
know them.

69 *of force* – "of necessity".

(II.iv) In this scene the Prince and his companions meet at the Boar's
Head tavern after the double robbery. We first see Hal and Poins making
fun of the dull-brained servant, Francis. Then the Prince thinks of acting
a play about Hotspur, but this plan is interrupted by the arrival of Falstaff. The latter accuses the Prince of running away and boastfully
describes his own fight against enemies, whose numbers he continually
increases. When the Prince and Poins reveal that they themselves were
his only opponents, Falstaff asserts that he had recognised them but ran
away for fear of hurting the Prince.

News of Hotspur's rebellion arrives, but despite the serious political
situation, Hal and Falstaff act out a play in which, at first, Falstaff represents Henry IV. As King he censures the Prince and praises Falstaff. But
then the two exchange parts, and Hal, speaking as King, rejects Falstaff
and banishes him. An officer of the law comes to arrest the thieves. The
Prince talks to him while Falstaff hides and falls asleep. As the scene ends,
Hal promises to pay back the stolen money and to make Falstaff a
captain of foot-soldiers in the coming war.

1 *fat* – "hot, airless".

2 *lend me . . . to laugh* – "help me to
carry out a joke".

3 *loggerheads . . . hogsheads.* The Prince
has been with stupid people *(loggerheads)*, i.e. the inn-servants, among
large barrels *(hogsheads)* in the cellar
of the tavern.

4 *I have sounded . . . humility* – "I have
reached the very lowest level of
humility". To sound the base string
usually means to play the lowest
notes on a stringed instrument.

Whither I must, I must; and, to conclude,
This evening must I leave you, gentle Kate.   100
I know[66] you wise, but yet no farther wise
Than Harry Percy's wife; constant you are,
But yet a woman; and for secrecy
No lady closer,[67] for I well believe
Thou wilt not utter what thou dost not know;   110
And so[68] far will I trust thee, gentle Kate.

LADY PERCY

How? so far?

HOTSPUR

Not an inch further. But hark you, Kate,
Whither I go, thither shall you go too:
Today will I set forth, tomorrow you.   115
Will this content you, Kate?

LADY PERCY

It must, of force.[69]

[*Exeunt*

Scene IV. Eastcheap. The Boar's Head Tavern.
Enter PRINCE *and* POINS.

PRINCE

Ned, prithee come out of that fat[1] room, and lend[2] me thy hand
to laugh a little.

POINS

Where hast been, Hal?

PRINCE

With three or four loggerheads,[3] amongst three or fourscore
hogsheads. I have sounded[4] the very base-string of humility.   5

5 *sworn brother*, one who has taken an oath to share all his goods and fortune with another according to the rules of knighthood. Hal uses the phrase jokingly.

6 *leash of drawers*, three men who serve drinks in the tavern; a *leash* is a set of three, usually three hounds.

7 *christen names*, first names.

8 *They take . . . salvation* – "They are prepared to swear by their hope of heaven".

9 *Prince of Wales*, Hal's title as eldest son of the King of England and Wales.

10 *king of courtesy*. Though only a prince, and not a king, Hal is the King in respect of courtesy, i.e. the most courteous of all men.

11 *flatly* – "without hesitation".

12 *Jack* – "fellow", the common name *Jack* used scornfully.

13 *Corinthian*, a gay but wild fellow, so called from the Greek city of Corinth, once famous for its luxury and vice.

14 *good boy* – "one of us".

15 *Eastcheap*, the part of London where the Board's Head Tavern stood.

16 *dyeing scarlet*. Those who drink too deeply become very red-faced.

17 *breathe in your watering* – "pause for breath in the middle of drinking".

18 *Play it off* – "Drink up".

19 *so good a proficient* – "so very expert".

20 *in his own language* – i.e. using the terms he had just learnt, which were commonly used by heavy drinkers among such people as tinkers.

21 *thou hast . . . action*. The Prince playfully describes his meeting with the drawers as if it were a military encounter *(action)*.

22 *sugar*. This was sold in taverns to sweeten the wine called "sack".

23 *clapped* – "thrust".

24 *underskinker* – "drink-server's assistant".

25 *Anon* – "Now". *Anon* was the word used by servants in reply to a call for service.

26 *Score . . . bastard* – "Write down the cost of a pint of sweet wine *(bastard)*". As the drawer served a drink he called out to the tavernkeeper to make a note of it, so that an account could be presented.

27 *Half-moon*. The rooms of an inn or tavern were given such names as *Half-moon* and *Pomgarnet* (see note 34) from the sign painted on the door. (Many people could not read.)

28 *drive* – "pass".

29 *some by-room* – "a room near to this one".

30 *to what end* – "for what purpose".

31 *do thou never leave* – "do not cease".

32 *that his . . . but "Anon"*. Hal's trick is to ask questions to which Francis's "Anon" ("now, at once") will be a funny answer.

33 *precedent* – "example".

Sirrah, I am sworn[5] brother to a leash[6] of drawers, and can call
them all by their christen[7] names, as Tom, Dick, and Francis.
They take[8] it already upon their salvation, that though I be but
Prince[9] of Wales, yet I am the king[10] of courtesy, and tell me
flatly[11] I am no proud Jack[12] like Falstaff, but a Corinthian,[13]   10
a lad of mettle, a good[14] boy (by the Lord, so they call me!),
and when I am King of England I shall command all the good
lads in Eastcheap.[15] They call drinking deep "dyeing[16] scarlet",
and when you breathe[17] in your watering they cry "Hem!"
and bid you "Play[18] it off!" To conclude, I am so good a   15
proficient[19] in one quarter of an hour that I can drink with any
tinker in his own language[20] during my life. I tell thee, Ned,
thou[21] hast lost much honour that thou wert not with me in
this action; but, sweet Ned – to sweeten which name of Ned I
give thee this penny-worth of sugar,[22] clapped[23] even now into   20
my hand by an underskinker,[24] one that never spake other
English in his life than "Eight shillings and sixpence", and "You
are welcome", with this shrill addition, "Anon,[25] anon, sir!
Score[26] a pint of bastard in the Half-moon",[27] or so. But Ned,
to drive[28] away the time till Falstaff come, I prithee do thou   25
stand in some by-room,[29] while I question my puny drawer to
what end[30] he gave me the sugar, and do[31] thou never leave
calling "Francis!", that[32] his tale to me may be nothing but
"Anon". Step aside, and I'll show thee a precedent.[33]

[*Exit* POINS

POINS *(calling from inside)*

Francis!   30

PRINCE

Thou art perfect.

POINS *(inside)*

Francis!

Enter FRANCIS, *a Drawer*

81

34 *Pomgarnet*, the name of a room at the tavern: "Pomegranate", a fruit.

35 *serve*. Francis was an apprentice, i.e. a boy who had agreed to serve his master for seven years while learning his trade.

36 *five years, and . . . to*, i.e. more than five years of apprenticeship remain to be served.

37 *lease*, usually the period of time for which a house is rented, here used of the remaining period of an apprenticeship.

38 *so valiant . . . heels* – "so brave as to turn your back on your apprenticeship contract *(indenture)* and run away from it".

39 *I'll be . . . books*, a reference to the custom of seeing that a man tells the truth by making him place his right hand on a Bible while speaking.

40 *I could . . . my heart* – "I would like to do it (i.e. to run away)".

Half-moon [27]   *Pomgarnet* [34]

FRANCIS

Anon, anon, sir. Look down into the Pomgarnet,[34] Ralph.

PRINCE

Come hither, Francis.

FRANCIS

My lord?   35

PRINCE

How long hast thou to serve,[35] Francis?

FRANCIS

Forsooth, five[36] years, and as much as to –

POINS *(inside)*

Francis!

FRANCIS

Anon, anon, sir.

PRINCE

Five years! By'r lady, a long lease[37] for the clinking of pewter;   40
but Francis, darest thou be so valiant[38] as to play the coward
with thy indenture, and show it a fair pair of heels, and run
from it?

FRANCIS

O Lord, sir, I 'll[39] be sworn upon all the books in England, I[40]
could find in my heart –   45

POINS *(inside)*

Francis!

FRANCIS

Anon, sir.

41 *a-Thursday* – "next Thursday".

PRINCE

How old art thou, Francis?

FRANCIS

Let me see, about Michaelmas next I shall be –

POINS *(inside)*

Francis!   50

FRANCIS

Anon, sir – pray stay a little, my lord.

PRINCE

Nay but hark you, Francis, for the sugar thou gavest me: 'twas
a pennyworth, was 't not?

FRANCIS

O Lord, I would it had been two!

PRINCE

I will give thee for it a thousand pound – ask me when thou   55
wilt, and thou shalt have it.

POINS *(inside)*

Francis!

FRANCIS

Anon, anon.

PRINCE

Anon, Francis? No, Francis, but tomorrow, Francis; or,
Francis, a-Thursday;⁴¹ or indeed, Francis, when thou wilt.   60
But Francis!

FRANCIS

My lord?

42 *rob.* By running away Francis would *rob* the inn-keeper of his service as an apprentice. From this point the Prince is trying to puzzle Francis, first with scraps of description of an inn-keeper in his fine clothes (lines 63 to 65) and then with mere nonsense (lines 67–69).

43 *not-pated* – "with short hair".

44 *agate-ring* – "(wearing) a ring with an agate stone in it".

45 *puke-stocking* – "(wearing) stockings of dark-coloured wool".

46 *caddis,* a coarse material for making garters.

47 *Spanish pouch,* a purse of Spanish leather.

48 *Why then . . . so much* (line 69). The general meaning of these lines is: You are not suited to anything better than the life you now lead. Although, the separate phrases refer to things that Francis understands, such as the wine *brown bastard* and sugar from *Barbary,* the whole speech is intended to perplex him.

49 *Vintner* – "Wine-seller", the tavern-keeper.

50 *Look to* – "Serve".

PRINCE

Wilt thou rob[42] this leather-jerkin, crystal-button, not-pated,[43] agate-ring,[44] puke-stocking,[45] caddis-garter,[46] smooth-tongue Spanish[47] pouch?

65

FRANCIS

O Lord, sir, who do you mean?

PRINCE

Why[48] then your brown bastard is your only drink: for look you, Francis, your white canvas doublet will sully. In Barbary, sir, it cannot come to so much.

FRANCIS

What, sir?

70

POINS (inside)

Francis!

PRINCE

Away, you rogue, dost thou not hear them call?
> [*They both call him; the* Drawer *stands amazed,
> not knowing which way to go*

Enter VINTNER[49]

VINTNER

What, standest thou still and hearest such a calling? Look[50] to the guests within. [*Exit* FRANCIS] My lord, old Sir John with half-a-dozen more are at the door – shall I let them in?

75

PRINCE

Let them alone awhile, and then open the door.
> [*Exit* VINTNER

Poins!

Re-enter POINS

51 *Anon.* Poins enters imitating Francis.

52 *what cunning match have you made* – "what clever trick have you played?"

53 *what's the issue* – "what success have you had?"

54 *humours* – "moods". The Prince is feeling very gay, willing to share any mood expressed during the whole history of mankind, though he later excepts Hotspur's passion for killing.

55 *Adam*, the first man, in the Bible story.

56 *pupil age* – "youth". At midnight the new day is just beginning and is therefore "young".

57 *What's o'clock* – "What time is it?"

58 *his eloquence . . . reckoning* – "his speech-making is limited to adding up".

59 *Some fourteen* – "About fourteen". Hal here imitates Hotspur. The audience has seen an example of Hotspur's delay in answering a question in the preceding scene.

60 *play* – "act". Informal plays often took place in inns.

61 *that damned brawn*, Falstaff.

62 *Dame Mortimer*, Hotspur's wife, who was Edmund Mortimer's sister.

63 *Rivo*, a cry used by drunkards.

64 *Ribs*, used with Tallow ("fat") and brawn ("flesh") to suggest Falstaff's fleshly bulk.

a dagger[79] *of lath*

88

POINS

Anon,[51] anon, sir.

PRINCE

Sirrah, Falstaff and the rest of the thieves are at the door; shall
we be merry?   80

POINS

As merry as crickets, my lad; but hark ye, what[52] cunning
match have you made with this jest of the drawer? come,
what 's[53] the issue?

PRINCE

I am now of all humours[54] that have showed themselves
humours since the old days of goodman Adam[55] to the pupil[56]   85
age of this present twelve o'clock at midnight.

Re-enter FRANCIS

What 's[57] o'clock, Francis?

FRANCIS

Anon, anon, sir.

[*Exit*

PRINCE

That ever this fellow should have fewer words than a parrot,
and yet the son of a woman! His industry is up-stairs and down-   90
stairs, his eloquence the parcel[58] of a reckoning. I am not yet of
Percy's mind, the Hotspur of the north, he that kills me some
six or seven dozen of Scots at a breakfast, washes his hands, and
says to his wife, "Fie upon this quiet life, I want work." "O my
sweet Harry," says she, "how many hast thou killed today?"   95
"Give my roan horse a drench," says he, and answers, "Some[59]
fourteen," an hour after, "a trifle, a trifle." I prithee call in Falstaff; I 'll play[60] Percy, and that damned[61] brawn shall play
Dame[62] Mortimer his wife. *Rivo!*[63] says the drunkard: call in
Ribs,[64] call in Tallow.   100

65 *a vengeance*. Falstaff's words are intended for Poins and the Prince, because they failed to help in the robbery. He does not yet directly call the Prince a coward, but speaks as if to himself, thus causing them to question him.

66 *sew nether-stocks . . . foot them too*. Falstaff vows, insincerely, to give up robbery and take up honest work; to make stockings *(nether-stocks)* and mend holes in the feet of them *(foot them)*.

67 *Titan kiss . . . that compound* (line 109). Before Falstaff's round red shining face his cup of sack disappears (as he drinks it) just as a dish of butter melts before the hot sun's loving kiss. *Titan*, the Greek Sungod.

68 *lime in this sack*. Lime was sometimes added to wine to improve its flavour and appearance, but the lime was popularly believed to cause disease.

69 *old Jack*, Falstaff is talking to himself, but intends the Prince to hear.

70 *good manhood* – "bravery".

71 *be not forgot* – "has not been forgotten".

72 *shotten herring*, a fish *(herring)* after releasing its eggs; such a fish is very thin.

73 *lives* – "live".

74 *one of them*, Falstaff himself.

75 *God help the while*, "may God improve the habits of this present age". An exclamation rather than a prayer.

76 *I would* – "I wish".

77 *weaver*. Many weavers sang as they worked, and those who were Puritans would sing only psalms. In this speech Falstaff speaks of *villainous man* as if he himself were a religious man speaking of "sinful" man.

78 *wool-sack*, a reference to Falstaff's being fat and shapeless.

79 *dagger of lath*. In older plays, the Vice or wicked character was armed with a short sword of thin wood *(dagger of lath)* with which he beat the other players. Falstaff is like the Vice in being both a tempter and a source of laughter.

80 *afore* – "before".

90

Enter FALSTAFF, GADSHILL, BARDOLPH, *and* PETO;
followed by FRANCIS, *with wine*

POINS

Welcome, Jack, where hast thou been?

FALSTAFF

A plague of all cowards, I say, and a vengeance[65] too, marry
and amen! Give me a cup of sack, boy. Ere I lead this life long,
I 'll sew nether-stocks,[66] and mend them and foot them too. A
plague of all cowards! Give me a cup of sack, rogue; is there 105
no virtue extant?   [*He drinks*

PRINCE

Didst thou never see Titan[67] kiss a dish of butter (pitiful-
hearted Titan!) that melted at the sweet tale of the sun's? If thou
didst, then behold that compound.

FALSTAFF

You rogue, here 's lime[68] in this sack too: there is nothing but 110
roguery to be found in villainous man, yet a coward is worse
than a cup of sack with lime in it. A villainous coward! Go thy
ways, old[69] Jack, die when thou wilt – if manhood, good[70]
manhood, be[71] not forgot upon the face of the earth, then am I
a shotten[72] herring: there lives[73] not three good men unhanged 115
in England, and one[74] of them is fat, and grows old, God[75] help
the while; a bad world I say. I would[76] I were a weaver;[77] I
could sing psalms, or anything. A plague of all cowards, I say still.

PRINCE

How now, wool-sack,[78] what mutter you?

FALSTAFF

A king's son! If I do not beat thee out of thy kingdom with a 120
dagger[79] of lath and drive all of thy subjects afore[80] thee like

91

81 *I'll never . . . face more* – "I'll shave off my beard".

82 *whoreson*, an insulting term – "son of unmarried woman".

83 *I'll see . . . coward*. A curse, which is also a refusal to call Poins (or Hal) a coward directly, though Falstaff continues his mockery about running away.

84 *backing* – "supporting". Falstaff has passed from one meaning of *back* ("move away") to another ("support").

85 *I am a rogue . . . today* – "You can call me a rogue if you can prove I have had a drink today".

86 *scarce* – "scarcely".

87 *All is one for that* – "That is not important".

88 *There be . . . morning* – "Four of us who are here have taken *(ta'en)* a thousand pounds this morning".

a flock of wild geese, I 'll never[81] wear hair on my face more.
You, Prince of Wales!

PRINCE

Why, you whoreson[82] round man, what 's the matter?

FALSTAFF

Are not you a coward? Answer me to that – and Poins there? 125

POINS

'Zounds, ye fat paunch, and ye call me coward by the Lord I 'll
stab thee.

FALSTAFF

I call thee coward? I 'll see[83] thee damned ere I call thee coward,
but I would give a thousand pound I could run as fast as thou
canst. You are straight enough in the shoulders, you care not 130
who sees your back. Call you that backing[84] of your friends? A
plague upon such backing; give me them that will face me!
Give me a cup of sack. I am a rogue[85] if I drunk today.

PRINCE

O villain! Thy lips are scarce[86] wiped since thou drunkest last.

FALSTAFF

All is one[87] for that. [*He drinks*] A plague of all cowards, still 135
say I.

PRINCE

What 's the matter?

FALSTAFF

What 's the matter? There[88] be four of us here have ta'en a
thousand pound this day morning.

93

89 *at half-sword*, fighting very close to the enemy, only half a sword's length away. Having, as a good story-teller, raised his audience's expectations, Falstaff now begins his account of his own glorious bravery.

90 *scaped* – "escaped".

91 *hose,* a trouser-like garment reaching from the waist to thigh or knee.

92 *ecce signum* – "see the sign", a Latin phrase which was in common use.

93 *dealt,* dealt blows with a sword.

94 *all would not do* – "all my efforts (to protect our stolen money) were in vain".

95 *sons of darkness,* Falstaff uses a phrase from the Bible (1 *Thessalonians* 5 v.5).

PRINCE

Where is it, Jack, where is it? 140

FALSTAFF

Where is it? Taken from us it is – a hundred upon poor four
of us.

PRINCE

What, a hundred, man?

FALSTAFF

I am a rogue if I were not at half-sword[89] with a dozen of them
two hours together. I have scaped[90] by miracle. I am eight times 145
thrust through the doublet, four through the hose,[91] my buckler
cut through and through, my sword hacked like a handsaw –
[*He shows his sword*] *ecce signum!*[92] I never dealt[93] better since I
was a man: all[94] would not do. A plague of all cowards! Let
them speak – if they speak more or less than truth, they are 150
villains, and the sons[95] of darkness.

PRINCE

Speak, sirs, how was it?

GADSHILL

We four set upon some dozen –

FALSTAFF

Sixteen at least, my lord.

GADSHILL

And bound them. 155

PETO

No, no, they were not bound.

95

96 *Ebrew*, i.e. Hebrew – "Jewish". *Jew* was used as a term of contempt. The general sense of the speech is "if you find that what I say is untrue, then you can call me a Jew".

97 *sharing*, i.e. sharing the stolen goods.

98 *other*, plural "others", i.e. some more of Falstaff's imaginary opponents.

99 *I am a bunch of radish*. Falstaff suggests that to doubt his word is as foolish as to believe he is a bunch of thin roots (*radish*).

100 *peppered* – "killed", by filling full of holes.

101 *paid* – "killed".

102 *ward*, a defensive move in sword-fighting.

103 *my point* – "the point of my sword".

104 *Four*. They have increased from the original two. The rapid increase of numbers in Falstaff's account is the chief source of amusement for Poins and the Prince.

FALSTAFF

You rogue, they were bound, every man of them, or I am a
Jew else: an Ebrew[96] Jew.

GADSHILL

As we were sharing,[97] some six or seven fresh men set upon us –

FALSTAFF

And unbound the rest, and then come in the other.[98]   160

PRINCE

What, fought you with them all?

FALSTAFF

All? I know not what you call all, but if I fought not with fifty
of them, I am a bunch[99] of radish: if there were not two or three
and fifty upon poor old Jack, then am I no two-legged creature.

PRINCE

Pray God you have not murdered some of them.   165

FALSTAFF

Nay, that 's past praying for: I have peppered[100] two of them.
Two I am sure I have paid,[101] two rogues in buckram suits. I
tell thee what, Hal, if I tell thee a lie, spit in my face, call me
horse. Thou knowest my old ward[102] – here I lay, and thus I
bore my point.[103] Four[104] rogues in buckram let drive at me –   170

PRINCE

What, four? Thou saidst but two even now.

FALSTAFF

Four, Hal, I told thee four.

POINS

Ay, ay, he said four.

105 *afront* – "from the front".
106 *mainly* – "violently".
107 *ado* – "fuss".
108 *target*, small round shield.
109 *these hilts* – "this hilt". The hilt (handle) of a sword, being shaped something like the Christian cross, was used as a sign of truth.

110 *points,* used in two senses: (i) Falstaff means "points of swords"; (ii) Poins thinks of another sense, "straps" for tying hose (lower garment) to an upper garment.

FALSTAFF

These four came all afront[105] and mainly[106] thrust at me; I
made me no more ado,[107] but took all their seven points in my 175
target,[108] thus!

PRINCE

Seven? Why, there were but four even now.

FALSTAFF

In buckram?

POINS

Ay, four, in buckram suits.

FALSTAFF

Seven, by these hilts,[109] or I am a villain else.   180

PRINCE

Prithee let him alone, we shall have more anon.

FALSTAFF

Dost thou hear me, Hal?

PRINCE

Ay, and mark thee too, Jack.

FALSTAFF

Do so, for it is worth the listening to. These nine in buckram
that I told thee of –   185

PRINCE

So, two more already.

FALSTAFF

Their[110] points being broken –

111 *give me ground* – "retreat a few steps before me".

112 *came in . . . paid* – "I not only attacked with my sword, but moved forward on foot and very quickly *(with a thought)* defeated *(paid)* seven of the eleven men.

113 *Kendal green*, green cloth often worn by poor people and favoured by robbers.

114 *at my back . . . at me* – "behind me and thrust (their swords) at me".

115 *begets* – "is father of".

116 *clay-brained guts* – "stupid fat fellow".

117 *knotty-pated* – "wooden-headed", i.e. foolish.

118 *tallow-catch* – "bundle of fat".

119 *upon compulsion* – "being compelled".

120 *strappado . . . racks*, forms of torture.

100

POINS

Down fell their hose.

FALSTAFF

Began to give[111] me ground; but I followed me close, came[112]
in, foot and hand, and, with a thought, seven of the eleven I 190
paid.

PRINCE

O monstrous! Eleven buckram men grown out of two!

FALSTAFF

But as the devil would have it, three misbegotten knaves in
Kendal[113] green came at my back[114] and let drive at me, for it
was so dark, Hal, that thou couldst not see thy hand. 195

PRINCE

These lies are like their father that begets[115] them, gross as a
mountain, open, palpable. Why, thou clay-brained[116] guts, thou
knotty-pated[117] fool, thou whoreson obscene greasy tallow-
catch[118] –

FALSTAFF

What, art thou mad? art thou mad? Is not the truth the truth? 200

PRINCE

Why, how couldst thou know these men in Kendal green when
it was so dark thou couldst not see thy hand? Come, tell us your
reason. What sayest thou to this?

POINS

Come, your reason, Jack, your reason.

FALSTAFF

What, upon compulsion?[119] 'Zounds, and I were at the strap- 205
pado[120] or all the racks in the world, I would not tell you on

101

121 *reasons*, spoken as if it were "raisins" (dried fruit), and so comparable with blackberries.

122 *this sin*, i.e. the sin of appearing to believe Falstaff.

123 *sanguine* now means "hopeful". In Shakespeare's day it described one of the four recognised types of character. A sanguine man was red-faced, fat, generous and merry, as well as hopeful.

124 *bed-presser*. This, like the following *horse-back-breaker*, is a reference to Falstaff's heavy weight.

125 *'Sblood*. The oath introduces Falstaff's list of insulting comparisons with Hal. All the items given are long and thin.

126 *starveling* – "thin hungry little fellow".

127 *neat* – "cow".

128 *bull's-pizzle*, whip made of dried bull's skin.

129 *stock-fish*, dried fish.

130 *tailor's-yard*, measuring stick, one yard long.

131 *bow-case*, long narrow cover for a soldier's bow.

132 *standing tuck*, stiff, thin sword.

133 *breathe* – "pause for breath".

134 *to it* – "begin".

135 *in base comparisons* – "in likening me to low things".

136 *and bound* – "and (you) bound".

137 *put you down* – "reveal your dishonesty".

138 *out-faced you* – "drove you away".

139 *guts* – "bowels". Here used scornfully of Falstaff's bulk.

140 *slave* – "vile, base fellow".

141 *starting-hole* – "hiding place".

compulsion. Give you a reason on compulsion? If reasons[121] were as plentiful as blackberries, I would give no man a reason upon compulsion, I.

PRINCE

I 'll be no longer guilty of this sin.[122] This sanguine[123] coward, 210 this bed-presser,[124] this horse-back-breaker, this huge hill of flesh –

FALSTAFF

'Sblood,[125] you starveling,[126] you eel-skin, you dried neat's[127]-tongue, you bull's-pizzle,[128] you stock-fish[129] – O for breath to utter what is like thee! – you tailor's-yard,[130] you sheath, 215 you bow-case,[131] you vile standing[132] tuck!

PRINCE

Well, breathe[133] awhile, and then to it[134] again, and when thou hast tired thyself in base comparisons,[135] hear me speak but this.

POINS

Mark, Jack.   220

PRINCE

We saw you four set on four, and bound[136] them and were masters of their wealth – mark now how a plain tale shall put[137] you down. Then did we two set on you four, and, with a word, out-faced[138] you from your prize, and have it, yea, and can show it you here in the house; and Falstaff, you carried your 225 guts[139] away as nimbly, with as quick dexterity, and roared for mercy, and still run and roared, as ever I heard bull-calf. What a slave[140] art thou to hack thy sword as thou hast done, and then say it was in fight! What trick, what device, what starting-hole[141] canst thou now find out, to hide thee from this open 230 and apparent shame?

103

142 *I knew ye.* Falstaff shows his usual skill in talking himself out of a difficult situation.

143 *turn upon,* attack one to whom loyalty is due.

144 *Hercules,* a very strong brave man in ancient Greek stories.

145 *the lion . . . true prince.* This was an old belief.

146 *Hostess, clap to* – "Mistress Quickly, shut".

147 *Watch* – "Remain awake". *Watch and pray,* in the Bible, *Matthew* 26 v.41 means "remain awake in order to pray", but Falstaff separates the two acts and suggests a wakeful night of enjoyment.

148 *pray tomorrow* can be taken in either of two senses: (i) *pray* – "say prayers"; (ii) *prey* – "rob".

149 *argument* – "subject" (of the play). Extempore plays were often acted in taverns. Hal had earlier suggested a play about Hotspur and his wife (line 98).

150 *O Jesu,* Mistress Quickly's favourite exclamation.

151 *would speak* – "who wants to speak".

152 *a royal man. Royal* and *noble* (*nobleman* at line 249) were not only titles of rank but also coins, a noble being worth 6s. 8d., a royal 10s. Playing on these meanings, the Prince suggests that a nobleman, given a little more money becomes *a royal man.*

royal 152

POINS

Come, let 's hear, Jack, what trick hast thou now?

FALSTAFF

By the Lord, I knew[142] ye as well as he that made ye. Why, hear
you, my masters, was it for me to kill the heir-apparent? Should
I turn[143] upon the true prince? Why, thou knowest I am as 235
valiant as Hercules[144] – but beware instinct: the lion[145] will not
touch the true prince. Instinct is a great matter; I was now a
coward on instinct. I shall think the better of myself, and thee,
during my life – I for a valiant lion, and thou for a true prince.
But by the Lord, lads, I am glad you have the money. Hostess,[146] 240
clap to the doors! Watch[147] tonight, pray[148] tomorrow! – Gal-
lants, lads, boys, hearts of gold, all the titles of good fellowship
come to you! What, shall we be merry, shall we have a play
extempore?

PRINCE

Content, and the argument[149] shall be thy running away. 245

FALSTAFF

Ah, no more of that, Hal, and thou lovest me.

Enter HOSTESS

HOSTESS

O Jesu,[150] my lord the Prince!

PRINCE

How now, my lady the hostess, what sayest thou to me?

HOSTESS

Marry, my lord, there is a nobleman of the court at door
would[151] speak with you: he says he comes from your father. 250

PRINCE

Give him as much as will make him a royal[152] man, and send
him back again to my mother.

105

153 *What doth gravity* - "What is a serious old man *(gravity)* doing".

154 *you fought fair . . . true prince.* The Prince is mocking Falstaff's excuses.

155 *he would swear . . . fight* - "he would make you believe that his sword was damaged in the fight even if he had to swear until his lies drove all truth out of England".

156 *the like* - "the same".

157 *spear-grass,* a kind of grass with sharp, cutting edges.

158 *beslubber* - "stain".

FALSTAFF

What manner of man is he?

HOSTESS

An old man.

FALSTAFF

What[153] doth gravity out of his bed at midnight? Shall I give 255
him his answer?

PRINCE

Prithee do, Jack.

FALSTAFF

Faith, and I 'll send him packing.

[*Exit*

PRINCE

Now, sirs: by 'r lady, you[154] fought fair, so did you, Peto,
so did you, Bardolph; you are lions too, you ran away upon 260
instinct, you will not touch the true prince, no, fie!

BARDOLPH

Faith, I ran when I saw others run.

PRINCE

Faith, tell me now in earnest, how came Falstaff's sword so
hacked?

PETO

Why, he hacked it with his dagger, and said he would swear[155] 265
truth out of England but he would make you believe it was
done in fight, and persuaded us to do the like.[156]

BARDOLPH

Yea, and to tickle our noses with spear-grass,[157] to make them
bleed, and then to beslubber[158] our garments with it, and swear

107

159 *I did . . . years before* – "I did something which I have not done for
seven years, i.e. *blushed,* became
red-faced from shame".

160 *taken with the manner* has two
meanings: (i) "caught in the act
(of stealing)"; (ii) "pleased with
the habit (of drinking)".

161 *instinct.* The Prince is still joking
about Falstaff's earlier excuse (lines
236–8).

162 *meteors . . . exhalations.* Bardolph
points to his shining red face which
he likens to *meteors* and *exhalations.*

163 *Hot livers, and cold purses.* The
Prince suggests that Bardolph's
redness of face is caused by too
much strong drink, which was
believed to heat the liver; and as
drink cost money, it caused the
drinker's purse to be empty *(cold).*

164 *Choler* now means only "anger".
In Shakespeare's day it indicated a
type of person. A choleric man
was red-faced, hot-tempered,
fierce, active, and fearless. Bardolph is trying to prove that he
cannot be a coward because his red
face shows that he is a brave
choleric character.

165 *taken* – "understood".

166 *halter. Choler* is pronounced like
"collar" and this leads to the idea
of a *halter,* i.e. Bardolph will be
hanged if caught *(taken).*

167 *lean . . . bombast.* The Prince mocks
Falstaff's fatness; *bombast* – "stuffing".

168 *about thy years* – "about as old as
you".

169 *not an eagle's talon* – "not as wide
as the curved nails *(talons)* on an
eagle's foot".

it was the blood of true men. I did[159] that I did not this seven 270
year before, I blushed to hear his monstrous devices.

PRINCE

O villain, thou stolest a cup of sack eighteen years ago, and wert
taken[160] with the manner; and ever since thou hast blushed
extempore. Thou hadst fire and sword on thy side, and yet thou
ranst away – what instinct[161] hadst thou for it? 275

BARDOLPH

My lord, do you see these meteors?[162] do you behold these
exhalations?

PRINCE

I do.

BARDOLPH

What think you they portend?

PRINCE

Hot livers,[163] and cold purses. 280

BARDOLPH

Choler,[164] my lord, if rightly taken.[165]

PRINCE

No, if rightly taken, halter.[166]

Re-enter FALSTAFF

Here comes lean[167] Jack, here comes bare-bone. How now, my
sweet creature of bombast, how long is 't ago, Jack, since thou
sawest thine own knee? 285

FALSTAFF

My own knee? When I was about[168] thy years, Hal, I was not an
eagle's[169] talon in the waist; I could have crept into any alderman's thumb-ring. A plague of sighing and grief, it blows a man

109

170 *abroad* – "publicly discussed".

171 *Percy*, Hotspur.

172 *he of Wales*, Owen Glendower. Falstaff gives a scornful account of Glendower's imaginary acts, and mocks his claim to have power over evil spirits (compare III.i. 11-15).

173 *gave Amamon the bastinado* – "gave Amamon (Amaimon, a chief devil) a beating on the soles of the feet *(bastinado)*".

174 *made Lucifer cuckold. Lucifer* is the name of the chief devil; *cuckold*, one whose wife is unfaithful. The whole phrase means "won the love of Lucifer's wife".

175 *swore . . . Welsh hook*. Swearing by the hilt of a sword, which was shaped like the Christian cross, was common practice. Glendower's Welsh hook, although also a weapon, had no cross-shaped part, and was therefore not a sign of truth; *liegeman* – "servant".

176 *son-in-law Mortimer*, Edmund Mortimer, who had married Glendower's daughter.

177 *old Northumberland*, Hotspur's father, the Earl of Northumberland.

178 *Scot of Scots* – "thoroughly Scottish Scot".

179 *a-horseback* – "on horseback".

180 *hit it* – "got it right".

181 *never*, i.e. never "hit", in the sense of "kill".

182 *mettle* – "courage" is pronounced like "metal". Both meanings are present here. A man of courage does not run away. Good metal does not melt *(run)*.

183 *cuckoo*, the name of the bird used to mean "foolish repeater of sounds".

184 *but afoot . . . budge a foot* – "but (when fighting) on the ground *(afoot)* he will not move one foot-length out of position".

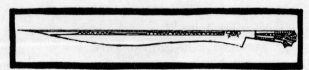

upon the cross of a Welsh hook [175]

up like a bladder. There 's villainous news abroad:[170] here was
Sir John Bracy from your father; you must to the court in the 290
morning. That same mad fellow of the north, Percy,[171] and he[172]
of Wales that gave Amamon[173] the bastinado, and made[174]
Lucifer cuckold, and swore[175] the devil his true liegeman upon
the cross of a Welsh hook – what a plague call you him?

POINS

O, Glendower. 295

FALSTAFF

Owen, Owen, the same; and his son-in-law[176] Mortimer, and
old Northumberland,[177] and that sprightly Scot[178] of Scots,
Douglas, that runs a-horseback[179] up a hill perpendicular –

PRINCE

He that rides at high speed and with his pistol kills a sparrow
flying. 300

FALSTAFF

You have hit[180] it.

PRINCE

So did he never[181] the sparrow.

FALSTAFF

Well, that rascal hath good mettle[182] in him, he will not run.

PRINCE

Why, what a rascal art thou then, to praise him so for running!

FALSTAFF

A-horseback, ye cuckoo,[183] but afoot[184] he will not budge a foot. 305

PRINCE

Yes, Jack, upon instinct.

185 *there,* with the rebels.

186 *blue-caps* – "Scots".

187 *is stolen away* – "has gone away secretly (to join the rebels)".

188 *you may buy land now.* If the rebels succeeded, they would divide the land among themselves and their supporters (see III.i.66–75), and the rights of the present owners would be ignored. Many people there-fore.offered their land for sale very cheaply rather than risk losing it altogether.

189 *it is like . . . hundreds* (line 313) – "it is likely if the coming summer is hot and if this civil war con-tinues *(holds)* that it will be as easy and as cheap to win the favours of girls as to buy shoe-nails *(hob-nails)*".

190 *good trading that way* – "good luck with the girls".

191 *horrible afeard* – "very much afraid".

192 *could the world* – "would it be possible to".

193 *thrill* – "run cold", i.e. Do you not feel fear running through you?

194 *Not a whit* – "Not the smallest bit".

195 *horribly chid* – "severely scolded".

196 *Content* – "All right; I agree".

FALSTAFF

I grant ye, upon instinct: well, he is there[185] too, and one Mordake, and a thousand blue-caps[186] more. Worcester is stolen[187]
away tonight; thy father's beard is turned white with the news;
you[188] may buy land now as cheap as stinking mackerel.   310

PRINCE

Why then, it is like,[189] if there come a hot June and this civil
buffeting hold, we shall buy maidenheads as they buy hob-
nails, by the hundreds.

FALSTAFF

By the mass, lad, thou sayest true; it is like we shall have good
trading[190] that way. But tell me, Hal, art not thou horrible   315
afeard?[191] Thou being heir apparent, could[192] the world pick
thee out three such enemies again as that fiend Douglas, that
spirit Percy, and that devil Glendower? Art thou not horribly
afraid? Doth not thy blood thrill[193] at it?

PRINCE

Not[194] a whit, i' faith, I lack some of thy instinct.   320

FALSTAFF

Well, thou wilt be horribly[195] chid tomorrow when thou
comest to thy father; if thou love me, practise an answer.

PRINCE

Do thou stand for my father and examine me upon the particulars of my life.

FALSTAFF

Shall I? Content![196] This chair shall be my state, this dagger my   325
sceptre, and this cushion my crown.
                    [*He places the cushion on his head*

197 *Thy state . . . dagger* – We accept a well-made stool as your throne and a dagger of lead as your golden sceptre". Blunt weapons of lead or wood were used instead of sharp ones in the theatre.

198 *crown,* in two senses: (i) "king's crown"; (ii) "top of the head".

199 *fire of grace* – "conscience".

200 *moved* – "made to feel shame".

201 *passion* – "grief".

202 *King Cambyses' vein.* Falstaff says he will imitate the manner *(vein)* of King Cambyses, a character in a well-known old tragedy by Thomas Preston, but in fact Shakespeare uses Falstaff's speeches to mock the style of some dramatists of his own day.

203 *leg* – "bow". Hal bows to Falstaff as if he were the King.

204 *nobility* – "nobles". He refers to those around him in the tavern. The hostess is amused at being spoken to in this way and at Falstaff's behaviour.

205 *Weep not . . . vain.* Falstaff uses the style of slightly old-fashioned stage tragedy and his phrases are very like those in actual plays.

206 *holds his countenance* – "looks serious".

207 *convey . . . her eyes* – "lead away my sad *(tristful)* Queen, for tears blind her eyes".

208 *harlotry players* – "worthless actors". Actors were not considered very respectable in Shakespeare's day.

PRINCE

Thy state is taken for a joint-stool, thy golden sceptre for a leaden dagger,[197] and thy precious rich crown for a pitiful bald crown.[198]

FALSTAFF

Well, an the fire[199] of grace be not quite out of thee, now shalt   330
thou be moved.[200] Give me a cup of sack to make my eyes look red, that it may be thought I have wept, for I must speak in passion,[201] and I will do it in King Cambyses'[202] vein.

PRINCE

Well, here is my leg.[203]

FALSTAFF

And here is my speech. Stand aside, nobility.[204]   335

HOSTESS

O Jesu, this is excellent sport, i' faith.

FALSTAFF

Weep[205] not, sweet Queen, for trickling tears are vain.

HOSTESS

O the Father, how he holds his countenance![206]

FALSTAFF

For God's sake, lords, convey[207] my tristful Queen,
For tears do stop the floodgates of her eyes.   340

HOSTESS

O Jesu, he doth it as like one of these harlotry[208] players as ever
I see!

209 *Peace* – "Be quiet".

210 *pint-pot,* suggests the small size of Mistress Quickly and *tickle-brain* ("strong drink") her work.

211 *though the camomile . . . wears* (line 347) – "though the camomile endures rough treatment, wasted youth is soon ended". In this speech Shakespeare is making fun of a passage in a well-known Elizabethan prose romance, Lyly's *Euphues.* This style is now known as Euphuistic writing. Two favourite devices were the use of strange similes from natural history and a series of questions that needed no answer.

212 *trick* – "characteristic expression".

213 *pointed at,* i.e. "noticed with scorn". Falstaff guesses correctly that the King is distressed by Hal's frequent appearance in bad company.

214 *micher* – "truant".

215 *son of England* – "son of Henry IV". The name of a country was sometimes used instead of the name of its king. *Son* and *sun* have the same sound, and the meanings of the two questions are closely related: should (i) the "sun" or (ii) the "Prince" leave his right place and abandon his duty for common lawless pleasures?

216 *pitch . . . doth defile,* an old saying from the Apocrypha (*Ecclesiasticus* 13 v.1); it also appears in a passage in *Euphues.*

217 *not . . . but in tears.* Falstaff, who had called for a cup of sack to make his eyes red (line 331), now, acting as the King, claims they are red not with drink but with weeping over the Prince's evil conduct.

218 *an it like* – "if it please".

219 *goodly portly* – "good, stately".

220 *carriage* – "behaviour".

221 *lewdly given* – "inclined to do evil".

222 *If then . . . fruit,* "If the outward appearance is a guide to the true quality of a tree (or a man)". A reference to the Bible (*Matthew* 12 v.33).

223 *peremptorily* – "in a resolved and determined manner".

224 *banish.* In fact the Prince, as Henry V, banishes Falstaff at the end of Shakespeare's play *Henry IV Part 2.*

225 *naughty varlet* – "wicked man".

FALSTAFF

Peace,[209] good pint-pot,[210] peace, good tickle-brain. – Harry,
I do not only marvel where thou spendest thy time, but also
how thou art accompanied. For though the camomile,[211] the 345
more it is trodden on the faster it grows, yet youth, the more it
is wasted the sooner it wears. That thou art my son I have partly
thy mother's word, partly my own opinion, but chiefly a villainous trick[212] of thine eye, and a foolish hanging of thy nether
lip, that doth warrant me. If then thou be son to me, here lies 350
the point – why, being son to me, art thou so pointed[213] at?
Shall the blessed sun of heaven prove a micher,[214] and eat blackberries? A question not to be asked. Shall the son[215] of England
prove a thief, and take purses? A question to be asked. There is
a thing, Harry, which thou hast often heard of, and it is known 355
to many in our land by the name of pitch. This pitch[216] (as
ancient writers do report) doth defile; so doth the company thou
keepest: for, Harry, now I do not[217] speak to thee in drink, but
in tears; not in pleasure, but in passion; not in words only, but
in woes also. And yet there is a virtuous man whom I have often 360
noted in thy company, but I know not his name.

PRINCE

What manner of man, an[218] it like your Majesty?

FALSTAFF

A goodly[219] portly man, i' faith, and a corpulent; of a cheerful
look, a pleasing eye, and a most noble carriage;[220] and, as I
think, his age some fifty, or by 'r lady inclining to threescore; 365
and now I remember me, his name is Falstaff. If that man should
be lewdly[221] given, he deceiveth me; for, Harry, I see virtue in
his looks. If[222] then the tree may be known by the fruit, as the
fruit by the tree, then peremptorily[223] I speak it, there is virtue
in that Falstaff; him keep with, the rest banish.[224] And tell me 370
now, thou naughty[225] varlet, tell me where hast thou been this
month?

117

226 *Dost thou . . . a king?* asked scornfully to suggest the meaning: "You do not speak like a king".

227 *Do thou stand for me.* Hal means that Falstaff is to act the part of Hal, while he himself acts the part of the King.

228 *If thou . . . poulter's hare* (line 377). Falstaff is always willing to make a joke about his own size and swear to his own excellence. Now he says that if Hal acts half as well as he, he will let himself be hung upside down as a very young rabbit (*rabbit-sucker*) or hare is hung up for sale in a poulterer's shop.

229 *set* – "seated".

230 *Judge, my masters,* i.e. judge which is the better actor, a remark addressed to the audience of actors on the stage and perhaps to the real audience as well.

231 *tickle . . . prince* – "show you how to act as a young prince".

232 *ungracious* – "wicked".

233 *grace* – "virtue".

234 *haunts* – "remains in your company". By copying Falstaff's trick of forgetting the man's name, Hal enables himself to give a very unflattering picture of Falstaff's great size and his faults of character, a picture expressed in descriptions of large containers for food and references to the stage figure of Vice (see note 243).

235 *tun,* a large barrel.

236 *converse with* – "associate with".

237 *trunk 'of humours* – "container of vile fluids".

238 *bolting-hutch,* a box in which the coarser parts of the flour remain when the finer parts have been sifted by the miller.

239 *bombard,* large leather jug.

and I'll play my father

118

PRINCE

Dost[226] thou speak like a king? Do[227] thou stand for me, and
I 'll play my father.

FALSTAFF

Depose me? If[228] thou dost it half so gravely, so majestically, 375
both in word and matter, hang me up by the heels for a rabbit-
sucker, or a poulter's hare.

PRINCE

Well, here I am set.[229]

[*He takes Falstaff's place on the stool*

FALSTAFF

And here I stand. Judge,[230] my masters.

PRINCE

Now, Harry, whence come you?   380

FALSTAFF

My noble lord, from Eastcheap.

PRINCE

The complaints I hear of thee are grievous.

FALSTAFF

'Sblood, my lord, they are false: nay, I 'll tickle[231] ye for a
young prince, i' faith.

PRINCE

Swearest thou, ungracious[232] boy? Henceforth ne'er look on 385
me. Thou art violently carried away from grace;[233] there is a
devil haunts[234] thee in the likeness of an old fat man; a tun[235] of
man is thy companion. Why dost thou converse[236] with that
trunk[237] of humours, that bolting-hutch[238] of beastliness, that
swollen parcel of dropsies, that huge bombard[239] of sack, that 390

119

240 *cloak-bag*, large travelling-bag.

241 *Manningtree ox*. An ox roasted whole formed part of many festivals, such as those at Manningtree, a town in a district of England famous for fat oxen.

242 *pudding* – "stuffing".

243 *reverend vice* – "wicked man old enough to be revered by the young". Here and in the following descriptive phrases Falstaff's age (worthy of respect) is contrasted with his lawless conduct. Falstaff is described as the figure of Vice (personified wickedness) who appeared in the old religious plays. In lines 400-1, as *misleader of youth*, he is likened to Satan (see note 249) who was also represented in plays that showed the struggle between good and evil for the possession of man's soul. Hal is joking, but Shakespeare intends us to see that Falstaff acts rather like the character, Vice.

244 *grey* – "grey-haired".

245 *father*, no longer young.

246 *vanity in years* – "worthlessness grown old".

247 *wherein cunning, but in craft?* – "in what *(wherein)* is he clever *(cunning)* except in deceit *(craft)*".

248 *I would . . . me with you* – "I wish your Majesty *(your Grace)* would explain *(take me with you)*". *Your Grace* was a suitable title of respect for Falstaff to use when acting as the Prince speaking to the King.

249 *Satan*, the name of the chief devil (also called *Lucifer*).

250 *the man I know* – "I (now) know the man (whom you mean)".

251 *harm* – "evil".

252 *were to . . . I know* – "would be to say something for which I have no evidence".

253 *saving your reverence*, a polite phrase of apology from a young man to an older one for an unpleasant word or phrase that follows.

254 *whoremaster*, one who goes with immoral women.

255 *old host* – "old innkeeper", with perhaps a reference to Mistress Quickly, the hostess.

256 *Pharaoh's lean kine*, a reference to the Bible (*Genesis* 41 v.19-21). The lean cows *(kine)* were to be hated rather than loved; they were a sign of seven years of starvation to come.

257 *banish not . . . world* – "do not banish him from your son Harry's company . . . if you banish Falstaff you might as well banish the whole world". As at line 370 the word *banish* looks forward to Falstaff's banishment at the end of *Henry IV Part 2*.

120

stuffed cloak-bag[240] of guts, that roasted Manningtree[241] ox
with the pudding[242] in his belly, that reverend[243] vice, that
grey[244] iniquity, that father[245] ruffian, that vanity[246] in years?
Wherein is he good, but to taste sack and drink it? wherein neat
and cleanly, but to carve a capon and eat it? wherein cunning,[247] 395
but in craft? wherein crafty, but in villainy? wherein villainous,
but in all things? wherein worthy, but in nothing?

FALSTAFF

I would your Grace[248] would take me with you: whom means
your Grace?

PRINCE

That villainous abominable misleader of youth, Falstaff, that 400
old white-bearded Satan.[249]

FALSTAFF

My lord, the man I know.[250]

PRINCE

I know thou dost.

FALSTAFF

But to say I know more harm[251] in him than in myself were[252]
to say more than I know. That he is old, the more the pity, his 405
white hairs do witness it; but that he is, saving[253] your reverence, a whoremaster,[254] that I utterly deny. If sack and sugar be
a fault, God help the wicked! If to be old and merry be a sin,
then many an old host[255] that I know is damned: if to be fat be
to be hated, then Pharaoh's[256] lean kine are to be loved. No, my 410
good lord; banish Peto, banish Bardolph, banish Poins – but for
sweet Jack Falstaff, kind Jack Falstaff, true Jack Falstaff, valiant
Jack Falstaff, and therefore more valiant, being as he is old Jack
Falstaff, banish[257] not him thy Harry's company, banish not
him thy Harry's company, banish plump Jack, and banish all 415
the world.

121

258 *monstrous watch* – "large number of street-guards". The *watch* were officers with power to arrest law-breakers; they walked about the streets during the hours of darkness.

259 *in* – "on". Though in grave danger of hanging, Falstaff wants to finish the play.

260 *Heigh,* a sigh.

261 *the devil . . . fiddle-stick.* These words were often said when there was a sudden noise or disturbance as if to suggest that this were caused by the devil flying by.

262 *Never call . . . seeming so* – "Do not mistake a true coin (i.e. Falstaff) for a false one: you, yourself, are truly royal *(essentially made)* though you do not behave like a prince". By using the image of a coin which may be real gold even though it appears no better than a worthless imitation, Falstaff suggests that both he and the Prince are better men than they seem to be.

263 *And thou . . . instinct* – "And you are a coward through natural fear not through natural (instinctive) respect for royalty".

264 *your major* – "the main part of your argument".

265 *deny the sheriff* – "refuse to admit the sheriff".

266 *so* – "good".

267 *If I become not a cart* – "If I do not look as fine in a cart". A cart was used to take condemned men to the gallows.

a most monstrous[258] *watch*

122

PRINCE

I do, I will.   [*A knocking is heard.*
                              Exeunt HOSTESS, FRANCIS, *and* BARDOLPH

Re-enter BARDOLPH, *running*

BARDOLPH

O my lord, my lord, the sheriff with a most monstrous[258] watch
is at the door.

FALSTAFF

Out, ye rogue! Play out the play! I have much to say in[259] the 420
behalf of that Falstaff.

Re-enter the HOSTESS

HOSTESS

O Jesu, my lord, my lord!

PRINCE

Heigh,[260] heigh, the devil[261] rides upon a fiddle-stick; what 's
the matter?

HOSTESS

The sheriff and all the watch are at the door; they are come to 425
search the house. Shall I let them in?

FALSTAFF

Dost thou hear, Hal? Never[262] call a true piece of gold a counterfeit: thou art essentially made without seeming so.

PRINCE

And[263] thou a natural coward without instinct.

FALSTAFF

I deny your major.[264] If you will deny[265] the sheriff, so;[266] if 430
not, let him enter. If[267] I become not a cart as well as another

123

268 *bringing up* – "education (in good public manners)".

269 *I hope . . . as another.* Falstaff jokes that his weight will cause his death on the gallows to be quicker than any other man's.

270 *Go hide . . . above.* While Falstaff hides behind the curtain *(arras)* at the back of the stage, the other thieves go upstairs *(above)*.

271 *their date is out* – "I no longer have them".

272 *what is your will with me* – "why do you want to see me?"

273 *hue and cry*, a crowd of people pursuing a suspected thief.

274 *engage* – "give".

man, a plague on my bringing[268] up! I[269] hope I shall as soon
be strangled with a halter as another.

PRINCE

Go[270] hide thee behind the arras, the rest walk up above. Now,
my masters, for a true face and good conscience.   435

FALSTAFF

Both which I have had, but their date[271] is out, and therefore
I 'll hide me.

[*Exeunt all but the* PRINCE *and* PETO

PRINCE

Call in the sheriff.

Enter SHERIFF *and* FIRST CARRIER

Now, master sheriff, what is your will[272] with me?

SHERIFF

First, pardon me, my lord. A hue[273] and cry   440
Hath followed certain men unto this house.

PRINCE

What men?

SHERIFF

One of them is well known, my gracious lord,
A gross fat man.

CARRIER

     As fat as butter.

PRINCE

The man I do assure you is not here,   445
For I myself at this time have employed him:
And sheriff, I will engage[274] my word to thee,

125

275 *marks,* a mark was an amount of money, 13s. 4d.
276 *good morrow* – "good morning".
277 *oily* – "fat".
278 *Paul's,* St Paul's Cathedral, a famous church in the centre of London, used as a meeting-place by lawyers, merchants and thieves.

279 *fetches* – "draws".

That I will by tomorrow dinner-time
Send him to answer thee, or any man,
For anything he shall be charged withal;   450
And so let me entreat you leave the house.

SHERIFF

I will, my lord: there are two gentlemen
Have in this robbery lost three hundred marks.[275]

PRINCE

It may be so: if he have robbed these men
He shall be answerable; and so, farewell.   455

SHERIFF

Good night, my noble lord.

PRINCE

I think it is good morrow,[276] is it not?

SHERIFF

Indeed, my lord, I think it be two o'clock.

[*Exit, with* CARRIER

PRINCE

This oily[277] rascal is known as well as Paul's.[278] Go call him
forth.   460

PETO

Falstaff! – Fast asleep behind the arras, and snorting like a
horse.

PRINCE

Hark how hard he fetches[279] breath. Search his pockets. [PETO
searches his pockets, and finds some papers] What hast thou
found?   465

127

280 *item a capon* – "For one fat chicken".
    Item was written before each entry
    in an account.
281 *ob*, Latin *obolus*, a halfpenny.
282 *intolerable* – "very great".
283 *close* – "secret".
284 *at more advantages* – "when we have
    more time".
285 *charge of foot*, command over a
    company of soldiers marching on
    foot (i.e. without horses).

286 *his death . . . twelve score* – "he will
    be killed by walking two hundred
    and forty (steps)".
287 *The money . . . advantage* – "I shall
    arrange for the money (stolen at
    Gad's Hill) to be paid back (to the
    men who were robbed) with some
    extra".
288 *betimes* – "early".

PETO

Nothing but papers, my lord.

PRINCE

Let 's see what they be; read them.

PETO *reads*

Item[280] a capon	..	..	..	..	..	..	2s. 2d.	
Item sauce	..	..	..	..	..	..	4d.	
Item sack two gallons	..	..	..	..	..	5s. 8d.	470
Item anchovies and sack after supper		..	..	2s. 6d.				
Item bread	..	..	..	..	..	..	ob.[281]	

PRINCE

O monstrous! but one halfpennyworth of bread to this intolerable[282] deal of sack? What there is else keep close,[283] we 'll read
it at more advantage.[284] There let him sleep till day; I 'll to the 475
court in the morning. We must all to the wars, and thy place
shall be honourable. I 'll procure this fat rogue a charge[285] of
foot, and I know his death[286] will be a march of twelve score.
The money[287] shall be paid back again with advantage. Be
with me betimes[288] in the morning; and so, good morrow, 480
Peto.

PETO

Good morrow, good my lord.

[*Exeunt*

129

(III.i) At a meeting in Wales, Hotspur, Mortimer and Glendower discuss the parts of Britain they will each govern after the rebellion. Hotspur, who is impatient and eager for action, thinks that Glendower is a wild, boastful dreamer and enjoys mocking him by playing on his quick temper. While the agreements are being written out, Mortimer and Hotspur see their wives for the last time. Lady Mortimer, who can speak no English, sings a Welsh song. Hotspur jokingly asks Lady Percy to sing.

1 *promises,* i.e. of help.

2 *parties sure* – "supporters dependable".

3 *our induction . . . hope* – "our beginning is full of hope for future success". An *induction* was an opening scene before the main action of a play.

4 *forgot the map.* This detail reveals Hotspur's impatient unpractical nature. Glendower, whom he despises as a mere dreamer, knows where the map is.

5 *Lancaster,* Henry IV, who was Duke of Lancaster before he became king.

6 *front* – "face". The appearance of the sky was thought to act as a warning of things to come, but here Glendower's boasts are foolish and are laughed at by Hotspur.

7 *cressets,* iron baskets on poles in which tarred rope was burnt to give a bright light in theatres and houses. The unnaturally bright stars, planets or meteors that were supposed to be seen in the sky at Glendower's birth are described as *cressets* here.

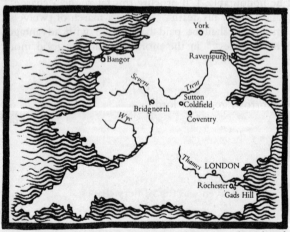

Map of England and Wales showing places named in the play

130

ACT THREE

Scene I. Bangor. The Archdeacon's House.

Enter HOTSPUR, WORCESTER, LORD MORTIMER,
OWEN GLENDOWER.

MORTIMER

These promises[1] are fair, the parties[2] sure,
And our induction[3] full of prosperous hope.

HOTSPUR

Lord Mortimer, and cousin Glendower, will you sit down?
And uncle Worcester. A plague upon it!
I have forgot the map.[4]

GLENDOWER

            No, here it is.   5
Sit, cousin Percy, sit, good cousin Hotspur;
For by that name as oft as Lancaster[5] doth speak of you
His cheek looks pale, and with a rising sigh
He wisheth you in heaven.

HOTSPUR

            And you in hell,
As oft as he hears Owen Glendower spoke of.   10

GLENDOWER

I cannot blame him: at my nativity
The front[6] of heaven was full of fiery shapes,
Of burning cressets;[7] and at my birth
The frame and huge foundation of the earth
Shaked like a coward.

131

8 *season* – "time".

9 *was not . . . it shook* – "did not have the same idea of you as I have, if you imagine it shook in fear of you".

10 *Diseased nature . . . passion shook* (line 32). Hotspur here refers to the belief that earthquakes were caused by a kind of sickness *(diseased nature)* when air tried to force itself from within the earth. This air shakes grandmother *(beldam* or *grandam)* earth and makes towers fall *(topples).* He jokes at Glendower's foolish boasts about his birth and suggests the shakings were caused by an earthquake. He picks up the idea of "birth" in his description of an earthquake – *teeming* ("fruitful"), *womb, enlargement* ("release" but also "birth") and perhaps suggests a connection between *unruly wind* ("violent hot air") and the birth of such a speaker of "hot air" (boastful talk) as Glendower. *Diseased, strange eruptions* ("breakings-out of spots on the skin"), *colic, distemperature* ("disorder"), *passion* ("bodily pain") develop the idea that an earthquake is a kind of sickness.

11 *of* – "from".

12 *crossings* – "arguments against me".

13 *Were strangely clamorous* – "made a strange loud noise".

14 *frighted* – "frightened".

15 *These signs . . . extraordinary* – "These special signs show that I am not an ordinary man".

HOTSPUR

Why, so it would have done   15
At the same season[8] if your mother's cat
Had but kittened, though yourself had never been born.

GLENDOWER

I say the earth did shake when I was born.

HOTSPUR

And I say the earth was[9] not of my mind,
If you suppose as fearing you it shook.   20

GLENDOWER

The heavens were all on fire, the earth did tremble –

HOTSPUR

O, then the earth shook to see the heavens on fire,
And not in fear of your nativity.
Diseased[10] nature oftentimes breaks forth
In strange eruptions; oft the teeming earth   25
Is with a kind of colic pinched and vexed
By the imprisoning of unruly wind
Within her womb, which for enlargement striving
Shakes the old beldam earth, and topples down
Steeples and moss-grown towers. At your birth   30
Our grandam earth, having this distemperature,
In passion shook.

GLENDOWER

Cousin, of[11] many men
I do not bear these crossings.[12] Give me leave
To tell you once again that at my birth
The front of heaven was full of fiery shapes,
The goats ran from the mountains, and the herds 35
Were strangely clamorous[13] to the frighted[14] fields.
These signs[15] have marked me extraordinary,

16 *courses* – "events".

17 *roll* – "list".

18 *Where is he living, clipped in* – "Who is there, surrounded".

19 *chides the banks* – "beats noisily and angrily against the shores".

20 *Which calls . . . to me* – "who can claim that I am his pupil or that he has been my teacher".

21 *And bring . . . experiments* (line 46) – "And show me the man *(And bring . . . woman's son)* who can follow my tracks *(trace)* in the long and difficult ways of magic and keep up with me *(hold me pace)* in experiments requiring great learning".

22 *speaks better Welsh* – in three senses: (i) "talks his own language better"; (ii) "talks more nonsense"; (iii) "boasts better".

23 *I'll to* – "I'll go to".

24 *I can call . . . for them* (line 52). Hotspur makes fun of Glendower's boasting by pointing out that any man can summon *(call)* spirits from boundless space *(vasty deep)*, but this is not proof of magical power unless the spirits come when they are called.

25 *command*, in two senses: (i) "order (him) to appear"; (ii) "rule".

26 *And I can . . . shame the devil* (line 55). Hotspur says that he will teach Glendower to make the devil feel shame by telling the truth, i.e. by ceasing to boast of his powers. The devil was considered the source of all lies, as in the common saying here: *tell truth and shame the devil*.

27 *I'll be sworn* – "I swear".

And all the courses[16] of my life do show
I am not in the roll[17] of common men.   40
Where[18] is he living, clipped in with the sea
That chides[19] the banks of England, Scotland, Wales,
Which[20] calls me pupil or hath read to me?
And[21] bring him out, that is but woman's son,
Can trace me in the tedious ways of art,   45
And hold me pace in deep experiments.

HOTSPUR

I think there 's no man speaks[22] better Welsh.
I 'll[23] to dinner.

MORTIMER

Peace, cousin Percy, you will make him mad.

GLENDOWER

I[24] can call spirits from the vasty deep.   50

HOTSPUR

Why, so can I, or so can any man;
But will they come when you do call for them?

GLENDOWER

Why, I can teach you, cousin, to command[25] the devil.

HOTSPUR

And[26] I can teach thee, coz, to shame the devil,
By telling truth: tell truth, and shame the devil.   55
If thou have power to raise him, bring him hither,
And I 'll be sworn[27] I have power to shame him hence:
O, while you live, tell truth, and shame the devil!

MORTIMER

Come, come, no more of this unprofitable chat.

135

28 *made head . . . my power* – "raised an army against my soldiers".

29 *Wye . . . Severn*, the names of two rivers on the border between England and Wales.

30 *Bootless* – "unsuccessful".

31 *without boots*, Hotspur pretends that he thought that Glendower meant "without boots" *(bootless)*. He also picks up *weather* in *weather-beaten* and makes it part of a joke. Almost everything Glendower says gives Hotspur a chance to make fun of him.

32 *How scapes he agues* – "How does he escape fevers *(agues)*".

33 *in the devil's name*. The phrase is used to add weight to what has been said, but it also refers back to Glendower's words about his command of the devil.

34 *According to . . . ta'en* – "according to the division into three parts that we have already made *(ta'en)*".

35 *Archdeacon*, the Archdeacon of Bangor in whose house the historical division of the kingdom took place.

36 *limits*, areas marked out by boundaries.

37 *off from* – "on the other side of".

38 *indentures tripartite*. An *indenture* was a written agreement with one edge cut (indented) in a wavy line, all copies having an exactly similar edge. *Indenture* here refers to the threefold *(tripartite)* copies of the agreement and also to the wavy lines on the map which marked the *tripartite* division of the kingdom.

39 *being sealéd interchangeably*. The seals of the three parties would be attached to each copy of the agreement; the copies would be exactly like each other and therefore *interchangeable*.

40 *this night may execute* – "may be done tonight".

41 *set forth* – "begin our journey".

42 *power* – "army".

43 *is appointed us* – "has been arranged for us".

44 *these fourteen days* – "for the next two weeks".

And our indentures[38] *tripartite are drawn*

GLENDOWER

Three times hath Henry Bolingbroke made head[28]   60
Against my power; thrice from the banks of Wye[29]
And sandy-bottomed Severn have I sent him
Bootless[30] home, and weather-beaten back.

HOTSPUR

Home without boots,[31] and in foul weather too!
How scapes he agues,[32] in the devil's[33] name?   65

GLENDOWER

Come, here is the map. Shall we divide our right
According[34] to our threefold order ta'en?

MORTIMER

The Archdeacon[35] hath divided it
Into three limits[36] very equally:
England, from Trent and Severn hitherto [*He points to the map*   70
By south and east is to my part assigned;
All westward, Wales beyond the Severn shore,
And all the fertile land within that bound,
To Owen Glendower; and, dear coz, to you
The remnant northward lying off[37] from Trent.   75
And our indentures[38] tripartite are drawn,
Which being sealéd[39] interchangeably,
(A business that this night[40] may execute)
Tomorrow, cousin Percy, you and I
And my good Lord of Worcester will set[41] forth   80
To meet your father and the Scottish power,[42]
As is appointed[43] us, at Shrewsbury.
My father Glendower is not ready yet,
Nor shall we need his help these fourteen[44] days.
[*To* GLENDOWER] Within that space you may have drawn
   together   85
Your tenants, friends, and neighbouring gentlemen.

45 *in my conduct* – "under my protection".

46 *steal . . . no leave* – "go secretly and not say good-bye", with a play on *take* and *steal*.

47 *world of water* – "immense amount of tears".

48 *moiety* – "share".

49 *one of yours* – "one of your shares".

50 *cranking* – "winding".

51 *cuts me . . . my land* – "cuts out the best of the land that would be mine (if the river flowed in a straight line)".

52 *cantle* – "corner".

53 *smug* – "smooth".

54 *indent* – "curve".

55 *so rich a bottom* – "so fertile a river-valley".

56 *mark how . . . from you* (line 107) – "see *(mark)* how the river *(he)* flows on and winds into my share *(runs me up)* with equal advantage to your side, cutting *(gelding)* as much away from the opposite bank *(opposed continent)* as he takes from you".

57 *a little charge will trench* – "it will not cost much to dig a (new) channel".

138

GLENDOWER

A shorter time shall send me to you, lords,
And in my conduct[45] shall your ladies come,
From whom you now must steal[46] and take no leave,
For there will be a world[47] of water shed   90
Upon the parting of your wives and you.

HOTSPUR

Methinks my moiety,[48] north from Burton here,
In quantity equals not one[49] of yours.
See how this river comes me cranking[50] in,
And cuts[51] me from the best of all my land –   95
A huge half-moon, a monstrous cantle[52] out.
I 'll have the current in this place dammed up,
And here the smug[53] and silver Trent shall run
In a new channel fair and evenly;
It shall not wind with such a deep indent,[54]   100
To rob me of so rich[55] a bottom here.

GLENDOWER

Not wind? It shall, it must – you see it doth.

                      [*He points to the map*

MORTIMER

Yea,
But mark[56] how he bears his course, and runs me up
With like advantage on the other side,   105
Gelding the opposed continent as much
As on the other side it takes from you.

WORCESTER

Yea, but a little charge[57] will trench him here,
And on this north side win this cape of land,
And then he runs straight and even.   110

HOTSPUR

I 'll have it so, a little charge will do it.

58 *say me nay* – "refuse me".

59 *I can speak English.* Glendower thinks that Hotspur is making fun of his way of speaking. Welsh and English are totally different languages and Welshmen often speak English with a strong rising and falling accent and irregular word order. Shakespeare probably had a good Welsh actor in mind when he wrote the part, as much humour arises from Glendower's "Welshness".

60 *trained up* – "educated".

61 *being but young* – "when I was still young". Glendower is pointing out that he has been using English for many years.

62 *framéd* – "fitted".

63 *lovely well* – "very well"; the use of the adjective *lovely* instead of an adverb such as *very* is an example of the "Welshness" Glendower is in fact denying.

64 *And gave . . . helpful ornament* – "and added beauty to the words (tongue) by music". Glendower is boasting that he learnt English so well that he was not only able to speak excellently but adorn the words with music – an ability (virtue) certainly not found in Hotspur.

65 *metre ballad-mongers.* Hotspur expresses his scorn for Glendower's musical and poetic education at the English court by speaking of street ballads – a low form of art. These ballads were stories about well-known characters, often living people, written in rough verse; they were sung and sold in the streets; *mongers* – "sellers".

66 *canstick,* a holder for a candle.

67 *axle-tree,* the rod on which a wheel turns.

68 *And that . . . mincing poetry* – "and that would not offend my ears nearly so much as poetry foolishly tripping (mincing) along".

GLENDOWER

I 'll not have it altered.

HOTSPUR

Will not you?

GLENDOWER

No, nor you shall not.

HOTSPUR

Who shall say[58] me nay?

GLENDOWER

Why, that will I.

HOTSPUR

Let me not understand you then; speak it in Welsh.   115

GLENDOWER

I[59] can speak English, lord, as well as you,
For I was trained[60] up in the English court,
Where, being but young,[61] I framéd[62] to the harp
Many an English ditty lovely[63] well,
And[64] gave the tongue a helpful ornament –   120
A virtue that was never seen in you.

HOTSPUR

Marry, and I am glad of it with all my heart!
I had rather be a kitten and cry "mew"
Than one of these same metre[65] ballad-mongers;
I had rather hear a brazen canstick[66] turned,   125
Or a dry wheel grate on the axle-tree,[67]
And[68] that would set my teeth nothing on edge,
Nothing so much as mincing poetry –
'T is like the forced gait of a shuffling nag.

141

69 *mark ye . . . part of a hair* – "listen to what I say, I'll argue *(cavil)* over the smallest details".

70 *drawn* – "written out in full".

71 *withal . . . departure hence* – "at the same time break the news to your wives that you are leaving (here)".

72 *moldwarp and the ant.* Holinshed's *Chronicles*, one of the books Shakespeare used for some of the historical details for this play, stated that some people thought that the rebels, in dividing the country, trusted in a foolish belief that the king was a *moldwarp* ("mole") cursed by God and that the rebels were dragon, lion and wolf that would divide the kingdom. Holinshed does not mention the other animals. Hotspur adds name after name to make fun of Glendower's endless talking and his faith in magic.

73 *Merlin,* a Welsh poet and magician.

74 *clip-winged griffin,* an imaginary animal with a lion's body and eagle's beak and wings – the wings clipped so that it could not fly *(clip-winged)*.

75 *moulten* – "having lost its feathers".

76 *couching lion . . . cat* – "a lion lying down with its head held up and a cat standing on its left back-leg, seen from the side". *Couching* and *ramping* are special words used to describe animals in these positions on knights' family shields. Hotspur uses the terms to make fun of Glendower's talk.

77 *such a . . . skimble-skamble stuff* – "such a lot of wild talk without meaning".

78 *puts . . . my faith* – "makes me doubt even my Christian faith".

79 *held me* – "kept me in conversation".

80 *several* – "different". Witches gave different names to the devils they could call upon to help them; they usually appeared in the form of animals.

81 *"Hum"* – "O, indeed!".

82 *go to* – " you don't say so", an expression of pretended surprise from Hotspur, who was trying to show interest although he was bored.

83 *marked him not* – "did not attend to him".

84 *railing* – "scolding".

85 *I had . . . windmill, far.* Hotspur says that he would rather live on the poorest food *(cheese and garlic)* in a noisy place *(windmill)* than listen to Glendower. The machinery for grinding the corn makes the inside of a windmill very noisy.

GLENDOWER

Come, you shall have Trent turned.   130

HOTSPUR

I do not care; I 'll give thrice so much land
To any well-deserving friend:
But in the way of bargain, mark[69] ye me,
I 'll cavil on the ninth part of a hair.
Are the indentures drawn?[70] Shall we be gone?   135

GLENDOWER

The moon shines fair; you may away by night:
I 'll haste the writer, and withal[71]
Break with your wives of your departure hence.
I am afraid my daughter will run mad,
So much she doteth on her Mortimer.   140

[*Exit*

MORTIMER

Fie, cousin Percy, how you cross my father!

HOTSPUR

I cannot choose; sometime he angers me
With telling me of the moldwarp[72] and the ant,
Of the dreamer Merlin[73] and his prophecies,
And of a dragon and a finless fish,   145
A clip-winged[74] griffin and a moulten[75] raven,
A couching[76] lion and a ramping cat,
And such[77] a deal of skimble-skamble stuff
As puts[78] me from my faith. I tell you what –
He held[79] me last night at least nine hours   150
In reckoning up the several[80] devils' names
That were his lackeys: I cried "Hum",[81] and "Well, go[82] to!"
But marked[83] him not a word. O, he is as tedious
As a tired horse, a railing[84] wife,
Worse than a smoky house. I[85] had rather live   155

143

86 *cates* – "fine tasty food".

87 *summer house.* Rich men had houses to go to in the country during the summer; there they could enjoy themselves. The quiet of such a house is contrasted with the noise of the inside of the windmill.

88 *profited . . . concealments* – "well-skilled in hidden mysteries".

89 *As mines of India.* India and the East generally were regarded as sources of great riches, particularly gold and jewels.

90 *He holds . . . respect* – "He respects your character *(temper)* very highly".

91 *curbs . . . his humour* – "keeps in check the natural expressions of his character when you oppose his mood".

92 *that man . . . alive* – "there is no one who".

93 *reproof* – "disgrace".

94 *too wilful-blame* – "to be blamed for too much self-will".

95 *put him . . . patience* – "make him lose his patience completely *(quite)*".

96 *You must needs* – "it is necessary that you should"

97 *blood* – "high spirits".

98 *the dearest grace it renders you* – "the best effect it has on you".

99 *defect* – "faultiness".

100 *want of government* – "lack of self-control".

101 *opinion,* too high an opinion of oneself.

102 *haunting* – "(if it is) characteristic of".

103 *Beguiling* – "robbing".

104 *schooled* – "taught a lesson".

105 *good manners . . . speed* – "let us hope good manners will bring you success".

griffin [74]

144

With cheese and garlic in a windmill, far,
Than feed on cates[86] and have him talk to me
In any summer[87] house in Christendom.

MORTIMER

In faith, he is a worthy gentleman,
Exceedingly well read, and profited[88]   160
In strange concealments, valiant as a lion,
And wondrous affable, and as bountiful
As[89] mines of India. Shall I tell you, cousin?
He[90] holds your temper in a high respect
And curbs[91] himself even of his natural scope   165
When you come 'cross his humour, faith he does:
I warrant you that[92] man is not alive
Might so have tempted him as you have done
Without the taste of danger and reproof:[93]
But do not use it oft, let me entreat you.   170

WORCESTER

In faith, my lord, you are too wilful-blame,[94]
And since your coming hither have done enough
To put[95] him quite beside his patience;
You must needs[96] learn, lord, to amend this fault.
Though sometimes it show greatness, courage, blood,[97]   175
– And that 's the dearest[98] grace it renders you –
Yet oftentimes it doth present harsh rage,
Defect[99] of manners, want[100] of government,
Pride, haughtiness, opinion,[101] and disdain,
The least of which, haunting[102] a nobleman,   180
Loseth men's hearts and leaves behind a stain
Upon the beauty of all parts besides,
Beguiling[103] them of commendation.   [Exit

HOTSPUR

Well, I am schooled[104] – good manners[105] be your speed!
Here come our wives, and let us take our leave.   185

106 *deadly spite* – "great cause of annoyance".

107 *aunt*. Lady Percy was Mortimer's sister, but Shakespeare confuses the two Mortimers as before. She was the *aunt* of the Mortimer who was historically heir to the throne.

108 *in your conduct* – "under your protection".

109 *peevish, self-willed harlotry*. – "stubborn, self-willed silly woman".

110 *no persuasion . . . good upon* – "no pleading will have a good effect upon".

111 *that pretty . . . swelling heavens* – "those pretty Welsh tears which you pour from your flooding eyes". As the sky *(heavens)* is the source of rain, so the eyes are thought of as like the sky, the tears being the rain.

112 *too perfect in* – "know too well from experience".

113 *such a parley* – "such speech", i.e. not words but tears.

114 *feeling disputation* – "contest in feelings (not words)".

115 *highly penned* – "written in a fine noble style".

116 *ravishing division,* a quick run of musical notes *(division)* giving musical delight *(ravishing)*.

Re-enter GLENDOWER *with the ladies*

MORTIMER

This is the deadly spite[106] that angers me;
My wife can speak no English, I no Welsh.

GLENDOWER

My daughter weeps, she 'll not part with you,
She 'll be a soldier too, she 'll to the wars.

MORTIMER

Good father, tell her that she and my aunt[107] Percy   190
Shall follow in your conduct[108] speedily.

> [GLENDOWER *speaks to her in Welsh, and she*
> *answers him in the same*

GLENDOWER

She is desperate here, a peevish,[109] self-willed harlotry, one that
no persuasion[110] can do good upon.

> [*The lady speaks in Welsh*

MORTIMER

I understand thy looks; that[111] pretty Welsh
Which thou pourest down from these swelling heavens   195
I am too perfect[112] in and, but for shame,
In such a parley[113] should I answer thee.

> [*The lady speaks again in Welsh*

I understand thy kisses, and thou mine,
And that 's a feeling[114] disputation;
But I will never be a truant, love,   200
Till I have learnt thy language, for thy tongue
Makes Welsh as sweet as ditties highly[115] penned,
Sung by a fair queen in a summer's bower
With ravishing[116] division to her lute.

147

117 *melt* – "weaken".

118 *O, I . . . this* – "O, I don't understand a word of this".

119 *wanton rushes*, fresh green plants used to cover the floors; a cheap form of covering that could be frequently changed.

120 *crown . . . sleep* – "make the god of sleep the only ruler". Glendower means that her song will put Mortimer pleasantly to sleep.

121 *charming* – "pleasing", as if she put a spell on you.

122 *As is . . . night.* An hour before the sun rises it is neither fully dark nor fully light; it is impossible to distinguish between day and night. Under the spell of Lady Mortimer's song, her husband will be unable to know whether he is awake or asleep because it will be so strangely beautiful.

123 *heavenly-harnessed team.* The sun-god (Phoebus) was often pictured as driving a chariot across the sky.

124 *progress*, a state journey made by a king. The sun's journey is referred to as a king's.

125 *book . . . drawn* – "agreement will be drawn up".

126 *Do so . . . and attend* (line 220). Glendower boasts of his magical knowledge and powers; he claims the power of summoning airy musicians to come from far distant skies and play for him immediately. In Elizabethan theatres the musicians often played from an upper part of the stage *(in the air)*.

127 *perfect* – "highly skilled".

128 *giddy goose* – "foolish fellow".

GLENDOWER

Nay, if you melt,[117] then will she run mad.   205

[*The lady speaks again in Welsh*

MORTIMER

O,[118] I am ignorance itself in this!

GLENDOWER

She bids you on the wanton[119] rushes lay you down,
And rest your gentle head upon her lap,
And she will sing the song that pleaseth you,
And on your eyelids crown[120] the god of sleep,   210
Charming[121] your blood with pleasing heaviness,
Making such difference 'twixt wake and sleep
As[122] is the difference betwixt day and night,
The hour before the heavenly-harnessed[123] team
Begins his golden progress[124] in the east.   215

MORTIMER

With all my heart I 'll sit and hear her sing;
By that time will our book[125] I think be drawn.

GLENDOWER

Do[126] so, and those musicians that shall play to you
Hang in the air a thousand leagues from hence,
And straight they shall be here: sit, and attend.   220

HOTSPUR

Come, Kate, thou art perfect[127] in lying down:
Come, quick, quick, that I may lay my head in thy lap.

LADY PERCY

Go, ye giddy[128] goose.

[*The music plays*

129 *Now I perceive . . . musician* (line 226). Throughout Hotspur has laughed at Glendower's boasts about his magic powers. He is now faced with proof – *the music plays*. Consequently he tries to dismiss the proof with a joke: "Now I see the devil understands the Welsh language (since he has obeyed your commands) and (if he understands your language) it is no wonder *(marvel)* he changes his mood so frequently *(is so humorous)*; certainly, he is a good musician (whose mood changes in accordance with the mood of the music)".

130 *governed by humours* – "ruled by changing moods".

131 *ye thief* – "you wretch".

132 *Lady . . . in Irish* – "Lady, my female hound, sing in Irish". The language spoken in Ireland would have sounded harsh to an English ear. *Lady* was the name of the hound.

133 *Neither . . . fault* – "I will do neither", i.e. neither allow my head to be broken nor be quiet – "to do so would make me appear a mere woman".

134 *Peace* – "Be quiet".

HOTSPUR

Now[129] I perceive the devil understands Welsh,
And 't is no marvel he is so humorous;   225
By 'r lady, he is a good musician.

LADY PERCY

Then should you be nothing but musical,
For you are altogether governed[130] by humours.
Lie still, ye thief,[131] and hear the lady sing in Welsh.

HOTSPUR

I had rather hear Lady[132] my brach howl in Irish.   230

LADY PERCY

Wouldst thou have thy head broken?

HOTSPUR

No.

LADY PERCY

Then be still.

HOTSPUR

Neither,[133] 't is a woman's fault.

LADY PERCY

Now God help thee!   235

HOTSPUR

To the Welsh lady's bed.

LADY PERCY

What 's that?

HOTSPUR

Peace,[134] she sings.   [*The lady sings a Welsh song*
Come, Kate, I 'll have your song too.

135 *in good sooth*, a mild oath meaning "indeed".

136 *comfit-maker*, a maker of sweets.

137 *"As true . . . day!"* Hotspur gives three more examples of mild oaths more suitable for a merchant's wife than a soldier's.

138 *givest . . . thy oaths.* Instead of using strong expressions as a pledge *(surety)*, Lady Percy uses delicate words; these Hotspur describes as *sarcenet* ("thin silk").

139 *Finsbury.* Finsbury fields was a favourite sports ground or public park for London merchants and their wives.

140 *lady* - "noble lady".

141 *such protest . . . gingerbread.* Pepper gingerbread, a kind of cake, would lie as lightly on the tongue as the mild oaths that Hotspur says suit only tradesmen's wives.

142 *velvet-guards . . . citizens*, people who wear fine clothes trimmed with velvet *(velvet-guards)* and city dwellers wearing their best *(Sunday)* clothes.

143 *'T is the next . . . teacher* - "Singing is the quickest way to change yourself into a tailor or a teacher of song-birds". Tailors often sang at their work.

144 *on fire* - "eager".

145 *By this* - "By this time".

146 *book* - "agreement".

147 *we'll but . . . horse immediately* - "we have only to put our seals on the agreement and then we will begin our journey at once".

LADY PERCY

Not mine, in good sooth.[135]   240

HOTSPUR

Not yours, in good sooth! Heart, you swear like a comfit-
maker's[136] wife – "Not you, in good sooth!", and "As[137] true
as I live!", and "As God shall mend me!", and "As sure as day!" –
And givest[138] such sarcenet surety for thy oaths
As if thou never walkest further than Finsbury.[139]   245
Swear me, Kate, like a lady[140] as thou art,
A good mouth-filling oath, and leave "In sooth",
And such protest[141] of pepper-gingerbread,
To velvet-guards,[142] and Sunday citizens.
Come, sing.   250

LADY PERCY

I will not sing.

HOTSPUR

'T is[143] the next way to turn tailor, or be redbreast teacher. And
the indentures be drawn, I 'll away within these two hours; and
so come in when ye will.

                                                      [*Exit*

GLENDOWER

Come, come, Lord Mortimer, you are as slow   255
As hot Lord Percy is on fire[144] to go.
By[145] this our book[146] is drawn – we 'll[147] but seal,
And then to horse immediately.

MORTIMER

                  With all my heart.

                                                      [*Exeunt*

153

(III.ii) In a private meeting with his son, Prince Hal, the King reveals his fear that Hal's unprincely conduct is a punishment for his own unlawful seizing of Richard II's throne. As a warning to Hal he describes how the common people treated Richard with contempt because he mixed too freely with them. He even suggests that Hal may prove a traitor and fight on the side of the rebels. In reply Hal promises to redeem his reputation by overcoming Hotspur in battle, a reformation looked forward to in his earlier soliloquy (I.ii.161-83) and fulfilled in v.iv. In the Prince's promise the King sees hope for the future.

Blunt arrives with news that Douglas and his men have joined the rebels. The King gives Hal command of part of the army and orders him to march through Gloucestershire and meet him later at Bridgnorth.

1 *give us leave* – "please leave us alone".

2 *presently . . . you* – "need you immediately".

3 *God will have it so* – "it is God's will".

4 *displeasing service* – "sin".

5 *doom* – "judgement"; *secret* because God may be working indirectly.

6 *out of . . . revengement* – "He will make my son an instrument of revenge".

7 *passages* – "courses".

8 *only marked . . . mistreadings* – "merely appointed (by God) to carry out his fiery *(hot)* revenge and punishment *(rod)* for my evil actions *(mistreadings)*".

9 *else . . . princely heart* (line 17) – "how otherwise could such low desires unworthy of princely rank *(inordinate)*, such poor, such wretched *(bare)*, such mean actions *(attempts)*, such empty pleasures, such rough and ignorant people as you mix with *(art matched withal)* and are attached to *(grafted to)*, accompany

your noble rank *(greatness of thy blood)* and put themselves on a level with your princely nature". To *graft* (line 15) means to put part of one plant into another to make the two grow as one; *grafted* therefore suggests that Hal is artificially and unnaturally attached to low actions and companions.

10 *Quit all offences* – "clear myself of all misdeeds".

11 *I am doubtless* – "I have no doubt".

12 *Yet . . . true submission* (line 28). The Prince explains that many of the charges are false and begs his father to excuse his few real faults.

13 *in reproof . . . newsmongers* – "to prove false many stories which a king must often necessarily hear, made up and told *(devised)* by flatterers *(pickthanks)* and people who make money from selling news *(newsmongers)*".

14 *Hath faulty . . . irregular* – "has strayed wrongly and lawlessly *(irregular)*".

15 *submission* – "confession".

Scene II. London. The Palace.

Enter the KING, PRINCE OF WALES, *and others.*

KING

Lords, give[1] us leave; the Prince of Wales and I
Must have some private conference: but be near at hand,
For we shall presently[2] have need of you.

[*Exeunt Lords*

I know not whether God[3] will have it so
For some displeasing[4] service I have done,   5
That in his secret doom[5] out[6] of my blood
He 'll breed revengement and a scourge for me;
But thou dost in thy passages[7] of life
Make me believe that thou art only marked[8]
For the hot vengeance and the rod of heaven,   10
To punish my mistreadings. Tell me else[9]
Could such inordinate and low desires,
Such poor, such bare, such lewd, such mean attempts,
Such barren pleasures, rude society,
As thou art matched withal, and grafted to,   15
Accompany the greatness of thy blood,
And hold their level with thy princely heart?

PRINCE

So please your Majesty, I would I could
Quit[10] all offences with as clear excuse
As well as, I am doubtless,[11] I can purge   20
Myself of many I am charged withal:
Yet[12] such extenuation let me beg
As, in reproof[13] of many tales devised,
Which oft the ear of greatness needs must hear,
By smiling pickthanks, and base newsmongers,   25
I may for some things true, wherein my youth
Hath[14] faulty wandered and irregular,
Find pardon on my true submission.[15]

16 *affections . . . flight of* – "desires which fly *(hold a wing)* in the opposite direction *(flight)*".

17 *Thy place . . . lost.* Shakespeare refers to the historical fact that Hal was dismissed from the king's council; though referred to, it is not included in the action of this play.

18 *younger brother,* Prince John of Lancaster.

19 *The hope . . . time* – "your hopeful and promising youth".

20 *soul . . . thy fall* – "everyone in his mind *(soul)* thinks of what will happen in the future *(forethink)* and expects your disgrace *(fall)*".

21 *common-hackneyed,* common and always seen, like a horse that is used for working every day, called a *hackney.*

22 *vulgar company* – "the company of common people".

23 *Opinion* – "public opinion".

24 *possession,* in two senses: (i) "the fact of possession"; (ii) "the possessor", i.e. Richard II.

25 *reputeless banishment* – "dishonour and exile".

26 *mark nor likelihood* – "importance nor promise of success". He says that if he had let himself be a common sight, the people would not have respected him, Richard II would have kept his throne, and he, Bolingbroke, would have remained in banishment.

27 *comet . . . wondered at, comets* were believed to be signs of some terrible event that was about to happen. Therefore they were viewed with surprise and fear *(wondered at).*

28 *stole . . . from heaven* – "assumed without right *(stole)* a kind and graceful manner as if it came from Heaven".

29 *person* – "royal character".

30 *Ne'er seen . . . at* – "never seen without being wondered at".

31 *won . . . such solemnity* – "won such dignity *(solemnity)* by being rarely seen".

32 *skipping king,* thoughtless King Richard who was like a child at play.

33 *rash bavin wits* – "thoughtless flashy young men". *Bavin* is brushwood that burns with a bright flame which soon goes out.

34 *carded . . . fools* – "lowered *(carded)* his dignity, mixed with dancing *(capering)* fools". To *card* was to mix drinks or to make them weaker.

KING

God pardon thee! Yet let me wonder, Harry,
At thy affections,[16] which do hold a wing   30
Quite from the flight of all thy ancestors.
Thy place[17] in Council thou hast rudely lost,
Which by thy younger[18] brother is supplied,
And art almost an alien to the hearts
Of all the court and princes of my blood: 35
The hope[19] and expectation of thy time
Is ruined, and the soul[20] of every man
Prophetically do forethink thy fall.
Had I so lavish of my presence been,
So common-hackneyed[21] in the eyes of men,   40
So stale and cheap to vulgar[22] company,
Opinion,[23] that did help me to the crown,
Had still kept loyal to possession,[24]
And left me in reputeless[25] banishment,
A fellow of no mark[26] nor likelihood.   45
By being seldom seen, I could not stir
But like a comet[27] I was wondered at,
That men would tell their children, "This is he!"
Others would say, "Where, which is Bolingbroke?"
And then I stole[28] all courtesy from heaven,   50
And dressed myself in such humility
That I did pluck allegiance from men's hearts,
Loud shouts and salutations from their mouths,
Even in the presence of the crownéd King.
Thus did I keep my person[29] fresh and new,   55
My presence, like a robe pontifical,
Ne'er[30] seen but wondered at; and so my state,
Seldom, but sumptuous, showed like a feast,
And won[31] by rareness such solemnity.
The skipping[32] King, he ambled up and down,   60
With shallow jesters and rash[33] bavin wits,
Soon kindled and soon burnt, carded[34] his state,
Mingled his royalty with capering fools,

157

35 *Had . . . their scorns* – "allowed his great name (of king) to be treated with disrespect". *Profane* means to treat something holy with disrespect. The king was thought of as God's agent on earth and was therefore "holy".

36 *gave his . . . his name,* in two senses: (i) "showed his face in a manner unsuited to his kingly title"; (ii) "by countenancing ('permitting') informality, reduced his kingly authority".

37 *gibing boys* – "boys who laugh disrespectfully".

38 *stand the push . . . comparative* – "submit to the rudeness of every young *(beardless)* vain insulting rival". *Comparative* is used in two senses: (i) "one who deals in insults"; (ii) "rival".

39 *Grew . . . common streets* – "was so often seen in the streets that they seemed his favourite place".

40 *enfeoffed* – "surrendered".

41 *That, being . . . too much* (line 73). The word. *swallowed* used here instead of "see" suggests that men saw too much of the king and like men who eat too much sweet food they soon grew sick from having too much *(surfeited)*.

42 *as the cuckoo . . . regarded.* The cuckoo, a bird, is noticed only when it first sings in April. Then its call, "cuckoo", is regarded as a sign of the beginning of spring; later nobody listens to it.

43 *sick . . . with community* – "tired and made less sharp *(blunted)* by seeing so often (just as a knife is blunted by too frequent use)".

44 *sun-like,* because the sun is the brightest of the stars and seems to "rule" the sky, it was thought of as a symbol for royalty.

45 *drowsed* – "became sleepy".

46 *Slept in his face . . . aspect* – "slept in his presence, and gave such a look".

47 *cloudy men,* in two senses: (i) "sullen"; (ii) "men opposed to the king *(sun-like majesty)*".

48 *glutted, gorged* – "over-fed", a return to the food metaphor of lines 70–73. Henry's contempt for the man he had deposed is shown in the imagery throughout this scene.

49 *very line* – "same class".

50 *vile participation* – "mixing too freely with the common people".

51 *Make blind . . . tenderness* – "no longer sees (the Prince's faults) as the result of my foolish warm feelings (towards him)". *Blind* also suggests that the king speaks of tears in his eyes which prevent him from seeing.

52 *Be more myself* – "act more like a prince"

53 *For all the world* – "Exactly".

Had[35] his great name profanéd with their scorns,
And gave[36] his countenance against his name   65
To laugh at gibing[37] boys, and stand[38] the push
Of every beardless vain comparative;
Grew[39] a companion to the common streets,
Enfeoffed[40] himself to popularity,
That,[41] being daily swallowed by men's eyes,   70
They surfeited with honey, and began
To loathe the taste of sweetness, whereof a little
More than a little is by much too much.
So, when he had occasion to be seen,
He was but as the cuckoo[42] is in June,   75
Heard, not regarded; seen, but with such eyes
As, sick[43] and blunted with community,
Afford no extraordinary gaze
Such as is bent on sun-like[44] majesty
When it shines seldom in admiring eyes,   80
But rather drowsed[45] and hung their eyelids down,
Slept in his face,[46] and rendered such aspect
As cloudy[47] men use to their adversaries,
Being with his presence glutted,[48] gorged, and full.
And in that very line,[49] Harry, standest thou,   85
For thou hast lost thy princely privilege
With vile participation.[50] Not an eye
But is a-weary of thy common sight,
Save mine, which hath desired to see thee more,
Which now doth that I would not have it do,   90
Make[51] blind itself with foolish tenderness.

PRINCE

I shall hereafter, my thrice gracious lord,
Be[52] more myself.

KING

                For[53] all the world
As thou art to this hour was Richard then

159

54 *from France . . . Ravenspurgh,* when
Bolingbroke arrived at the English
port of Ravenspurgh after his exile
in France, where he had been sent
by Richard II.

55 *even as I . . . now.* Hotspur is now
like the Bolingbroke of earlier years
in two ways: he is now trying to
take the throne; and he is respected
because he has not made himself a
common sight.

56 *to boot* – "as well".

57 *He hath . . . succession* – "his merits
give him a stronger claim to the
throne than your own hope through
an uncertain right of inheritance".

58 *colour* – "excuse".

59 *harness* – "armed soldiers".

60 *Turns head . . . jaws* – "uses his
forces to fight against the King's
army".

61 *no more in debt to years* – "no older".

62 *bruising arms* – "battles causing
wounds".

63 *Douglas,* Hotspur's victory over
Douglas is mentioned in I.i.67–72.

64 *high . . . hot incursions* – "brave deeds
and fierce attacks".

65 *Holds from . . . majority* – "take away
from all other soldiers the claim to
be the best fighter".

66 *capital* – "chief".

67 *Thrice,* (i) on 19 August 1388 at
Otterburn, where Douglas won; (ii) on 22 June 1402 at Nisbet; (iii)
on 14 September 1402 at Holmedon.

68 *Mars . . . clothes* – "god of war in
baby clothes", i.e. very young victorious general.

69 *discomfited* – "matched in battle".

70 *ta'en him once, Enlargéd him* – "captured him once (i.e. at Holmedon)
and set him free".

71 *To fill . . . defiance up,* either (i) "to
increase the sound of rebellion", or
(ii) "to feed the appetite for rebellion full".

72 *Capitulate . . . are up* – "draw up an
agreement against us and are ready
for war".

73 *these news* – "these items of information".

74 *dearest,* in two senses: (i) "most
loved"; (ii) "worst".

75 *vassal fear . . . spleen* – "slavish fear,
attraction towards the low, and the
action of ill-temper".

76 *dog his heels,* follow him as a dog
follows his master's heels.

77 *curtsy at his frowns* – "bow humbly
when he looks stern".

When I from[54] France set foot at Ravenspurgh,   95
And even as I was then is Percy[55] now.
Now by my sceptre and my soul to boot,[56]
He[57] hath more worthy interest to the state
Than thou the shadow of succession.
For of no right, nor colour[58] like to right,   100
He doth fill fields with harness[59] in the realm,
Turns[60] head against the lion's arméd jaws,
And, being no[61] more in debt to years than thou,
Leads ancient lords and reverend bishops on
To bloody battles and to bruising[62] arms.   105
What never-dying honour hath he got
Against renownéd Douglas![63] whose high[64] deeds,
Whose hot incursions and great name in arms,
Holds[65] from all soldiers chief majority
And military title capital[66]   110
Through all the kingdoms that acknowledge Christ.
Thrice[67] hath this Hotspur, Mars[68] in swathling clothes,
This infant warrior, in his enterprises
Discomfited[69] great Douglas, ta'en[70] him once,
Enlargéd him, and made a friend of him,   115
To fill[71] the mouth of deep defiance up,
And shake the peace and safety of our throne.
And what say you to this? Percy, Northumberland,
The Archbishop's Grace of York, Douglas, Mortimer,
Capitulate[72] against us and are up.   120
But wherefore do I tell these[73] news to thee?
Why, Harry, do I tell thee of my foes,
Which art my nearest and dearest[74] enemy?
Thou that art like enough, through vassal[75] fear,
Base inclination, and the start of spleen,   125
To fight against me under Percy's pay,
To dog[76] his heels, and curtsy[77] at his frowns,
To show how much thou art degenerate.

161

78 *I will redeem*. This whole speech looks forward to Hal's victory over Hotspur at Shrewsbury (v.iv).

79 *favours*, in two senses: (i) "face"; (ii) "the object, such as a scarf worn on a knight's helmet in battle". Hal speaks of shedding blood and being washed afterwards as if it were a form of religious purification to redeem his misspent past.

80 *lights* – "happens".

81 *unthought-of* – "not highly esteemed".

82 *helm* – "helmet".

83 *Would they were multitudes* – "I wish they were even greater in number than they are".

84 *indignities* – "unworthy actions".

85 *factor* – "agent".

86 *engross up* – "acquire great quantities of".

87 *shall render . . . up*. A knight who overcomes another in a battle takes over all the honours his opponent has already won. Hotspur refers to this custom when he is dying (v.iv).

88 *slightest worship . . . time* – "even the smallest honour paid him during his life".

89 *if He be pleased* – "if God wills".

90 *salve . . . my intemperance* – "heal the injuries caused over a long period by my unrestrained behaviour *(intemperance)*"; *wounds* carries on the metaphor of *salve* ("heal").

91 *bands* – "bonds", i.e. "vows".

92 *parcel* – "part".

93 *in this* – "as the result of this (speech)".

94 *Thou shalt . . . herein* – "You shall have command *(charge)* over an army and highest *(sovereign)* trust in this battle *(herein)*".

PRINCE

Do not think so; you shall not find it so;
And God forgive them that so much have swayed   130
Your Majesty's good thoughts away from me!
I[78] will redeem all this on Percy's head,
And in the closing of some glorious day
Be bold to tell you that I am your son,
When I will wear a garment all of blood,   135
And stain my favours[79] in a bloody mask,
Which, washed away, shall scour my shame with it;
And that shall be the day, whene'er it lights,[80]
That this same child of honour and renown,
This gallant Hotspur, this all-praised knight,   140
And your unthought-of[81] Harry chance to meet.
For every honour sitting on his helm,[82]
Would[83] they were multitudes, and on my head
My shames redoubled! For the time will come
That I shall make this northern youth exchange   145
His glorious deeds for my indignities.[84]
Percy is but my factor,[85] good my lord,
To engross[86] up glorious deeds on my behalf;
And I will call him to so strict account
That he shall[87] render every glory up,   150
Yea, even the slightest[88] worship of his time,
Or I will tear the reckoning from his heart.
This in the name of God I promise here,
The which if[89] He be pleased I shall perform,
I do beseech your Majesty may salve[90]   155
The long-grown wounds of my intemperance:
If not, the end of life cancels all bands,[91]
And I will die a hundred thousand deaths
Ere break the smallest parcel[92] of this vow.

KING

A hundred thousand rebels die in[93] this –   160
Thou[94] shalt have charge and sovereign trust herein.

95 *are full of speed* – "suggest the need for haste".

96 *So hath . . . business* – "So does my business (require immediate attention)".

97 *Lord Mortimer.* George Dunbar, Earl of March. Shakespeare wrongly assumed that the Scottish Earls of March were Mortimers like the English Earls of March.

98 *fearful head* – "army to be feared (*fearful*)".

99 *foul play* – "unlawful action".

100 *advertisement* – "information".

101 *by which account . . . valuéd* – "by which reckoning, having estimated (*valuéd*) the time our business will take".

102 *him* – "himself". The general sense of this line is that those who seize a favourable opportunity when others hold back will succeed.

(III.iii) At the Boar's Head Tavern Falstaff begins to speak of repenting and reforming. He then asks the Hostess if she has found out who picked his pocket. She replies angrily, suspecting that he is trying to avoid paying his old bills for food and drink. In the argument that follows, Falstaff speaks disrespectfully of the Prince. Hal arrives and encourages Falstaff to describe his loss in detail. He claims he has lost far more than the Prince has taken from his pocket. Both the Prince and the Hostess treat his story with mocking scorn and the latter reports Falstaff's remarks about the Prince. When the Hostess is out of the room, the Prince relates that the stolen money has been paid back. He reports that he is friends with his father again and has obtained a command of foot-soldiers for Falstaff.

1 *fallen away vilely* – "become terribly thin".

2 *last action.* Falstaff refers to the robbery at Gad's Hill and its results and he speaks of it as if it were a military "action".

3 *bate* – "grow smaller".

4 *loose gown*, a shapeless garment worn by old women.

5 *apple-john*, an apple with skin that wrinkles if it is kept for a time.

6 *suddenly* – "at once".

7 *I am . . . liking*, in two senses: (i) "while I feel like doing so"; (ii) "while I still have some flesh on me".

8 *out of heart*, in two senses: (i) "disinclined"; (ii) "in poor condition"

Enter BLUNT

How now, good Blunt? Thy looks are full[95] of speed.

BLUNT

So[96] hath the business that I come to speak of.
Lord[97] Mortimer of Scotland hath sent word
That Douglas and the English rebels met   165
The eleventh of this month at Shrewsbury.
A mighty and a fearful[98] head they are,
If promises be kept on every hand,
As ever offered foul[99] play in a state.

KING

The Earl of Westmoreland set forth today,   170
With him my son, Lord John of Lancaster,
For this advertisement[100] is five days old.
On Wednesday next, Harry, you shall set forward,
On Thursday we ourselves will march.
Our meeting is Bridgnorth; and, Harry, you   175
Shall march through Gloucestershire, by which account,[101]
Our business valuéd, some twelve days hence
Our general forces at Bridgnorth shall meet.
Our hands are full of business, let 's away;
Advantage feeds him[102] fat while men delay.   [*Exeunt* 180

Scene III. Eastcheap. The Boar's Head Tavern.

Enter FALSTAFF *and* BARDOLPH.

FALSTAFF

Bardolph, am I not fallen[1] away vilely since this last[2] action?
Do I not bate?[3] Do I not dwindle? Why, my skin hangs about
me like an old lady's loose[4] gown. I am withered like an old
apple-john.[5] Well, I 'll repent, and that suddenly,[6] while I am
in some liking;[7] I shall be out of heart[8] shortly, and then I shall   5

9 *a peppercorn, a brewer's horse.* A peppercorn is very small; a brewer's horse was usually thin from over-work. One of Falstaff's favourite ways of asserting the truth of what he is saying is to invite his hearers to call him something strange if he is telling a lie.

10 *hath been the spoil* – "has ruined".

11 *fretful,* in two senses: (i) "inclined to worry"; (ii) "wearing away".

12 *there is it* – "that's it". Falstaff's mood soon changes; he forgets his thoughts of repentance. This comic treatment of Falstaff's repentance, following immediately after the grave treatment of Hal's vow to redeem his faults (III.ii), reveals Shakespeare's skill in relating and contrasting serious and humorous scenes in the play.

13 *was as virtuously given* – "behaved as virtuously". In this speech Falstaff jokingly describes his far from virtuous life.

14 *bawdy-house,* house of vice where men pay to be received by women.

15 *quarter* – "quarter of a year", but Falstaff immediately changes the meaning when he adds *of an hour.*

16 *good compass* – "within bounds", i.e. lived an orderly life. This and other references to disorder describe Falstaff's life, but they also link him to the characters who represented the spirit of "disorder" and "misrule" in the old religious plays in which man's virtues and vices were represented by dramatic characters.

17 *out of all . . . compass.* Bardolph makes a joke about Falstaff's fat stomach which has grown beyond its normal limits *(compass).*

18 *admiral . . . nose of thee.* In a navy, other ships followed the light *(lantern)* in the back *(the poop)* of the *admiral* (the leading ship). Bardolph's "lantern" is his red nose.

19 *Knight of the Burning Lamp.* Falstaff jokingly remembers Amadis, the Knight of the Burning Sword, a hero of a famous Spanish story.

20 *No, I'll be sworn* – "No, I agree".

21 *death's-head, or a memento mori,* a skull, or any object used or worn as a reminder of death.

22 *Dives.* The reference is to the story of Dives, the rich man, and Lazarus, the beggar, in the Bible *(Luke* 16 v.19–31). Dives wore fine purple robes when alive; afterwards he suffered the fires of hell.

23 *given to virtue* – "virtuous".

24 *God's angel,* angels were believed to appear flaming.

have no strength to repent. An I have not forgotten what the
inside of a church is made of, I am a peppercorn,[9] a brewer's
horse – the inside of a church! Company, villainous company,
hath[10] been the spoil of me.

BARDOLPH

Sir John, you are so fretful[11] you cannot live long.   10

FALSTAFF

Why, there[12] is it. Come, sing me a bawdy song, make me
merry. I was as virtuously[13] given as a gentleman need to be:
virtuous enough; swore little; diced not above seven times –
a week; went to a bawdy-house[14] not above once in a quarter[15]
– of an hour; paid money that I borrowed – three or four times;   15
lived well, and in good compass;[16] and now I live out of all
order, out of all compass.

BARDOLPH

Why, you are so fat, Sir John, that you must needs be out of all
compass, out[17] of all reasonable compass, Sir John.

FALSTAFF

Do thou amend thy face, and I 'll amend my life: thou art our   20
admiral,[18] thou bearest the lantern in the poop, but 't is in the
nose of thee: thou art the Knight[19] of the Burning Lamp.

BARDOLPH

Why, Sir John, my face does you no harm.

FALSTAFF

No,[20] I 'll be sworn, I make as good use of it as many a man doth
of a death's-head,[21] or a *memento mori*. I never see thy face but I   25
think upon hell-fire, and Dives[22] that lived in purple, for there
he is in his robes, burning, burning. If thou wert any way
given[23] to virtue, I would swear by thy face: my oath should be
"By this fire, that 's God's[24] angel!" But thou art altogether

25 *thou art altogether . . . utter darkness* – "you are altogether inclined to evil *(given over)* and if you had not that light (the red nose) in your face, you would be a man living in the outer *(utter)* darkness (of evil)".

26 *ignis fatuus*, a light that leads travellers out of their way.

27 *ball of wildfire*, in two senses: (i) "a flaming ball of explosive powder"; (ii) "lightning".

28 *no purchase in money* – "money is of no value".

29 *triumph* – "public festival". Torches and bright lights were used at festivals.

30 *marks*. A mark was 13s. 4d.

31 *links*, burning lights on the ends of sticks, carried to show the way by night.

32 *the sack . . . as good cheap* – "the money I have spent on the amount of sack you have drunk would have bought enough candles to give me just as good a light".

33 *maintained . . . thirty years* – "kept your nose *(that salamander)* fiery red (by providing free drink) for the whole of thirty-two years". A salamander is a small animal that was once thought able to live in fire.

34 *I would . . . your belly* – "I wish my face were in your stomach (where there is always a good supply of sack)".

35 *heartburnt*. To suit Bardolph, Falstaff picks on a bodily disorder that contains the idea of "burning". *Heartburn* is a burning pain in the throat or breast.

36 *Dame Partlet*, a common name for a hen and so for a scolding woman.

37 *picked my pocket* – "stole goods out of my pocket".

38 *shaved and lost many a hair*. In speaking of the *tithe* (one-tenth) *of a hair*, Mistress Quickly meant that not even the smallest, most unimportant thing had ever been lost in her house, but Falstaff pretends to believe that she was really talking about hairs.

39 *Go to* – "I don't believe a word of it".

40 *never called so*, Mistress Quickly takes Falstaff's *you are a woman* to mean "you are a bad woman".

that salamander of yours[33]

168

given[25] over; and wert indeed, but for the light in thy face, the 30
son of utter darkness. When thou ranst up Gad's Hill in the
night to catch my horse, if I did not think thou hadst been an
ignis fatuus,[26] or a ball[27] of wildfire, there 's no purchase[28] in
money. O, thou art a perpetual triumph,[29] an everlasting
bonfire-light! Thou hast saved me a thousand marks[30] in links[31] 35
and torches, walking with thee in the night betwixt tavern and
tavern; but the sack[32] thou hast drunk me would have bought
me lights as good cheap as the dearest chandler's in Europe. I
have maintained[33] that salamander of yours with fire any time
this two and thirty years, God reward me for it! 40

BARDOLPH

'Sblood, I would[34] my face were in your belly!

FALSTAFF

God-a-mercy! so should I be sure to be heartburnt.[35]

Enter HOSTESS

How now, Dame Partlet[36] the hen, have you enquired yet who
picked[37] my pocket?

HOSTESS

Why, Sir John, what do you think, Sir John, do you think I 45
keep thieves in my house? I have searched, I have enquired, so
has my husband, man by man, boy by boy, servant by servant
– the tithe of a hair was never lost in my house before.

FALSTAFF

Ye lie, hostess; Bardolph was shaved[38] and lost many a hair,
and I 'll be sworn my pocket was picked. Go[39] to, you are a 50
woman, go.

HOSTESS

Who, I? No, I defy thee: God's light, I was never[40] called so in
mine own house before.

41 *beguile me* – "rob me by deceit".

42 *to your back* – "for you to wear on your back".

43 *Dowlas,* a coarse linen cloth. Falstaff suggests that the material was of poor quality, full of fine holes, so that it could make cloths for sifting flour *(bolters)* but was not good enough for shirts.

44 *holland . . . an ell* – "good linen cloth *(holland)* which cost eight shillings an ell (1¼ yards)".

45 *diet, and by-drinkings* – "food, and drink between meals".

46 *He,* Bardolph.

47 *What call . . . rich?* Falstaff points to Bardolph's richly-coloured nose.

48 *coin* – "make money from".

49 *denier,* a small copper coin worth 1/10 of a penny.

50 *younker,* in two senses: (i) "a waster"; (ii) "an inexperienced youth".

51 *take mine ease* – "rest and enjoy myself".

52 *seal-ring,* a ring bearing a man's official seal, used to impress his mark in wax on a letter.

53 *How?* – "What do you say?"

54 *Jack, a sneak-up* – "dishonest fellow, a cowardly creeping fellow".

55 *cudgel,* beat with a thick stick *(cudgel)*.

FALSTAFF

Go to, I know you well enough.

HOSTESS

No, Sir John, you do not know me, Sir John, I know you, Sir   55
John, you owe me money, Sir John, and now you pick a quarrel to
beguile[41] me of it. I bought you a dozen of shirts to[42] your back.

FALSTAFF

Dowlas,[43] filthy dowlas. I have given them away to bakers'
wives; they have made bolters of them.

HOSTESS

Now as I am a true woman, holland[44] of eight shillings an ell!   60
You owe money here besides, Sir John, for your diet,[45] and by-
drinkings, and money lent you, four and twenty pound.

FALSTAFF

He[46] had his part of it; let him pay.

HOSTESS

He? Alas, he is poor, he hath nothing.

FALSTAFF

How? Poor? Look upon his face. What[47] call you rich? Let   65
them coin[48] his nose, let them coin his cheeks, I 'll not pay a
denier.[49] What, will you make a younker[50] of me? Shall I not
take[51] mine ease in mine inn but I shall have my pocket picked?
I have lost a seal-ring[52] of my grandfather's worth forty mark.

HOSTESS

O Jesu, I have heard the Prince tell him, I know not how oft,   70
that that ring was copper.

FALSTAFF

How?[53] the Prince is a Jack,[54] a sneak-up. 'Sblood, and he were
here I would cudgel[55] him like a dog if he would say so.

56 *fife* – "flute".
57 *Is the wind . . . door* – "Is the wind blowing from that quarter, i.e. is it now time for us to be soldiers marching off to war?"
58 *Newgate fashion,* as prisoners are taken to Newgate prison, fastened together in twos.

59 *list* – "listen"
60 *arras,* curtain used as a screen.
61 *bonds,* written promises to pay money to the bearer of the paper.

Enter the PRINCE *marching, with* PETO, *and* FALSTAFF
meets him, playing upon his truncheon like a fife.[56]

How now, lad? Is[57] the wind in that door, i' faith; must we all
march?   75

BARDOLPH

Yea, two and two, Newgate[58] fashion.

HOSTESS

My lord, I pray you hear me.

PRINCE

What sayest thou, Mistress Quickly? How doth thy husband?
I love him well, he is an honest man.

HOSTESS

Good my lord, hear me.   80

FALSTAFF

Prithee let her alone, and list[59] to me.

PRINCE

What sayest thou, Jack?

FALSTAFF

The other night I fell asleep here, behind the arras,[60] and had
my pocket picked. This house is turned bawdy-house, they pick
pockets.   85

PRINCE

What didst thou lose, Jack?

FALSTAFF

Wilt thou believe me, Hal, three or four bonds[61] of forty pound
apiece, and a seal-ring of my grandfather's.

62 *eightpenny matter* - "matter of no importance".

63 *What! he did not,* the Prince pretends to be surprised.

64 *else* - "if I have not told the truth".

65 *stewed prune* - "a bad woman"; stewed prunes were connected with "bawdy houses".

66 *drawn fox,* fox that has been drawn out of hiding. It is then more than usually cunning.

67 *and for womanhood . . . thee* - "and Maid Marian would be a perfect example of womanly virtue *(the deputy's wife of the ward)* compared to you". Maid Marian was a character in country dances and as she was often played by a man the name became connected with improper behaviour. *Ward* is a division of a city; the deputy was its most responsible citizen and hence his wife should normally be a model of virtue.

68 *you thing* - "you creature", a term of abuse.

69 *what thing?* the Hostess protests against being spoken to so scornfully.

70 *setting . . . aside* - "taking no notice of the fact that you are a knight". A knight, being a man of high rank, would not be expected to behave like a low common fellow *(knave)*.

PRINCE

A trifle, some eightpenny[62] matter.

HOSTESS

So I told him, my lord, and I said I heard your Grace say so: 90
and, my lord, he speaks most vilely of you, like a foul-mouthed
man as he is, and said he would cudgel you.

PRINCE

What![63] he did not?

HOSTESS

There 's neither faith, truth, nor womanhood in me else.[64]

FALSTAFF

There 's no more faith in thee than in a stewed[65] prune, nor no   95
more truth in thee than in a drawn[66] fox – and for womanhood,[67] Maid Marian may be the deputy's wife of the ward to
thee. Go, you thing,[68] go!

HOSTESS

Say, what[69] thing, what thing?

FALSTAFF

What thing? Why, a thing to thank God on.   105

HOSTESS

I am no thing to thank God on, I would thou shouldst know it;
I am an honest man's wife, and setting[70] thy knighthood aside,
thou art a knave to call me so.

FALSTAFF

Setting thy womanhood aside, thou art a beast to say otherwise.

HOSTESS

Say, what beast, thou knave, thou?   110

71 *where to have her* – "how to understand her".

72 *where to have me* – "that he can trust me".

73 *ought* – "owed".

74 *Sirrah.* The Prince speaks to Falstaff not as an equal but as an inferior; his tone here becomes more severe.

75 *thy love . . . million.* Falstaff tries to escape from a difficult position by using humorous flattery.

FALSTAFF

What beast? Why, an otter.

PRINCE

An otter, Sir John? Why an otter?

FALSTAFF

Why? She's neither fish nor flesh; a man knows not where[71] to
have her.

HOSTESS

Thou art an unjust man in saying so; thou or any man knows 115
where to have[72] me, thou knave, thou.

PRINCE

Thou sayest true, hostess, and he slanders thee most grossly.

HOSTESS

So he doth you, my lord, and said this other day you ought[73]
him a thousand pound.

PRINCE

Sirrah,[74] do I owe you a thousand pound? 120

FALSTAFF

A thousand pound, Hal? A million, thy[75] love is worth a
million, thou owest me thy love.

HOSTESS

Nay, my lord, he called you Jack, and said he would cudgel you.

FALSTAFF

Did I, Bardolph?

BARDOLPH

Indeed, Sir John, you said so. 125

76 *if he . . . fear thee* (line 129). Falstaff admits that he said he would strike the Prince, but skilfully suggests that his threat was conditional – if he said the ring was copper. Then when the Prince fulfils the condition *(I say 't is copper)* Falstaff gives the situation a new twist by reminding the Prince that they are not equals and that it is this inequality, not any cowardice, that prevents him from carrying out his threat to beat him.

77 *lion's whelp,* the young of a lion. The lion is used here as a symbol for the king.

78 *dost thou . . . father.* Falstaff again skilfully and humorously turns the argument to his own advantage by pleading higher loyalty to the king.

79 *bosom* – "breast", first thought of as the centre of the feelings (of *faith* and *truth*) and then as part of Falstaff's gross body.

80 *midriff* – "stomach"

81 *whoreson,* a term of contempt.

82 *embossed* – "swollen".

83 *long-winded,* fighting cocks were given sugar to give them longer breath.

84 *injuries,* objects of whose loss Falstaff complains as an injury.

85 *stand to it* – "insist that your story is true".

86 *pocket up wrong,* accept a wrong done to one without protest.

87 *Adam fell,* a reference to the Fall of Man as recorded in the first book of the Bible, *Genesis.* Falstaff here returns to religious language, and claims that, as Adam committed a sin when the world was innocent, it is much more difficult for himself, Falstaff, to be virtuous now that the world had become wicked *(in the days of villainy).*

88 *therefore more frailty,* Falstaff refers to the saying "the flesh is frail", based on the Bible (*Matthew* 26 v.41 and *Mark* 14 v.38), "the flesh is weak".

178

FALSTAFF

Yea, if[76] he said my ring was copper.

PRINCE

I say 't is copper, darest thou be as good as thy word now?

FALSTAFF

Why, Hal, thou knowest as thou art but man I dare, but as thou art prince, I fear thee as I fear the roaring of the lion's whelp.[77]

PRINCE

And why not as the lion?   130

FALSTAFF

The King himself is to be feared as the lion: dost[78] thou think I 'll fear thee as I fear thy father? Nay, and I do, I pray God my girdle break.

PRINCE

O, if it should, how would thy guts fall about thy knees! But sirrah, there 's no room for faith, truth, nor honesty in this 135 bosom[79] of thine; it is all filled up with guts and midriff.[80] Charge an honest woman with picking thy pocket? Why, thou whoreson[81] impudent embossed[82] rascal, if there were anything in thy pocket but tavern reckonings, memorandums of bawdy-houses, and one poor pennyworth of sugar-candy to make thee 140 long-winded,[83] if thy pocket were enriched with any other injuries[84] but these, I am a villain; and yet you will stand[85] to it, you will not pocket[86] up wrong! Art thou not ashamed?

FALSTAFF

Dost thou hear, Hal? Thou knowest in the state of innocency Adam[87] fell, and what should poor Jack Falstaff do in the days 145 of villainy? Thou seest I have more flesh than another man, and therefore[88] more frailty. You confess then, you picked my pocket?

179

89 *I forgive thee . . . guests.* Falstaff's
shamelessness and quick humour
make him pretend that it is he who
is sinned against. His phrases about
duties to husband, servants and
guests are Biblical (*Ephesians* 5 and
6); *look to* – "attend to".

90 *tractable to* – "willing to act according to".

91 *pacified still* – "always ready to be
peaceful (after a quarrel)".

92 *answered* – "dealt with".

93 *beef* – "ox", referring to Falstaff's
gross flesh.

94 *good angel* – "a good influence on".

95 *paying back . . . labour.* Stealing the
money was one labour; paying it
back doubles the amount of labour.

96 *do it . . . hands too* – "do it immediately".

97 *charge of foot,* position of officer-in-
charge of foot soldiers.

98 *I would . . . horse.* Falstaff immediately wishes that he had been put in
charge of soldiers on horseback so
that he would have had a horse to
carry his heavy weight.

99 *laud* – "praise".

PRINCE

It appears so by the story.

FALSTAFF

Hostess, I forgive[89] thee, go make ready breakfast, love thy 150
husband, look to thy servants, cherish thy guests, thou shalt find
me tractable[90] to any honest reason; thou seest I am pacified[91]
still, nay prithee be gone. [*Exit* HOSTESS] Now, Hal, to the
news at court: for the robbery, lad, how is that answered?[92]

RINCE

O my sweet beef,[93] I must still be good angel[94] to thee – the 155
money is paid back again.

FALSTAFF

O, I do not like that paying[95] back, 't is a double labour.

PRINCE

I am good friends with my father and may do anything.

FALSTAFF

Rob me the exchequer the first thing thou dost, and do[96] it with
unwashed hands too.   160

BARDOLPH

Do, my lord.

PRINCE

I have procured thee, Jack, a charge[97] of foot.

FALSTAFF

I[98] would it had been of horse. Where shall I find one that can
steal well? O for a fine thief of the age of two and twenty or
thereabouts: I am heinously unprovided. Well, God be thanked 165
for these rebels, they offend none but the virtuous; I laud[99]
them, I praise them.

100 *Temple Hall*, Inner Temple Hall in London, a common meeting place.
101 *thy charge* – "soldiers you are in charge of".
102 *furniture*, things necessary to fit soldiers ready for battle.

103 *burning* – "full of fiery passions".
104 *were my drum* – "were the place where my soldiers would assemble".

PRINCE

Bardolph!

BARDOLPH

My lord?

PRINCE

Go bear this letter to Lord John of Lancaster,   170
To my brother John, this to my Lord of Westmoreland.

[*Exit* BARDOLPH

Go, Peto, to horse, to horse, for thou and I
Have thirty miles to ride ere dinner-time.

[*Exit* PETO

Jack, meet me tomorrow in the Temple[100] Hall
At two o'clock in the afternoon: 175
There shalt thou know thy charge,[101] and there receive
Money and order for their furniture.[102]
The land is burning,[103] Percy stands on high,
And either we or they must lower lie.

[*Exit*

FALSTAFF

Rare words! Brave world! Hostess, my breakfast, come!   180
O, I could wish this tavern were my drum.[104]

[*Exit*

183

(IV.i) The scene opens in the middle of a conversation between Hotspur and Douglas in which they speak confidently of their chance of success. A messenger brings news that Hotspur's father, Northumberland, is ill and will not bring his army to join the rebels. After a moment's anxiety, Hotspur regains confidence, but Worcester fears that Northumberland's absence will discourage their supporters. More news is brought by Sir Richard Vernon: the King's forces are well prepared for war, and Prince Hal has shown himself as the perfect knight in arms, eager for battle. Hotspur vows to meet him in a fight to the death. Vernon adds one further piece of bad news: Glendower's army will not be ready for another two weeks.

1 *Well said*. The scene opens in the middle of a conversation. Douglas has suggested a course of action that meets with Hotspur's approval.

2 *fine*, used ironically. Hotspur does not think it is a very good age.

3 *attribution* – "praise".

4 *As not . . . current* – "that no soldier living in this age would be more honoured".

5 *defy* – "despise".

6 *soothers* – "flatterers".

7 *braver* – "more excellent".

8 *task me . . . approve me* – "test me to see that my actions fit my word, put me to the proof".

9 *king of honour* – "chief man of honour among us".

10 *No man . . . beard him* – "There is no man living *(breathes)* anywhere on earth so powerful *(potent)* that I will not oppose him face to face *(beard)*". *But* – "that . . . not".

11 *Do so, and 't is well*. Hotspur probably refers to something said before the scene begins.

12 *I can but thank you*, probably spoken to Douglas.

13 *grievous* – "very".

184

ACT FOUR

Scene I. Shrewsbury. The Rebel Camp.

Enter HOTSPUR, WORCESTER, *and* DOUGLAS.

HOTSPUR

Well[1] said, my noble Scot! If speaking truth
In this fine[2] age were not thought flattery,
Such attribution[3] should the Douglas have
As[4] not a soldier of this season's stamp
Should go so general current through the world.   5
By God, I cannot flatter; I do defy[5]
The tongues of soothers,[6] but a braver[7] place
In my heart's love hath no man than yourself.
Nay, task[8] me to my word, approve me, lord.

DOUGLAS

Thou art the king[9] of honour.   10
No[10] man so potent breathes upon the ground
But I will beard him.

HOTSPUR

Do[11] so, and 't is well.

Enter a Messenger *with letters*

What letters hast thou there? – I can[12] but thank you.

MESSENGER

These letters come from your father.

HOTSPUR

Letters from him? Why comes he not himself?   15

MESSENGER

He cannot come, my lord, he is grievous[13] sick.

185

14 *how has he the leisure* – "how can he find time". Hotspur does not show the grief of a son for a sick father, but the anger of a commander whose supporter fails to arrive.

15 *justling time* – "unsettled time", when people are shaken and pushed one against another.

16 *power* – "army".

17 *government* – "command".

18 *bear his mind* – "convey his meaning".

19 *keep his bed* – "stay in bed".

20 *He was . . . physicians* – "his doctors feared that he might not recover".

21 *I would . . . whole* – "I wish the situation had been normal *(whole)*".

22 *better worth* – "of more value".

23 *Sick.* Throughout this and following speeches the state of the rebel's cause is expressed in terms of health and sickness. The figure of speech comes naturally after the news that Northumberland is sick and cannot therefore march with his army to aid the rebels.

24 *Droop* – "Grow weak".

25 *catching* – "infectious". Hotspur speaks as if his father's sickness had a direct effect on the success *(health)* of their attempt.

26 *inward,* affecting the interior organs of the body. Hotspur here breaks off what he has begun to say and passes quickly to another detail in the letter.

27 *his friends . . . drawn* – "his friends could not so soon be assembled *(drawn)* by a substitute leader *(by deputation)*".

28 *meet* – "fit".

29 *dear* – "important".

30 *On any . . . own* – "on any person less directly concerned than himself".

31 *advertisement* – "counsel".

32 *with our small conjunction . . . to us* – "with our small combined forces *(conjunction)* we should march ahead to see whether fortune will bring us success".

33 *possessed . . . our purposes* – "informed of all our plans".

HOTSPUR

'Zounds, how[14] has he the leisure to be sick
In such a justling[15] time? Who leads his power?[16]
Under whose government[17] come thy along?

MESSENGER

His letters bear[18] his mind, not I, my lord.   20

WORCESTER

I prithee tell me, doth he keep[19] his bed?

MESSENGER

He did, my lord, four days ere I set forth,
And at the time of my departure thence
He[20] was much feared by his physicians.

WORCESTER

I[21] would the state of time had first been whole   25
Ere he by sickness had been visited:
His health was never better[22] worth than now.

HOTSPUR

Sick[23] now? Droop[24] now? This sickness doth infect
The very life-blood of our enterprise;
'T is catching[25] hither, even to our camp.   30
He writes me here that inward[26] sickness –
And that his friends[27] by deputation could not
So soon be drawn, nor did he think it meet[28]
To lay so dangerous and dear[29] a trust
On[30] any soul removed but on his own.   35
Yet doth he give us bold advertisement[31]
That with our small conjunction[32] we should on
To see how fortune is disposed to us;
For, as he writes, there is no quailing now,
Because the King is certainly possessed[33]   40
Of all our purposes. What say you to it?

34 *maim* – "wound".

35 *A perilous .... lopped off.* Hotspur describes his father's absence through sickness as a deep cut in their side and as a loss of limb.

36 *His present . . . more* – "The loss of him at this present moment seems more serious".

37 *Were it good . . . doubtful hour* (line 48) – "Would it be wise to risk *(set)* the whole *(exact)* wealth of all our fortunes at one throw *(cast)* of the dice? To risk so valuable a store *(main)* on the evenly-balanced chance *(nice hazard)* of a single occasion *(hour)* when there is doubt of success?" Hotspur compares fighting with playing games for money, and unwisely concludes that, because a gamester does not risk all his money at one throw, a commander should not put all his soldiers into one battle.

38 *therein . . . fortunes* (line 52) – "in a single battle *(therein)* we should see plainly on what our hope depends, the bottom, the limit *(very list)*, the farthest extent of all our fortunes".

39 *where* – "but".

40 *sweet reversion,* an inheritance to which one looks forward eagerly.

41 *boldly spend . . . come in,* boldly use our present strength, knowing that a new supply of soldiers will come in later (from Northumberland).

42 *A comfort . . . in this* – "A retreat to which we can retire for support lies in this hope *(in this)*".

43 *rendezvous* – "a place to retreat to".

44 *devil . . . big Upon* – "danger and bad luck threaten".

45 *maidenhead* – "beginning".

46 *hair of our attempt* – "character of our adventure".

47 *Brooks no* – "will not endure".

48 *mere* – "absolute".

49 *apprehension* – "thought".

50 *may turn . . . cause* – "may cause timid supporters of the rebellion to change their minds and return to the king's side and may encourage people to wonder if our party is a good one and likely to succeed".

WORCESTER

Your father's sickness is a maim[34] to us.

HOTSPUR

A perilous[35] gash, a very limb lopped off –
And yet, in faith, it is not! His present[36] want
Seems more than we shall find it. Were[37] it good   45
To set the exact wealth of all our states
All at one cast? to set so rich a main
On the nice hazard of one doubtful hour?
It were not good, for therein[38] should we read
The very bottom and the soul of hope,   50
The very list, the very utmost bound
Of all our fortunes.

DOUGLAS

Faith, and so we should, where[39] now remains
A sweet[40] reversion – we may boldly[41] spend
Upon the hope of what is to come in.   55
A comfort[42] of retirement lives in this.

HOTSPUR

A rendezvous,[43] a home to fly unto,
If that the devil[44] and mischance look big
Upon the maidenhead[45] of our affairs.

WORCESTER

But yet I would your father had been here: 60
The quality and hair[46] of our attempt
Brooks[47] no division. It will be thought,
By some that know not why he is away,
That wisdom, loyalty, and mere[48] dislike
Of our proceedings kept the Earl from hence;   65
And think how such an apprehension[49]
May[50] turn the tide of fearful faction,
And breed a kind of question in our cause:

51 *offering side* – "attacking side".

52 *strict arbitrement* – "too close examination of the rightness of their cause".

53 *stop all . . . upon us* – "close up all openings, every narrow window *(loop)* through which thoughtful people *(the eye of reason)* may examine us". Worcester is anxious to keep the rebel's plans as secret as a closed-up house, because he does not want the weakness of their forces to become known.

54 *draws . . . dreamt of* – "moves aside a curtain and allows those who do not know us *(the ignorant)* to see a kind of fear that they had not imagined before".

55 *strain too far* – "place too much importance on these events".

56 *make this use* – "see it having this use".

57 *opinion* – "reputation".

58 *larger dare* – "greater boldness".

59 *make a head* – "form an army".

60 *topsy-turvy down* – "upside down".

61 *Yet* – "Up to this present moment".

62 *all our joints are whole* – "our army is strongly united".

63 *As heart can think* – "(As whole) as anyone can imagine".

64 *Pray God . . . lord* – "I wish to God the news (I bring) deserved the warm welcome you have given me".

65 *seven thousand strong* – "with an army of seven thousand men".

All furnished,[71] *all in arms;*
All plumed[72] *like estridges*

For well you know we of the offering[51] side
Must keep aloof from strict[52] arbitrement,   70
And stop[53] all sight-holes, every loop from whence
The eye of reason may pry in upon us.
This absence of your father's draws[54] a curtain
That shows the ignorant a kind of fear
Before not dreamt of.

HOTSPUR

You strain[55] too far.   75
I rather of his absence make[56] this use:
It lends a lustre and more great opinion,[57]
A larger dare[58] to our great enterprise,
Than if the Earl were here; for men must think
If we without his help can make[59] a head   80
To push against a kingdom, with his help
We shall o'erturn it topsy-turvy[60] down.
Yet[61] all goes well, yet all[62] our joints are whole.

DOUGLAS

As[63] heart can think: there is not such a word
Spoke of in Scotland as this term of fear.   85

Enter SIR RICHARD VERNON

HOTSPUR

My cousin Vernon! Welcome, by my soul!

VERNON

Pray[64] God my news be worth a welcome, lord.
The Earl of Westmoreland, seven[65] thousand strong,
Is marching hitherwards, with him Prince John.

HOTSPUR

No harm, what more?

191

66 *hitherwards . . . mighty preparation* –
"setting out *(intended)* speedily towards this place *(hitherwards)* with
a large army all prepared for battle".

67 *shall be welcome.* Hotspur means
that they are ready to meet the
King's army in battle.

68 *nimble-footed.* Accounts of Hal by
historians noted his swift running
when hunting.

69 *daft the world aside* – "waved aside
the opinions of others in the world".

70 *bid it pass* – "treated the world as of
no consequence".

71 *furnished* – "dressed for battle". In
this speech, Vernon describes Hal
through a series of images of birds
and animals, young, strong, beautiful, and finally god-like as he rides
his horse.

72 *All plumed . . . bathed* – "all adorned
with feathers *(plumed)* like ostriches
(estridges) that beat *(bated)* their
wings in the wind like eagles which
have just come from bathing".
Other explanations of this difficult
passage have been given: *estridges*
might mean another kind of bird;
with may have read *wing* in the text
of the play; *bait* could mean "re-
freshed".

73 *spirit* – "energy".

74 *Wanton as* – "as full of life as".

75 *beaver* – "helmet".

76 *cushes,* armour for the thigh.

77 *Mercury,* the flying messenger of
the Roman gods, pictured with
winged shoes *(feathered)*.

78 *with such ease.* It would be extremely
difficult to leap straight into the
saddle because of the weight of the
full armour.

79 *wind* – "wheel about".

80 *Pegasus,* an imaginary horse with
wings.

81 *witch* – "cast a spell on".

82 *Worse than . . . blood* (line 117). The
March sun was believed to cause
people to shake with fevers *(agues)*:
praise of the Prince causes Hotspur's
men to shake with dismay. In order
to change dismay to pleasure, Hotspur compares the Prince's fine
appearance with that of animals
decorated *(in their trim)* ready to be
sacrificed; and says that he will
sacrifice them to Bellona, the
Roman goddess of war *(the fire-
eyed maid of smoky war)* and Mars,
the war-god, in his armour *(mailéd)*,
i.e. he will kill the Prince and his
companions in battle.

192

VERNON

And further, I have learned,   90
The King himself in person is set forth,
Or hitherwards[66] intended speedily,
With strong and mighty preparation.

HOTSPUR

He shall[67] be welcome too. Where is his son,
The nimble-footed[68] madcap Prince of Wales,   95
And his comrades that daft[69] the world aside
And bid[70] it pass?

VERNON

All furnished,[71] all in arms;
All plumed[72] like estridges that with the wind
Bated, like eagles having lately bathed,
Glittering in golden coats like images,   100
As full of spirit[73] as the month of May,
And gorgeous as the sun at midsummer;
Wanton[74] as youthful goats, wild as young bulls.
I saw young Harry with his beaver[75] on,
His cushes[76] on his thighs, gallantly armed,   105
Rise from the ground like feathered Mercury,[77]
And vaulted with[78] such ease into his seat
As if an angel dropped down from the clouds
To turn and wind[79] a fiery Pegasus,[80]
And witch[81] the world with noble horsemanship.   110

HOTSPUR

No more, no more! Worse[82] than the sun in March,
This praise doth nourish agues. Let them come!
They come like sacrifices in their trim,
And to the fire-eyed maid of smoky war
All hot and bleeding will we offer them: 115
The mailéd Mars shall on his altar sit
Up to the ears in blood. I am on fire

83 *reprisal* – "prize".

84 *nigh* – "near".

85 *taste* – "test".

86 *bosom* – "person".

87 *Harry to Harry* – "Hotspur to Prince Hal".

88 *hot horse to horse* – "one eager horse against another".

89 *corse* – "dead body".

90 *He cannot . . . fourteen days* – "Glendower cannot collect his forces in less than fourteen days".

91 *bears a frosty sound* – "chills the heart", i.e. the news is so bad it discourages Worcester.

92 *What may . . . unto* – "What (number) does the King's whole army *(battle)* amount to?"

93 *Forty let it be* – "Even if it were forty (thousand it would make no difference)".

94 *The powers . . . serve* – "our forces will be sufficient".

95 *take a muster* – "count the number of our forces".

96 *Doomsday* – "Day of judgement", i.e. the day on which, as Christians believed, all men that had ever lived would be brought before God to be judged.

97 *die all, die merrily* – "if we all die together then we die happy in good company".

98 *out of fear* – "not afraid".

To hear this rich reprisal[83] is so nigh,[84]
And yet not ours! Come, let me taste[85] my horse,
Who is to bear me like a thunderbolt   120
Against the bosom[86] of the Prince of Wales.
Harry[87] to Harry shall, hot[88] horse to horse,
Meet and ne'er part till one drop down a corse.[89]
O that Glendower were come!

VERNON

                    There is more news:
I learned in Worcester as I rode along   125
He cannot[90] draw his power this fourteen days.

DOUGLAS

That 's the worst tidings that I hear of yet.

WORCESTER

Ay, by my faith, that bears[91] a frosty sound.

HOTSPUR

What[92] may the King's whole battle reach unto?

VERNON

To thirty thousand.

HOTSPUR

                    Forty[93] let it be: 130
My father and Glendower being both away,
The powers[94] of us may serve so great a day.
Come, let us take[95] a muster speedily –
Doomsday[96] is near; die[97] all, die merrily.

DOUGLAS

Talk not of dying, I am out[98] of fear   135
Of death or death's hand for this one half year.

                                              [*Exeunt*

(IV.ii) Falstaff, now a captain and on his way to join the King at Shrewsbury, sends Bardolph to buy some wine. In his absence he gives a humorous explanation of why all his soldiers are so poor. At first he carefully chose men with enough money to pay for their release from military service. Only those too poor to pay have remained. Prince Hal and Westmoreland arrive. Falstaff jokes with Hal, but is reminded by Westmoreland that they are eagerly expected at Shrewsbury.

1 *get thee before* – "go ahead of me".

2 *Sutton Co'fil'*, Sutton Coldfield is 20 miles beyond Coventry.

3 *Lay out* – "Pay with your own money".

4 *This . . . angel* – "The price of this bottle brings the total I have spent for you up to an angel". An *angel* was a coin with the figure of an angel on it, worth 6s. 8d.

5 *An if it do.* Falstaff pretends to misunderstand Bardolph, speaking as if Bardolph had said that the bottle could be made into a coin.

6 *I'll answer the coinage* – "I'll be responsible for the coins". It was against the law for private persons to make coins.

7 *soused gurnet*, a small fish preserved in very salty water. Its size is in humorous contrast to Falstaff's. Its use here suggests Falstaff's continuous thought of food. *Gurnet* was sometimes used as a word of contempt.

8 *King's press.* Officers were given a commission by the king to force *(press)* men to serve as soldiers.

9 *of* – "for".

10 *and odd* – "and a few more".

11 *press me . . . householders* – "I force into service only wealthy *(good)* householders".

12 *yeomen's sons,* the sons of small farmers who owned their own land.

13 *contracted . . . the banns,* single men who had already made plans for their marriage. The names of the man and woman intending to marry are read in the church on three occasions before the wedding. If this notice *(banns)* has been read twice, the day of the wedding is near.

14 *such a commodity . . . drum* – "such a quantity of comfortable cowards *(warm slaves)* who would rather *(as lief)* hear the devil (calling them to hell) than a drum (calling them to battle)".

15 *caliver*, a gun.

16 *struck* – "wounded".

17 *toasts-and-butter*, city-dwellers who enjoyed every comfort in life and who would therefore be most unwilling to exchange such a life for the dangers and hardship of the army.

18 *bellies* – "bodies".

19 *bought out . . . services,* paid a sum of money in order to be freed from having to serve as soldiers.

Scene II. A public road near Coventry.

Enter FALSTAFF *and* BARDOLPH.

FALSTAFF

Bardolph, get[1] thee before to Coventry; fill me a bottle of sack. Our soldiers shall march through; we 'll to Sutton[2] Co'fil' tonight.

BARDOLPH

Will you give me money, captain?

FALSTAFF

Lay out,[3] lay out.

BARDOLPH

This[4] bottle makes an angel.

FALSTAFF

An[5] if it do, take it for thy labour – an if it make twenty, take them all, I 'll[6] answer the coinage. Bid my lieutenant Peto meet me at town's end.

BARDOLPH

I will, captain: farewell.   [*Exit* 10

FALSTAFF

If I be not ashamed of my soldiers, I am a soused[7] gurnet; I have misused the King's[8] press damnably. I have got in exchange of[9] a hundred and fifty soldiers three hundred and odd[10] pounds. I press[11] me none but good householders, yeomen's[12] sons, inquire me out contracted[13] bachelors, such as had been asked   15 twice on the banns, such a commodity[14] of warm slaves as had as lief hear the devil as a drum, such as fear the report of a caliver[15] worse than a struck[16] fowl or a hurt wild duck. I pressed me none but such toasts-and-butter,[17] with hearts in their bellies[18] no bigger than pins' heads, and they have bought[19]   20

197

20 *charge* – "company", i.e. those under his *charge*.

21 *ancients*, officers of lowest rank.

22 *gentlemen of companies,* these were placed in rank between the ordinary soldiers and the officers.

23 *as ragged . . . his sores.* Falstaff compares his company's clothes to those of the beggar, Lazarus, in a picture *(painted cloth).* The beggar's sores were licked by the dogs of the rich man, Dives, called *the glutton* ("the man who eats too much"). The story is told in the Bible *(Luke 16 vv.19–31).*

24 *unjust serving-men* – "dishonest servants".

25 *younger sons . . . brothers* – "men with no fortunes". The oldest son inherited his father's property. A younger son could expect very little, especially if the father had himself been a younger brother.

26 *revolted,* those who have run away and have thus broken their contracts to their masters.

27 *trade-fallen* – "out of work".

28 *cankers* – "the evil (effects)".

29 *more dishonourable . . . ancient* – "more ragged in a dishonourable way than an old ragged flag (i.e. a flag honourably worn out in battle)".

30 *rooms of them as* – "the places of those who".

31 *prodigals* – "wasters". The story of a prodigal who spent all his money and had to eat pig's food *(draff and husks)* is told in the Bible *(Luke 15).*

32 *mad fellow,* a man with a sense of humour.

33 *gibbets,* gallows.

34 *flat* – "certain".

35 *wide betwixt the legs* – "with their legs wide apart as if they had chains *(gyves)* on". Prisoners often wore chains.

36 *not,* it is typical of Falstaff to say almost the opposite in his next few words.

37 *herald,* an officer who proclaimed the beginning of a procession, festival or play. He wore a sleeveless coat.

38 *host* – "inn-keeper".

39 *that 's all one* – "that does not matter at all".

40 *find linen . . . hedge,* Falstaff is suggesting that his men will be able to steal clothes from the washing left out to dry on the hedges.

41 *blown,* in two senses: (i) "swollen"; (ii) "short of wind".

42 *Jack.* As well as being a short form of John (Falstaff's Christian name), *Jack* was a word for a soldier's padded coat.

43 *quilt,* a padded bed-cover. The word continues Hal's joke about Falstaff's fatness.

44 *mad wag* – "joking fellow".

45 *I cry you mercy* – "I beg you to forgive me". Falstaff uses this polite phrase before slyly suggesting that Westmoreland should already be at Shrewsbury. He does this to stop Westmoreland from asking why he has not marched further towards the King's camp.

46 *powers* – "forces".

47 *looks for* – "expects".

out their services; and now my whole charge[20] consists of
ancients,[21] corporals, lieutenants, gentlemen[22] of companies –
slaves as ragged[23] as Lazarus in the painted cloth, where the
glutton's dogs licked his sores: and such as indeed were never
soldiers, but discarded unjust[24] serving-men, younger[25] sons to 25
younger brothers, revolted[26] tapsters, and ostlers trade-fallen,[27]
the cankers[28] of a calm world and a long peace, ten times more[29]
dishonourable-ragged than an old fazed ancient. And such have
I to fill up the rooms[30] of them as have bought out their services,
that you would think that I had a hundred and fifty tattered 30
prodigals[31] lately come from swine-keeping, from eating draff
and husks. A mad[32] fellow met me on the way, and told me I
had unloaded all the gibbets[33] and pressed the dead bodies. No
eye hath seen such scarecrows. I'll not march through Coventry
with them, that's flat:[34] nay, and the villains march wide[35] 35
betwixt the legs as if they had gyves on, for indeed I had the
most of them out of prison. There's not[36] a shirt and a half in
all my company, and the half shirt is two napkins tacked together and thrown over the shoulders like a herald's[37] coat
without sleeves; and the shirt to say the truth stolen from my 40
host[38] at Saint Albans, or the red-nose innkeeper of Daventry.
But that's[39] all one, they'll find[40] linen enough on every hedge.

Enter the PRINCE *and the* LORD OF WESTMORELAND

PRINCE

How now, blown[41] Jack?[42] How now, quilt?[43]

FALSTAFF

What, Hal! How now, mad[44] wag? What a devil dost thou in
Warwickshire? My good Lord of Westmoreland, I[45] cry you 45
mercy; I thought your honour had already been at Shrewsbury.

WESTMORELAND

Faith, Sir John, 't is more than time that I were there, and you
too, but my powers[46] are there already; the King, I can tell you,
looks[47] for us all; we must away all night.

48 *never fear me* – "do not fear (that I shall fail to arrive)".

49 *already made thee butter* – "already made you fat". Butter is made from cream.

50 *good enough . . . mortal men* (line 58) – "good enough to throw away (*toss*), fit to be shot (*powder* – "gunpowder"); their bodies will fill a grave (*pit*) as well as better men's; . . . being men they must die at some time (are *mortal*)". Falstaff reveals his practical view of the common soldier's miserable part in war; in contrast to the ideal of military glory shared by many of the other characters, he sees that ordinary soldiers are something to be fed to the guns.

51 *bare* – "dressed in rags".

52 *bareness* – "Falstaff pretends to take the word "bare" to mean "lean".

53 *No, I'll be sworn* – "No, I'll swear that it is true".

54 *three fingers*, a finger is a measure of ¾-inch. Hal says there is three times this amount of fat on Falstaff's ribs.

55 *field* – "battle-field".

*like a herald's*³⁷ *coat without sleeves*

FALSTAFF

Tut, never[48] fear me; I am as vigilant as a cat to steal cream.　　50

PRINCE

I think, to steal cream indeed, for thy theft hath already made thee butter;[49] but tell me, Jack, whose fellows are these that come after?

FALSTAFF

Mine, Hal, mine.

PRINCE

I did never see such pitiful rascals.　　55

FALSTAFF

Tut, tut, good[50] enough to toss, food for powder, food for powder; they 'll fill a pit as well as better; tush man, mortal men, mortal men.

WESTMORELAND

Ay, but, Sir John, methinks they are exceeding poor and bare,[51] too beggarly.　　60

FALSTAFF

Faith, for their poverty I know not where they had that; and for their bareness[52] I am sure they never learned that of me.

PRINCE

No,[53] I 'll be sworn, unless you call three[54] fingers in the ribs bare. But sirrah, make haste; Percy is already in the field.[55]

[*Exit*

FALSTAFF

What, is the King encamped?　　65

201

56 *Well . . . keen guest* – "To arrive at
the end of a fight *(fray)* and the
beginning of a feast suits an unwilling fighter and an eager guest".
Falstaff's words repeat a common
saying.

(IV.iii) The rebels are in camp near the King's army. Hotspur and
Douglas urge an immediate attack, but Vernon and Worcester want to
wait until their horses are rested and all their men have arrived. Blunt
brings a promise of pardon from the King, but Hotspur reminds Blunt
of other promises that Henry has broken, and of wrongs done to the
Percy family. Hotspur decides to send Worcester next morning with his
reply to the King.

1 *with him* – "against the King".
2 *then*, i.e. if you do not fight tonight.
Douglas is addressing Worcester.
3 *Not a whit* – "Not the smallest
amount (of advantage)".

4 *supply*, more soldiers to join his
army.
5 *His is . . . doubtful* – "His (the King's)
added forces will certainly arrive
but it is doubtful if ours will".

WESTMORELAND

He is, Sir John, I fear we shall stay too long.

[*Exit*

FALSTAFF

Well,[56]
To the latter end of a fray, and the beginning of a feast
Fits a dull fighter and a keen guest.

[*Exit*

Scene III. Shrewsbury. The Rebel Camp.

Enter HOTSPUR, WORCESTER, DOUGLAS, VERNON.

HOTSPUR

We 'll fight with[1] him tonight.

WORCESTER

It may not be.

DOUGLAS

You give him then[2] advantage.

VERNON

Not[3] a whit.

HOTSPUR

Why say you so, looks he not for supply?[4]

VERNON

So do we.

HOTSPUR

His[5] is certain, ours is doubtful.

WORCESTER

Good cousin, be advised, stir not tonight.

5

6 *cold heart* – "lack of courage".
7 *Do me no slander* – "Do not speak against my honour".
8 *dare well maintain . . . life* – "and I will prove my courage at the risk of my life (by challenging anyone who doubts my courage)".
9 *well respected honour* – "carefully considered honour", compared with the wild boasting about honour heard from Hotspur and Douglas.
10 *I hold . . . fear* – "my plans are as little affected by cowardly fear".
11 *Content* – "I agree", but Vernon's wisdom returns when Hotspur once again takes up the idea of fighting that night.

12 *such great leading* – "such wide experience in leading armies".
13 *Drag . . . expedition* – "prevent our moving fast".
14 *horse,* this (plural) word here includes the soldiers trained to fight on horseback as well as the animals.
15 *asleep* – "inactive".
16 *tame* – "without spirit".
17 *not a horse . . . himself* – "the horses have only a small part of their usual powers and strength".

VERNON

Do not, my lord.

DOUGLAS

You do not counsel well.
You speak it out of fear and cold[6] heart.

VERNON

Do[7] me no slander, Douglas; by my life,
And I dare[8] well maintain it with my life,
If well-respected[9] honour bid me on,   10
I hold[10] as little counsel with weak fear
As you, my lord, or any Scot that this day lives;
Let it be seen tomorrow in the battle
Which of us fears.

DOUGLAS

Yea, or tonight.

VERNON

Content.[11]

HOTSPUR

Tonight, say I.   15

VERNON

Come, come, it may not be. I wonder much,
Being men of such[12] great leading as you are,
That you foresee not what impediments
Drag[13] back our expedition: certain horse[14]
Of my cousin Vernon's are not yet come up,   20
Your uncle Worcester's horse came but today,
And now their pride and mettle is asleep,[15]
Their courage with hard labour tame[16] and dull,
That not[17] a horse is half the half himself.

18 *journey-bated . . . low* – "made weak and low-spirited by a long journey".

19 *better part* – "the majority".

20 *King* – "King's army".

21 *sounds a parley* – "is sounded as a signal that a messenger has arrived to speak for the other army".

22 *respect* – "attention".

23 *determination* – "mind", i.e. Hotspur wishes Blunt were on the rebels' side in the fight.

24 *deservings* – "merits".

25 *are not . . . against us* – "are not of our party *(quality)* but oppose us".

26 *God defend* – "may God forbid (any other course of action)".

27 *limit* – "bounds (of loyalty)".

28 *But to my charge* – "But now I must do my duty (tell you what I was sent to tell you)".

29 *griefs* – "complaints".

30 *and whereupon . . . hostility* – "and upon what grounds *(whereupon)* you arouse as if by magic *(conjure)* feelings of daring opposition from hearts *(breasts)* obedient to the government *(of civil peace)*".

31 *duteous land* – "country which has been obedient (to the King)".

32 *good deserts* – "good actions that should have been rewarded".

33 *Which*, the deserts.

HOTSPUR

So are the horses of the enemy   25
In general journey-bated[18] and brought low.
The better[19] part of ours are full of rest.

WORCESTER

The number of the King[20] exceedeth ours:
For God's sake, cousin, stay till all come in.
                              [*The trumpet sounds a parley*[21]

Enter SIR WALTER BLUNT

BLUNT

I come with gracious offers from the King,   30
If you vouchsafe me hearing and respect.[22]

HOTSPUR

Welcome, Sir Walter Blunt: and would to God
You were of our determination![23]
Some of us love you well, and even those some
Envy your great deservings[24] and good name,   35
Because you are not[25] of our quality,
But stand against us like an enemy.

BLUNT

And God[26] defend but still I should stand so,
So long as out of limit[27] and true rule
You stand against anointed majesty.   40
But[28] to my charge. The King hath sent to know
The nature of your griefs,[29] and whereupon[30]
You conjure from the breast of civil peace
Such bold hostility, teaching his duteous[31] land
Audacious cruelty. If that the King   45
Have any way your good[32] deserts forgot,
Which[33] he confesseth to be manifold,
He bids you name your griefs, and with all speed

34 *You shall . . . interest* – "you will have what you wish and more added".

35 *absolute*, without conditions attached.

36 *suggestion* – "temptation".

37 *King is kind*, said ironically as can be seen from the following words which refer back to Bolingbroke's ingratitude after the Percys had helped him. These events appear in *Richard II*.

38 *well we . . . pay* (lines 52-3), Hotspur is suggesting that the King is a cunning schemer.

39 *same royalty he wears* – "his position as King".

40 *Sick . . . world's regard* – "lowered in people's opinion".

41 *unminded* – "unnoticed".

42 *Duke of Lancaster*. On his return to England from exile Bolingbroke told the Percys that he intended only to reclaim the title that he had lost during his banishment.

43 *sue his livery*, a term used in the laws of the Middle Ages; it meant the process of recovering possession of lands that had passed into the king's hands.

44 *terms of zeal* – "declarations of loyalty".

45 *in kind . . . moved* – "out of the kindness of his heart and affected by pity".

46 *lean to* – "favour".

47 *more and less* – "high and low".

48 *cap and knee*. To take off one's cap and to kneel were both signs of respect. Hotspur adds this and later details to express his contempt for the excessive and perhaps not very sincere honour paid to Bolingbroke at the time.

49 *Attended* – "waited for".

50 *in lanes* – "in rows", through which Bolingbroke passed.

51 *oaths*, of loyalty.

52 *golden*, in two senses: (i) "finely dressed in gold"; (ii) "promising success".

53 *He presently . . . vow* – "Immediately (presently)*, as the ambitious man discovers the greatness that he believes lies within him, he begins to have higher hopes than those in his vow (that he came only to reclaim his lands)".

54 *blood was poor*, perhaps in two senses: (i) "when he had not yet discovered royal blood in his veins"; (ii) "when his courage and ambition were low".

55 *naked* – "bare".

56 *Ravenspurgh*, the Yorkshire port where Bolingbroke landed from exile.

57 *forsooth* – "in truth", said in scorn.

58 *strait* – "strict".

59 *Cries out upon* – "exposes".

You[34] shall have your desires with interest,
And pardon absolute[35] for yourself and these   50
Herein misled by your suggestion.[36]

HOTSPUR

The King[37] is kind, and well[38] we know the King
Knows at what time to promise, when to pay:
My father, and my uncle, and myself
Did give him that same[39] royalty he wears;   55
And when he was not six and twenty strong,
Sick[40] in the world's regard, wretched and low,
A poor unminded[41] outlaw sneaking home,
My father gave him welcome to the shore;
And when he heard him swear and vow to God   60
He came but to be Duke[42] of Lancaster,
To sue[43] his livery, and beg his peace
With tears of innocency, and terms[44] of zeal,
My father, in kind[45] heart and pity moved,
Swore him assistance, and performed it too.   65
Now when the lords and barons of the realm
Perceived Northumberland did lean[46] to him,
The more[47] and less came in with cap[48] and knee,
Met him in boroughs, cities, villages,
Attended[49] him on bridges, stood in lanes,[50]   70
Laid gifts before him, proffered him their oaths,[51]
Gave him their heirs as pages, followed him
Even at the heels in golden[52] multitudes.
He presently,[53] as greatness knows itself,
Steps me a little higher than his vow   75
Made to my father while his blood[54] was poor
Upon the naked[55] shore at Ravenspurgh;[56]
And now forsooth[57] takes on him to reform
Some certain edicts and some strait[58] decrees
That lie too heavy on the commonwealth;   80
Cries[59] out upon abuses, seems to weep
Over his country's wrongs; and by this face,

60 *seeming brow of justice* – "appearance of being just".

61 *angle for* – "fish for". As the fisherman uses tasty food to tempt the fishes to bite, so Bolingbroke has practised deceit in attracting the people towards him.

62 *In deputation . . . Irish war* – "left behind him here as substitute (to rule for him) when he was present himself *(personal)* in the war in Ireland. It was while Richard II was in Ireland that Henry Bolingbroke was able to gather followers ready to depose Richard on his return to England.

63 *in the neck . . . tasked* – "immediately after that, taxed".

64 *suffered . . . in Wales* (line 95) – "allowed his relation, the Earl of March, who is, if everyone possessed his proper title and place, the king in fact, to be held prisoner *(engaged)* in Wales".

65 *There . . . lie forfeited* – "there to remain unclaimed *(lie forfeited)* as no money *(ransom)* had been paid for his release".

66 *happy* – "splendid".

67 *intelligence* – "by means of secret agents".

68 *Rated* – "drove away my uncle (Worcester) with angry words". This refers back to the action in I.iii.14–20.

69 *head of safety* – "army for protecting ourselves".

70 *withal* – "also".

71 *indirect*, in two senses: (i) "not in direct line"; (ii) "morally corrupt", referring to the means by which Bolingbroke gained the crown.

72 *let there . . . return* – "let some important person (from the King's army) remain with us as a pledge (that my uncle will be allowed) to return safely (tomorrow)".

This seeming[60] brow of justice, did he win
The hearts of all that he did angle[61] for;
Proceeded further – cut me off the heads   85
Of all the favourites that the absent King
In deputation[62] left behind him here,
When he was personal in the Irish war.

BLUNT

Tut, I came not to hear this.

HOTSPUR

        Then to the point.
In short time after he deposed the King,   90
Soon after that deprived him of his life,
And in the neck[63] of that, tasked the whole state;
To make that worse, suffered[64] his kinsman March
(Who is, if every owner were well placed,
Indeed his King) to be engaged in Wales,   95
There[65] without ransom to lie forfeited;
Disgraced me in my happy[66] victories,
Sought to entrap me by intelligence,[67]
Rated[68] mine uncle from the Council-board,
In rage dismissed my father from the court,   100
Broke oath on oath, committed wrong on wrong,
And in conclusion drove us to seek out
This head[69] of safety, and withal[70] to pry
Into his title, the which we find
Too indirect[71] for long continuance.   105

BLUNT

Shall I return this answer to the King?

HOTSPUR

Not so, Sir Walter. We 'll withdraw awhile.
Go to the King, and let[72] there be impawned
Some surety for a safe return again,

73 *Bring . . . purposes* – "tell him what
   we have decided to do".
74 *grace* – "the King's favour".
75 *And may . . . shall*. This is an un-
   expectedly mild answer from Hotspur, but he answers thus in one of
   Shakespeare's sources, Holinshed's
   Chronicles.

(IV.iv) In this scene the Archbishop of York is sending letters to his friends
asking them for help. He has heard that the rebels, divided and weak, are
likely to be defeated at Shrewsbury, and fears that the King will march
against York as soon as Hotspur is overthrown.

1 *Hie . . . Michael* – "Go, good Sir
   Michael". *Sir* was a title given to
   both knights and priests. The Archbishop's messenger is probably a
   priest.
2 *brief* – "letter".
3 *wingèd haste* – "as quickly as if you
   had wings to fly".
4 *Lord Marshall,* Thomas Mowbray,
   Duke of Norfolk.

5 *cousin Scroop,* probably Sir Stephen
   Scroop, a character in Shakespeare's
   Richard II.
6 *directed* – "addressed".
7 *How much . . . import* – "how important they are".
8 *tenor* – "general meaning".
9 *Like enough* – "It is probable that".
10 *bide the touch* – "stand the test".

an Archbishop

212

And in the morning early shall mine uncle   110
Bring[73] him our purposes – and so, farewell.

BLUNT

I would you would accept of grace[74] and love.

HOTSPUR

And[75] may be so we shall.

BLUNT

    Pray God you do.

            [*Exeunt*

Scene IV. York. The Archbishop's Palace.

Enter the ARCHBISHOP OF YORK *and* SIR MICHAEL.

ARCHBISHOP

Hie,[1] good Sir Michael, bear this sealéd brief[2]
With wingéd[3] haste to the Lord Marshall,[4]
This to my cousin[5] Scroop, and all the rest
To whom they are directed.[6] If you knew
How[7] much they do import you would make haste.   5

SIR MICHAEL

My good lord,
I guess their tenor.[8]

ARCHBISHOP

    Like[9] enough you do.
Tomorrow, good Sir Michael, is a day
Wherein the fortune of ten thousand men
Must bide[10] the touch; for sir, at Shrewsbury,   10
As I am truly given to understand,
The King with mighty and quick-raiséd power

11 *Lord Harry*, Hotspur.
12 *Whose power . . . proportion* – "whose army was larger than any other".
13 *rated sinew* – "valued source of strength".
14 *o'er-ruled by prophecies*. York suggests that Glendower had not joined the rebels at Shrewsbury because he thought that signs showed that fate was against him. In III.i Glendower's faith in magic is shown.

15 *instant* – "immediate".
16 *head* – "army".
17 *special head . . . land* – "the whole army of the crown (as opposed to the forces of the rebels)".
18 *many mo . . . of estimation* – "many more partners *(corrivals)* and men highly valued for their honour".
19 *needful 'tis* – "it is necessary".
20 *speed* – "make haste".
21 *thrive not* – "does not succeed".

Meets with Lord Harry:[11] and I fear, Sir Michael,
What with the sickness of Northumberland,
Whose power[12] was in the first proportion,   15
And what with Owen Glendower's absence thence,
Who with them was a rated[13] sinew too,
And comes not in, o'er-ruled[14] by prophecies,
I fear the power of Percy is too weak
To wage an instant[15] trial with the King.   20

SIR MICHAEL

Why, my good lord, you need not fear,
There is Douglas, and Lord Mortimer.

ARCHBISHOP

No, Mortimer is not there.

SIR MICHAEL

But there is Mordake, Vernon, Lord Harry Percy,
And there is my Lord of Worcester, and a head[16]   25
Of gallant warriors, noble gentlemen.

ARCHBISHOP

And so there is: but yet the King hath drawn
The special[17] head of all the land together:
The Prince of Wales, Lord John of Lancaster,
The noble Westmoreland, and warlike Blunt,   30
And many mo[18] corrivals and dear men
Of estimation and command in arms.

SIR MICHAEL

Doubt not, my lord, they shall be well opposed.

ARCHBISHOP

I hope no less, yet needful[19] 't is to fear;
And to prevent the worst, Sir Michael, speed.[20]   35
For if Lord Percy thrive[21] not, ere the King

215

22 *he . . . confederacy* – "he (the King) has heard of our plotting together".

23 *make strong . . . him* – "prepare strong defences against him".

Dismiss his power he means to visit us,
For he[22] hath heard of our confederacy,
And 't is but wisdom to make[23] strong against him:
Therefore make haste – I must go write again   40
To other friends; and so, farewell, Sir Michael.

[*Exeunt*

(v.i) As the sun rises, Worcester brings Hotspur's last message to the King: that King Henry's ill-treatment has forced the Percys to fight in self-defence. The King replies that this is the usual false excuse of rebels; he repeats his offer of free pardon but, knowing it is unlikely to be accepted, prepares for battle. Prince Hal offers to meet Hotspur in single combat. Falstaff, left alone, considers the value of "honour". He decides that, since honour is useless to those who die in winning it, he prefers to live without it.

1 *peer . . . hill* – "come into sight over that bushy *(yon busky)* hill".

2 *distemperature* – "disorder", a medical term; it here refers to the unusual blood-red colour of the sun, which, taken as a sign of the coming slaughter, makes the day look pale with fear.

3 *Doth play . . . purposes* – "makes a sound like a trumpet to show its intentions (as a trumpet is used by an army as a signal that an important announcement is to be made)".

4 *doff* – "take off (clothing)".

5 *crush . . . ungentle steel* – "put on war-armour in my old age".

6 *unknit . . . abhorréd war* – "untie this stiff *(churlish)* knot of war which is hated by everyone", i.e. send away the forces that have become united like the threads in a tightly tied knot.

7 *And move . . . exhaled meteor* (line 19) – "and move more obediently in your proper place (in society) again, where your actions showed your loyalty *(did give a fair and natural light)*, and do not behave any longer like something unnatural that is to be feared *(exhaled meteor)*". The imagery is suggested by the imagery at the beginning of the scene *(sun, distemperature)*. It continues the connection between the idea of disorder in nature and in man. In the old view of the universe it was believed that the planets and stars each moved in an orderly way in its own *orb* (path through the sky). The description of Worcester as a *meteor*, a part that has fallen from its proper place, strengthens the idea that disobedience to a king is contrary to the natural order; *exhaled*, in two senses: (i) "created by vapours from the sun"; (ii) "dragged from the proper heavenly order".

8 *prodigy of fear* – "fearful sign of what will happen in the future".

9 *broachéd . . . unborn times* – "misfortune just begun (which will affect) the future *(unborn times)*".

218

ACT FIVE

Scene I. Shrewsbury. The King's Camp.

Enter the KING, PRINCE OF WALES, LORD JOHN OF LANCASTER,
SIR WALTER BLUNT, FALSTAFF

KING

How bloodily the sun begins to peer[1]
Above yon busky hill! The day looks pale
At his distemperature.[2]

PRINCE

        The southern wind
Doth[3] play the trumpet to his purposes,
And by his hollow whistling in the leaves
Foretells a tempest and a blustering day.   5

KING

Then with the losers let it sympathise,
For nothing can seem foul to those that win.

                  [The trumpet sounds

Enter WORCESTER *and* VERNON

How now, my Lord of Worcester! 'T is not well
That you and I should meet upon such terms   10
As now we meet. You have deceived our trust,
And made us doff[4] our easy robes of peace
To crush[5] our old limbs in ungentle steel:
This is not well, my lord, this is not well.
What say you to it? Will you again unknit[6]   15
This churlish knot of all-abhorréd war,
And move[7] in that obedient orb again
Where you did give a fair and natural light,
And be no more an exhaled meteor,
A prodigy[8] of fear, and a portent   20
Of broachéd[9] mischief to the unborn times?

10 *For mine own part* – "as far as I am concerned".

11 *entertain the lag-end* – "spend the last days".

12 *day of this dislike* – "this day of dispute".

13 *Peace, chewet* – "Silence, jackdaw (a noisy chattering bird)". The Prince sees that this is no moment for Falstaff's jokes and silences him immediately.

14 *looks of favour* – "signs of friendship".

15 *remember* – "remind".

16 *staff of . . . break,* a reference to the time before Henry Bolingbroke became king. Worcester, who was the chief officer of Richard II's household, broke the staff which was the sign of his official position, and rode to join Bolingbroke.

17 *posted* – "rode".

18 *in place . . . so strong* – "in position in society, and in people's opinion not nearly so strong".

19 *brought you home,* used in two senses: (i) "brought you back from banishment"; (ii) "helped you to succeed".

20 *outdare* – "defy".

21 *that oath,* Bolingbroke swore to the Percys at Doncaster that he would demand only the lands that were his through his father, John of Gaunt. These lands had been unlawfully seized by Richard while Bolingbroke was in exile.

22 *did . . . 'gainst* – "did not intend to do anything against".

23 *new-fall'n right . . . Gaunt* – "newly inherited right to possess the title and estate *(seat)* of John of Gaunt".

24 *in short space* – "in a short time".

at market[40] *crosses*

WORCESTER

Hear me, my liege:
For[10] mine own part, I could be well content
To entertain[11] the lag-end of my life
With quiet hours: for I protest   25
I have not sought the day[12] of this dislike.

KING

You have not sought it? How comes it, then?

FALSTAFF

Rebellion lay in his way, and he found it.

PRINCE

Peace,[13] chewet, peace!

WORCESTER

It pleased your Majesty to turn your looks[14]   30
Of favour from myself and all our house;
And yet I must remember[15] you, my lord,
We were the first and dearest of your friends;
For you my staff[16] of office did I break
In Richard's time, and posted[17] day and night   35
To meet you on the way, and kiss your hand,
When yet you were in place[18] and in account
Nothing so strong and fortunate as I.
It was myself, my brother, and his son,
That brought[19] you home, and boldly did outdare[20]   40
The dangers of the time. You swore to us,
And you did swear that oath[21] at Doncaster,
That you did[22] nothing purpose 'gainst the state,
Nor claim no further than your new-fallen[23] right,
The seat of Gaunt, dukedom of Lancaster.   45
To this we swore our aid: but in short[24] space
It rained down fortune showering on your head,
And such a flood of greatness fell on you,

25 *What with . . . absent King* – "partly as a result of our help, partly as a result of the King's absence". Richard II was in Ireland when Bolingbroke returned from exile.

26 *wanton* – "disordered".

27 *seeming sufferances* – "apparent sufferings".

28 *contrarious* – "contrary".

29 *repute him dead* – "think that he was dead".

30 *took occasion . . . sway* – "seized the opportunity to be quickly persuaded *(wooed)* to grasp *(gripe)* the government of the state *(general sway)*".

31 *fed* – "supported"; the word introduces a comparison between Bolingbroke and the baby cuckoo *(cuckoo's bird)*. The mother cuckoo puts her eggs into another bird's (sparrow's) nest and later the young cuckoo, fed by the mother sparrow, grows rapidly and pushes the young sparrows out of the nest *(did oppress our nest*, line 61); *useth* – "treats".

32 *gull*, a very young bird without feathers.

33 *swallowing* – "being swallowed".

34 *this present head* – "this army which is at present in the field".

35 *by such means* – "as a result of such causes (of offence)".

36 *unkind usage, dangerous countenance* – "unnatural action, threatening looks".

37 *troth* – "pledged word".

38 *in your younger enterprise* – "earlier in your adventure".

39 *articulate* – "written down as separate items (in a list of complaints)".

40 *at market crosses*, i.e. in the centre of towns and villages. Crosses or buildings, with no surrounding walls but with a roof and cross above, were built in the centre of towns and villages as places where holy men could preach. The market crosses became favourite places for meetings, and public announcements were made from them or placed on them.

41 *To face . . . colour* – "to make the rebellion seem a fine thing by providing it with an excuse". To *face* a garment is a way of adorning and strengthening it. *Colour* has its usual sense and also a second sense, "excuse".

42 *changelings . . . discontents*, people who frequently change sides in politics and poor people discontented with their fortune and place in society.

43 *rub the elbow*, a sign of their satisfaction.

44 *hurly-burly innovation* – "noisy, riotous disturbance".

45 *never yet . . . his cause* – "at no time *(never yet)* did rebellion lack *(want)* similar weak excuses *(water-colours)* to justify itself". *Colour* has the second meaning of "excuse"; *water-colours* are colours that soon wash off and so suggest "poor excuses"; the image of painting is continued with the verb *impaint* – "make (rebellion's cause) seem better than it really is". The image of *colour*, suggesting false appearance, follows on from *fine colour* (line 75).

46 *moody*, either (i) "sullen" or (ii) "angry".

47 *starving*, hungry for, i.e. "eager for".

48 *pell-mell* – "disorderly".

What[25] with our help, what with the absent King,
What with the injuries of a wanton[26] time,   50
The seeming[27] sufferances that you had borne,
And the contrarious[28] winds that held the King
So long in his unlucky Irish wars
That all in England did repute[29] him dead:
And from this swarm of fair advantages   55
You took[30] occasion to be quickly wooed
To gripe the general sway into your hand,
Forgot your oath to us at Doncaster,
And being fed[31] by us, you used us so
As that ungentle gull[32] the cuckoo's bird   60
Useth the sparrow – did oppress our nest,
Grew by our feeding to so great a bulk
That even our love durst not come near your sight
For fear of swallowing;[33] but with nimble wing
We were enforced for safety sake to fly   65
Out of your sight, and raise this present[34] head,
Whereby we stand opposéd by such[35] means
As you yourself have forged against yourself
By unkind[36] usage, dangerous countenance,
And violation of all faith and troth[37]   70
Sworn to us in your younger[38] enterprise.

KING

These things indeed you have articulate,[39]
Proclaimed at market[40] crosses, read in churches,
To face[41] the garment of rebellion
With some fine colour that may please the eye   75
Of fickle changelings[42] and poor discontents,
Which gape and rub[43] the elbow at the news
Of hurly-burly[44] innovation;
And never[45] yet did insurrection want
Such water-colours to impaint his cause,   80
Nor moody[46] beggars starving[47] for a time
Of pell-mell[48] havoc and confusion.

223

49 *your armies*, Prince Hal refers to the King's army and that of the rebels.

50 *encounter* – "armed meeting".

51 *join in trial* – "engage in battle to test who shall win".

52 *by my hopes*, an oath, "by my hopes of heaven".

53 *This present . . . head* – "provided that this rebellious act *(present enterprise)* is not counted against him".

54 *valiant-young* – "courageous for one so young".

55 *grace this latter age* – "confer honour on this late age". In Shakespeare's time men often spoke of their own age as a "late" or "final" one, in contrast to earlier "golden" or "silver" ages which were supposed to have been more splendid.

56 *I have . . . account me too* – "I have absented myself *(a truant been)* from my duties as a knight and, I hear, he values me as a neglecter of such duties *(so)* too".

57 *Yet this . . . majesty* – "yet I make this offer before my father's royal person".

58 *take the odds* – "take advantage".

59 *estimation* – "reputation".

60 *save the blood . . . side* – "prevent bloodshed in the rival armies".

61 *Try fortune with him* – "see which of us is favoured by fortune".

62 *venture thee* – "risk your life".

63 *Do make against it* – "argue against it".

64 *even those we love* – "We (the King) love even those".

65 *cousin's*, i.e. Hotspur's.

66 *And will they . . . grace* – "and if they will accept the offer of my mercy *(grace)*".

67 *Rebuke . . . their office* (line 112) – "judgement and fearful punishment are at my command and they will perform their proper actions (of dealing severely with the offenders)".

68 *take it advisedly* – "think carefully of the offer we make".

PRINCE

In both your[49] armies there is many a soul
Shall pay full dearly for this encounter[50]
If once they join[51] in trial. Tell your nephew,   85
The Prince of Wales doth join with all the world
In praise of Henry Percy: by[52] my hopes,
This[53] present enterprise set off his head,
I do not think a braver gentleman,
More active-valiant or more valiant-young,[54]   90
More daring or more bold, is now alive
To grace[55] this latter age with noble deeds.
For my part, I may speak it to my shame,
I[56] have a truant been to chivalry,
And so I hear he doth account me too;   95
Yet[57] this before my father's majesty –
I am content that he shall take[58] the odds
Of his great name and estimation,[59]
And will, to save[60] the blood on either side,
Try[61] fortune with him in a single fight.   100

KING

And, Prince of Wales, so dare we venture[62] thee,
Albeit, considerations infinite
Do[63] make against it. No, good Worcester, no,
We love our people well, even[64] those we love
That are misled upon your cousin's[65] part,   105
And[66] will they take the offer of our grace,
Both he, and they, and you, yea, every man
Shall be my friend again, and I 'll be his.
So tell your cousin, and bring me word
What he will do. But if he will not yield,   110
Rebuke[67] and dread correction wait on us,
And they shall do their office. So, be gone;
We will not now be troubled with reply:
We offer fair, take[68] it advisedly.

[*Exit* WORCESTER, *with* VERNON

69 *on my life* – "I am certain".

70 *confident . . . in arms* – "are confident of their ability to overcome all those who fight against them, however many they may be".

71 *charge* – "command".

72 *on their answer . . . on them* – "when we receive their reply we will attack".

73 *bestride me, so* – "stand over me (with one leg on each side of me) in this fashion *(so)*", with Falstaff standing as if over a fallen soldier to show Hal what he wants him to do.

74 *point* – "sign".

75 *Colossus,* a very large statue supposed to have stood with one leg on each side of the entrance to the harbour at Rhodes.

76 *bed-time.* Hal's joking command to Falstaff to say his prayers suggests prayers before sleeping *(bed-time)* and leads to Falstaff's wish that the day were over and the battle finished.

77 *death.* There is word play on "death" and "debt"; therefore *owest.*

78 *what need . . . forward* – "why should I be so eager".

79 *honour pricks me on* – "the pursuit of military glory *(honour)* urges me on". Throughout the following questions and answers Falstaff shows that the *honour* awarded to a valiant soldier is enjoyed by neither the living nor the dead. His humorous speech gives a practical common-sense view of honour, which is in strong contrast to Hotspur's earlier in the play. Hal's idea of honour lies between the two extremes and this fact is stressed by the dramatic action of the play.

80 *prick me off* – "ticks me off a list", i.e. "what if I die in the cause of honour?" Falstaff uses similar words, *pricks me on* and *prick me off* to make his joke about honour more humorous.

81 *set to a leg* – "put back a leg that has been cut off".

82 *grief* – "pain".

83 *Honour hath . . . surgery then?* – "Honour has none of the doctor's skill then?"

84 *Air,* i.e. nothing more substantial than the breath used in saying the word.

85 *trim* – "fine", used mockingly.

86 *He that . . . a-Wednesday.* No particular man is intended. Falstaff is reminding himself that *honour* is often won by dying bravely; *a-Wednesday* – "on Wednesday".

87 *insensible,* not to be recognised by any of the senses.

PRINCE

It will not be accepted, on[69] my life.   115
The Douglas and the Hotspur both together
Are confident[70] against the world in arms.

KING

Hence, therefore, every leader to his charge;[71]
For on their answer[72] will we set on them,
And God befriend us as our cause is just!   120
                    [*Exeunt all but the* PRINCE *and* FALSTAFF

FALSTAFF

Hal, if thou see me down in the battle and bestride[73] me, so,
't is a point[74] of friendship.

PRINCE

Nothing but a Colossus[75] can do thee that friendship. Say thy
prayers, and farewell.

FALSTAFF

I would 't were bed-time,[76] Hal, and all well.   125

PRINCE

Why, thou owest God a death.[77]   [*Exit*

FALSTAFF

'T is not due yet, I would be loath to pay him before his day –
what[78] need I be so forward with him that calls not on me?
Well, 't is no matter, honour[79] pricks me on. Yea, but how if
honour prick[80] me off when I come on, how then? Can honour 130
set[81] to a leg? No. Or an arm? No. Or take away the grief[82] of
a wound? No. Honour[83] hath no skill in surgery then? No.
What is honour? A word. What is in that word honour? What
is that honour? Air.[84] A trim[85] reckoning! Who hath it? He[86]
that died a-Wednesday. Doth he feel it? No. Doth he hear it? 135
No. 'T is insensible,[87] then? Yea, to the dead. But will it not

227

88 *Detraction . . . suffer it* – "Slander
   will not allow it".
89 *scutcheon,* a painted banner which
   was hung up in churches at funerals
   of gentlemen.

(v.ii) Worcester decides not to report the King's offer of mercy, for
he is afraid that, if it is accepted, his own life will be in danger. After
Worcester's false report of his interview with the King, the rebels send
a message of defiance to the royal army. Hotspur accepts the Prince's
challenge to combat, but not as a substitute for battle between the two
armies.

1 *my nephew,* Hotspur.
2 *'T were best he did* – "He ought to be
   told".
3 *undone* – "ruined".
4 *It is not possible . . . loving us* – "It is
   impossible to believe that the King
   will keep his promise to us".
5 *still . . . other faults* – "(suspect us)
   continually, and delay the punishment for this offence until he can
   find other faults as an excuse for
   heavy punishment".
6 *stuck full of eyes* – "always watch-
   ing".
7 *treason . . . his ancestors* (line 11) –
   "those who have already committed treason once will be trusted
   no more than a pet fox which,
   although seeming tame, still has
   some natural characteristics of his
   wild ancestors".
8 *Look how we can, or* – "It will
   make no difference how we look,
   whether".

9 *Interpretation . . . our looks* – "those
   who try to understand *(our looks)*
   will come to false conclusions".
10 *we shall feed . . . death* – "we shall
   receive kind treatment such as oxen
   enjoy which are fed better and
   better the nearer they are to being
   killed".
11 *My nephew's . . . blood* – "My
   nephew's fault may be completely
   forgotten, it will be excused on
   account of his youth and angry
   excitement *(heat of blood)*".
12 *adopted name,* i.e. the name "Hotspur", meaning "rash" or "quick to
   anger". The use of this name seems
   to give Harry Percy the privilege of
   being governed by his quick temper
   (spleen).
13 *All his offences . . . him on* – "I and
   his father will be held responsible
   for all his offences; we led *(did
   train)* him".

live with the living? No. Why? Detraction[88] will not suffer it.
Therefore I 'll none of it. Honour is a mere scutcheon[89] – and
so ends my catechism.   [*Exit*

Scene II. *Shrewsbury. The Rebel Camp.*

Enter WORCESTER *and* SIR RICHARD VERNON.

WORCESTER

O no, my nephew[1] must not know, Sir Richard,
The liberal and kind offer of the King.

VERNON

'T were[2] best he did.

WORCESTER

Then are we all undone.[3]
It[4] is not possible, it cannot be,
The King should keep his word in loving us;   5
He will suspect us still,[5] and find a time
To punish this offence in other faults:
Suspicion all our lives shall be stuck[6] full of eyes,
For treason[7] is but trusted like the fox,
Who, never so tame, so cherished and locked up,   10
Will have a wild trick of his ancestors.
Look[8] how we can, or sad or merrily,
Interpretation[9] will misquote our looks,
And we[10] shall feed like oxen at a stall,
The better cherished still the nearer death.   15
My[11] nephew's trespass may be well forgot,
It hath the excuse of youth and heat of blood,
And an adopted[12] name of privilege –
A hare-brained Hotspur, governed by a spleen
All[13] his offences live upon my head   20
And on his father's; we did train him on;

229

14 *his corruption . . . for all* – "his disloyalty he copied from us; we as the
source of all, shall be punished for
all".

15 *Deliver what you will* – "Give any
message you please".

16 *Lord of Westmoreland.* The "surety"
of IV.iii.109, who must now be
returned to the King.

17 *presently* – "now".

18 *and shall* – "I will".

19 *no seeming mercy* – "no sign of
mercy". Thus Worcester begins
his false report of his meeting with
the King.

20 *God forbid* – "May God forbid it",
meaning "that is not what I want",
a strong expression still in use.

21 *mended,* spoken with scorn. Worcester reports that Henry did not
"mend" his broken oath, but made
it worse.

And, his[14] corruption being ta'en from us,
We, as the spring of all, shall pay for all:
Therefore, good cousin, let not Harry know
In any case the offer of the King.   25

VERNON

Deliver[15] what you will; I 'll say 't is so.
Here comes your cousin.

Enter HOTSPUR *and* DOUGLAS

HOTSPUR

              My uncle is returned;
Deliver up my Lord[16] of Westmoreland.
Uncle, what news?

WORCESTER

The King will bid you battle presently.[17]   30

DOUGLAS

Defy him by the Lord of Westmoreland.

HOTSPUR

Lord Douglas, go you and tell him so.

DOUGLAS

Marry, and shall,[18] and very willingly.   [*Exit*

WORCESTER

There is no[19] seeming mercy in the King.

HOTSPUR

Did you beg any? God[20] forbid!   35

WORCESTER

I told him gently of our grievances,
Of his oath-breaking; which he mended[21] thus,

231

22 *forswearing . . . forsworn* – "falsely denying that he has broken an oath". To *forswear* could mean "deny", "swear falsely", or "break an oath".

23 *scourge* – "punish severely".

24 *hateful name,* i.e. "rebels" and "traitors". Worcester pretends to be angered by the use of these words, feeling that as the King himself came to the throne by treason and rebellion, he has no right to demand loyalty from others.

25 *for I have thrown . . . teeth,* I have sent a bold message to the King, as insulting as a blow on the face (which would be a call to battle).

26 *engaged* – "held (by Hotspur) as a pledge (of Worcester's safe return from taking Hotspur's reply to the King)".

27 *Which cannot . . . quickly on* – "and this will certainly cause him to attack immediately".

28 *single fight,* fight of one man against another.

29 *would the quarrel . . . Monmouth* (line 49) – "I wish the fight were our responsibility and that no man need become breathless today (from fighting), except the Prince and myself". *Monmouth* was the town where the Prince was born.

30 *How showed his tasking* – "in what manner did he deliver the challenge *(tasking)*"

31 *urged* – "put forward".

32 *proof* – "contest".

33 *all the duties of a man* – "all the honour due from one man to another".

34 *deservings* – "praises deserved".

35 *Making you . . . valued with you* – "making your merits even better than his praise by repeatedly saying that no words were good enough to describe your worth".

36 *blushing cital* – "modest account".

37 *instantly* – "at the same time".

By now forswearing[22] that he is forsworn:
He calls us rebels, traitors, and will scourge[23]
With haughty arms this hateful[24] name in us.   40

Re-enter DOUGLAS

DOUGLAS

Arm, gentlemen, to arms! for I have thrown[25]
A brave defiance in King Henry's teeth,
And Westmoreland that was engaged[26] did bear it,
Which[27] cannot choose but bring him quickly on.

WORCESTER

The Prince of Wales stepped forth before the King,   45
And, nephew, challenged you to single[28] fight.

HOTSPUR

O, would[29] the quarrel lay upon our heads,
And that no man might draw short breath today
But I and Harry Monmouth! Tell me, tell me,
How[30] showed his tasking? Seemed it in contempt?   50

VERNON

No, by my soul, I never in my life
Did hear a challenge urged[31] more modestly,
Unless a brother should a brother dare
To gentle exercise and proof[32] of arms.
He gave you all[33] the duties of a man,   55
Trimmed up your praises with a princely tongue,
Spoke your deservings[34] like a chronicle,
Making[35] you even better than his praise
By still dispraising praise valued with you,
And, which became him like a prince indeed,   60
He made a blushing[36] cital of himself,
And chid his truant youth with such a grace
As if he mastered there a double spirit
Of teaching and of learning instantly.[37]

233

38 *envy* – "hatred".

39 *owe* – "own".

40 *wantonness* – "wild behaviour".

41 *Of any prince . . . liberty* – "that any prince spent his time of freedom (from the cares of kingship) so wildly".

42 *embrace him.* Hotspur speaks ironically; he does not mean that he will hold Hal lovingly in his arms *(embrace)* but "meet him in battle".

43 *courtesy* – "gentle manners", following the ironic use of *embrace*, is here used mockingly for "sword-play".

44 *Better consider . . . persuasion* (line 78). Hotspur is speaking quickly and without much attention to grammar. The general sense is clearly: "It is better for you to consider what you have to do than for me (without much skill in speaking) to try raising your courage with persuasion". It was the custom for a commander to raise his men's courage and fill them with self-confidence by addressing them in an exciting and persuasive speech just before battle. Hotspur fails to do this, because he dislikes fine speaking.

45 *the time . . . an hour* (line 84) – "life is short; but if it lasted only one hour by the clock, it could be too long, lived basely"; i.e. a brave life is better than a cowardly one of any length.

46 *dial's point* – "clock-hand".

47 *tread on* – "triumph over".

48 *If die, brave death* – "if we die, what a fine death it will be".

49 *intent* – "purpose".

50 *apace* – "quickly".

There did he pause: but let me tell the world –   65
If he outlive the envy[38] of this day,
England did never owe[39] so sweet a hope
So much misconstrued in his wantonness.[40]

HOTSPUR

Cousin, I think thou art enamoured
On his follies: never did I hear   70
Of[41] any prince so wild a liberty.
But be he as he will, yet once ere night
I will embrace[42] him with a soldier's arm,
That he shall shrink under my courtesy.[43]
Arm, arm with speed! And fellows, soldiers, friends,   75
Better[44] consider what you have to do
Than I, that have not well the gift of tongue,
Can lift your blood up with persuasion.

Enter a Messenger

MESSENGER

My lord, here are letters for you.

HOTSPUR

I cannot read them now.   80
O gentlemen, the time[45] of life is short!
To spend that shortness basely were too long
If life did ride upon a dial's[46] point,
Still ending at the arrival of an hour.
And if we live, we live to tread[47] on kings,   85
If die,[48] brave death when princes die with us!
Now, for our consciences, the arms are fair
When the intent[49] of bearing them is just.

Enter another Messenger

MESSENGER

My lord, prepare, the King comes on apace.[50]

51 *cuts me . . . tale* – "stops me from saying more".

52 *profess not talking* – "do not claim to be a good speaker". Hotspur wishes to be thought a man of action, but in spite of his contempt for fine speaking, words come pouring from him when he is excited.

53 *temper* – "sharp edge".

54 *Esperance,* the Percy war-cry, see II.iii, note 49.

55 *For, heaven . . . courtesy* – "for the chances are as great as heaven is greater than earth that some of us will never again embrace as friends", i.e. they will die in the battle. Thus, bravely, but without giving his men confidence in their power and without prayer, Hotspur goes into battle.

(v.iii) In this and the following scenes, a number of rapid actions and encounters follow one another on the stage to represent the fighting of a battle.

Blunt, dressed like the King, is killed by Douglas. The Prince finds that Falstaff carries wine instead of a gun on the battlefield.

1 *The King.* The King and his army pass across the stage to show the audience that the battle has begun and that the disguised Blunt, who enters as the King leaves, is not in fact the King.

2 *Upon my head* – "by killing me". To kill the leader of the enemies is the greatest honour in battle. Douglas mistakes Blunt for the King because he is one of the several men who are dressed like King Henry in order to draw attacks away from the real King.

3 *haunt* – "remain close to".

4 *dear . . . Thy likeness* – "has paid heavily *(dear)* for looking too like you *(thy likeness)*", i.e. Douglas has killed him.

HOTSPUR

I thank him that he cuts[51] me from my tale,   90
For I profess[52] not talking: only this –
Let each man do his best; and here draw I
A sword whose temper[53] I intend to stain
With the best blood that I can meet withal
In the adventure of this perilous day.   95
Now, Esperance![54] Percy! and set on.
Sound all the lofty instruments of war,
And by that music let us all embrace,
For,[55] heaven to earth, some of us never shall
A second time do such a courtesy.   100

        [They embrace. The trumpets sound. Exeunt

Scene III. Shrewsbury. The Field of Battle.

The KING[1] *enters with his army. The trumpets sound the call
to battle. Exeunt. Then enter* DOUGLAS, *and* SIR WALTER
BLUNT *disguised as the King.*

BLUNT

What is thy name that in the battle thus
Thou crossest me? What honour dost thou seek
Upon[2] my head?

DOUGLAS

        Know then my name is Douglas,
And I do haunt[3] thee in the battle thus
Because some tell me that thou art a king.   5

BLUNT

They tell thee true.

DOUGLAS

The Lord of Stafford dear[4] today hath bought
Thy likeness, for instead of thee, King Harry,

237

5 *I was not born* – "I am not by nature".

6 *hadst thou . . . triumphed* – "if you had fought at Holmedon like this I should never have triumphed"; Hotspur defeated Douglas at Holmedon; see 1.i.70.

7 *breathless* – "dead".

8 *Semblably furnished like* – similarly clothed to".

9 *A fool . . . soul* – "May the name of *fool* stay with you after your death"

10 *A borrowed title*, the title of "King".

11 *coats* – "surcoats", worn over armour. The surcoat was a loose garment with a large device (design) on it, by which the wearer could easily be recognised, even when his face was covered by his helmet. Each knight had his own device, but those wearing the King's coats would have the royal device.

in his coats[11]

This sword hath ended him: so shall it thee
Unless thou yield thee as my prisoner.   10

BLUNT

I was not born[5] a yielder, thou proud Scot,
And thou shalt find a king that will revenge
Lord Stafford's death.

> [*They fight.* DOUGLAS *kills* BLUNT

Then enter HOTSPUR

HOTSPUR

O Douglas, hadst[6] thou fought at Holmedon thus
I never had triumphed upon a Scot.   15

DOUGLAS

All's done, all's won: here breathless[7] lies the King.

HOTSPUR

Where?

DOUGLAS

Here.

HOTSPUR

This, Douglas? No, I know this face full well:
A gallant knight he was; his name was Blunt,   20
Semblably[8] furnished like the King himself.

DOUGLAS

A fool[9] go with thy soul, whither it goes!
A borrowed[10] title hast thou bought too dear.
Why didst thou tell me that thou wert a king?

HOTSPUR

The King hath many marching in his coats.[11]   25

12 *stand full . . . day* – "have a fair chance of winning the day's battle".

13 *shot-free,* used in two senses: (i) "without having to pay" (from *shot* meaning "an item in an account"); (ii) "without being shot at". Using double meanings Falstaff contrasts his easy London tavern-life with his danger·on the battle-field.

14 *scoring,* used in two senses: (i) "entering an account" to be paid later; (ii) "cutting".

15 *pate* – "head".

16 *there's honour for you.* Falstaff shows contempt for Blunt's *honour* that led to death. He has already, in v.i, given his views of honour. The sight of the dead man confirms his opinion that honour is useless.

17 *Here's no vanity* – "This (death) was not in vain", spoken mockingly to suggest the opposite meaning: "How useless this honour is".

18 *lead,* lead-shot from a gun.

19 *I have led . . . peppered,* Falstaff may have led his band of ragged soldiers into danger, but .he has not remained with them; he is more concerned for his own safety than for the success of the battle; *peppered* is used in two senses: (i) "filled with holes"; (ii) "killed".

20 *for the town's end, to beg,* i.e. so badly wounded they will never be able to work. The main road, at the point where travellers entered or left the town, was a favourite place for beggars.

21 *stark and stiff* – "motionless in death".

22 *Turk Gregory.* The Turks had a reputation for cruelty. "Turk" could be used as a name for any cruel man. Gregory was probably Pope Gregory XIII (1572-85) who was an enemy of the English Church.

23 *paid Percy . . . sure* – "killed Hotspur, I have made him harmless *(sure)*". Falstaff is clearly lying, as the Prince quickly points out. Hotspur is *sure* in its other meaning "safe".

DOUGLAS

Now, by my sword, I will kill all his coats;
I 'll murder all his wardrobe, piece by piece,
Until I meet the King.

HOTSPUR

Up and away!
Our soldiers stand[12] full fairly for the day.

[*Exeunt*

A trumpet sounds. Enter FALSTAFF *alone*

FALSTAFF

Though I could scape shot-free[13] at London, I fear the shot here;   30
here 's no scoring[14] but upon the pate.[15] Soft! who are you? Sir
Walter Blunt – there 's[16] honour for you! Here 's[17] no vanity!
I am as hot as molten lead, and as heavy too. God keep lead[18]
out of me; I need no more weight than mine own bowels. I
have led[19] my ragamuffins where they are peppered: there 's not   35
three of my hundred and fifty left alive, and they are for[20] the
town 's end, to beg during life. But who comes here?

Enter the PRINCE

PRINCE

What, stand'st thou idle here? Lend me thy sword:
Many a nobleman lies stark[21] and stiff
Under the hoofs of vaunting enemies,   40
Whose deaths are yet unrevenged. I prithee lend me thy sword.

FALSTAFF

O Hal, I prithee give me leave to breathe awhile – Turk
Gregory[22] never did such deeds in arms as I have done this day;
I have paid[23] Percy, I have made him sure.

PRINCE

He is indeed, and living to kill thee: I prithee lend me thy   45
sword.

24 *hot*. Still lying, Falstaff claims that his pistol has been fired so many times that it is too hot to hold and must be carried in its case.

25 *sack*, used in two senses: (i) *sack* a city – "rob a defeated city"; (ii) "white wine" (which Falstaff carried in his pistol-case).

26 *make a carbonado of me* – "cut me all over and cook me". A *carbonado* was a piece of meat with deep cuts made across it before being cooked.

27 *grinning*, with the lips drawn back from the teeth, in death.

28 *so* – "good".

FALSTAFF

Nay, before God, Hal, if Percy be alive thou gets not my sword,
but take my pistol if thou wilt.

PRINCE

Give it me. What? Is it in the case?

FALSTAFF

Ay, Hal, 't is hot,[24] 't is hot; there 's that will sack[25] a city.   50
        [*The* PRINCE *draws it out, and finds it to be a bottle of sack*

PRINCE

What, is it a time to jest and dally now?
                        [*He throws the bottle at him. Exit*

FALSTAFF

Well, if Percy be alive, I 'll pierce him. If he do come in my
way, so: if he do not, if I come in his willingly, let him make a
carbonado[26] of me. I like not such grinning[27] honour as Sir
Walter hath. Give me life, which if I can save, so:[28] if not,   55
honour comes unlooked for, and there 's an end.
                                            [*Exit*

Scene IV. The Same.

A trumpet sounds. Soldiers cross the stage fighting. Enter the
KING, *the* PRINCE, LORD JOHN OF LANCASTER, EARL
OF WESTMORELAND.

KING

I prithee, Harry, withdraw thyself, thou bleedest too much.
Lord John of Lancaster, go you with him.

LANCASTER

Not I, my lord, unless I did bleed too.

(v.iv) In this scene Prince Hal shows his true nature and regains his princely reputation. Though wounded, he will not retire from the battle; he generously praises his young brother's courage; he saves his father from being killed by Douglas; and when at last Hal meets Hotspur face to face, the Prince is the better fighter, and Hotspur is killed.

Meanwhile Douglas returns and attacks Falstaff, who falls, pretending to be dead. After Hal's departure, Falstaff rises, stabs Hotspur's dead body, and claims to have killed him, hoping for a rich reward.

1 *I beseech . . . make up* – "I beg your Majesty to go up to the battle-front".

2 *amaze* – "dismay".

3 *lead* – "help".

4 *stained nobility,* used in two senses: (i) "wounded (blood-*stained*) men of high rank"; (ii) "men of high character now disgraced".

5 *breathe* – "take rest".

6 *I did. . . spirit* – "I did not think you had such courage".

7 *I saw . . . warrior* (line 22) – "I saw him keep Hotspur a sword's length away, holding his position more strongly *(with lustier maintenance)* than I expected *(did look for)* of such a young soldier".

PRINCE

I beseech[1] your Majesty, make up,
Lest your retirement do amaze[2] your friends.   5

KING

I will do so. My Lord of Westmoreland,
Lead[3] him to his tent.

WESTMORELAND

Come, my lord, I'll lead you to your tent.

PRINCE

Lead me, my lord? I do not need your help,
And God forbid a shallow scratch should drive   10
The Prince of Wales from such a field as this,
Where stained[4] nobility lies trodden on,
And rebels' arms triumph in massacres!

LANCASTER

We breathe[5] too long. Come, cousin Westmoreland,
Our duty this way lies: for God's sake, come.   15
            [*Exeunt* LANCASTER *and* WESTMORELAND

PRINCE

By God, thou hast deceived me, Lancaster,
I[6] did not think thee lord of such a spirit:
Before, I loved thee as a brother, John,
But now I do respect thee as my soul.

KING

I saw[7] him hold Lord Percy at the point   20
With lustier maintenance than I did look for
Of such an ungrown warrior.

PRINCE

                    O, this boy
Lends mettle to us all!   [*Exit*

8 *Hydra's heads.* The Hydra, a creature in classical stories, grew two heads for each one cut off.

9 *person* – "appearance".

10 *So many . . . very King* – "that you have met so many people dressed up to look like him, and not the true *(very)* King".

11 *Seek* – "who seek for".

12 *seeing . . . assay thee* – "since you came upon me by chance, I will test your courage".

13 *counterfeit,* man dressed to look like the King.

14 *bearest thee* – "carry yourself", i.e. "behave".

15 *mine* – "my victim".

16 *art like Never to* – "are unlikely ever to".

17 *Shirley, Stafford, Blunt,* all three, dressed as the King, had been killed by Douglas.

18 *Cheerly,* a cry of encouragement.

like Hydra's[8] heads

246

Enter DOUGLAS

DOUGLAS

Another king! They grow like Hydra's[8] heads.
I am the Douglas, fatal to all those   25
That wear those colours on them. What art thou
That counterfeit'st the person[9] of a king?

KING

The King himself, who, Douglas, grieves at heart
So many[10] of his shadows thou hast met,
And not the very King. I have two boys   30
Seek[11] Percy and thyself about the field,
But seeing[12] thou fall'st on me so luckily
I will assay thee; so defend thyself.

DOUGLAS

I fear thou art another counterfeit,[13]
And yet, in faith, thou bearest[14] thee like a king;
But mine[15] I am sure thou art, whoe'er thou be,   35
And thus I win thee.

                              [*They fight and the* KING *is in danger*

Re-enter PRINCE

PRINCE

Hold up thy head, vile Scot, or thou art[16] like
Never to hold it up again! The spirits
Of valiant Shirley,[17] Stafford, Blunt are in my arms.   40
It is the Prince of Wales that threatens thee,
Who never promiseth but he means to pay.

                                        [*They fight:* DOUGLAS *runs away*

Cheerly,[18] my lord, how fares your grace?
Sir Nicholas Gawsey hath for succour sent,
And so hath Clifton – I 'll to Clifton straight.   45

247

19 *breathe* – "rest".
20 *Thou hast redeemed . . . my life* – "you have regained your lost reputation *(opinion)* and shown that you have some regard for *(makest some tender of)* my life". The King is remembering his suspicion that Hal might betray him, and Hal's promise to prove his loyalty on the battle-field (III.ii.122–32).
21 *hearkened* – "waited for".
22 *insulting* – "triumphing".
23 *as speedy . . . end* – "as quick in bringing about your death".
24 *treacherous labour*, the action Hal had been suspected of planning to cause his father's death.

25 *Make up to* – "Go to help".
26 *Two stars . . . one sphere*. The importance of this moment in the play, the only time Hal and Hotspur meet, is strengthened by the imagery. It used to be believed that each planet *(star)* had its own sphere, in which it moved (see v.i, note 7); for two to occupy one sphere would be against the laws of the natural universe. For Hal and Hotspur to reign is equally impossible: one of the two must die.
27 *brook* – "endure".

KING

Stay and breathe[19] a while:
Thou hast redeemed[20] thy lost opinion,
And showed thou makest some tender of my life,
In this fair rescue thou hast brought to me.

PRINCE

O God, they did me too much injury
That ever said I hearkened[21] for your death.   50
If it were so, I might have let alone
The insulting[22] hand of Douglas over you,
Which would have been as[23] speedy in your end
As all the poisonous potions in the world,
And saved the treacherous[24] labour of your son.   55

KING

Make[25] up to Clifton, I 'll to Sir Nicholas Gawsey.   [*Exit*

Enter HOTSPUR

HOTSPUR

If I mistake not, thou art Harry Monmouth.

PRINCE

Thou speakst as if I would deny my name.

HOTSPUR

My name is Harry Percy.

PRINCE

Why then I see   60
A very valiant rebel of the name.
I am the Prince of Wales, and think not, Percy,
To share with me in glory any more:
Two[26] stars keep not their motion in one sphere,
Nor can one England brook[27] a double reign   65
Of Harry Percy and the Prince of Wales.

28 *To end* – "that will put an end to (i.e. kill) one of us".

29 *and would . . . mine.* Hotspur says boastingly that it is a pity Hal is not his equal and therefore a suitable opponent.

30 *And all . . . my head.* Hotspur's youthful fame is described as a *budding* plant that is *cropped* ("cut") too early in order to make a crown of flowers for Hal's victorious head. *Honours* is used in two senses: (i) "military reputation", in which sense Hal, by defeating Hotspur, will take over all his fame; (ii) "coloured feathers or scarf by which a knight might be recognised", and which might be cut off by anyone who defeated him.

31 *vanities* – "proud foolish talk".

32 *Well said* – "Well done".

33 *no boy's play* – "nothing that a mere child can do".

34 *my youth* – "the glory of my youthful deeds".

35 *I better . . . me* – "I can more patiently endure (*brook*) the loss of my life, which is easily destroyed (*brittle*), than the loss of my victorious reputation (*those proud titles*) which you have won from me".

36 *They wound my thoughts* – "the loss of these honours injures my pride (*wound my thoughts*)".

37 *thoughts . . . have a stop* (line 82) – "thoughts, which end when life ends, life itself, which is mocked by time, and time, which holds all things in the world under its rule, must in the end cease to exist". Hotspur here envies the victorious Prince, and looks for comfort in these thoughts.

38 *O, I could prophesy.* It was believed that at death a good man was given power to see into the future.

39 *food for –.* He was perhaps going to say "worms". i.e. in the earth after his death.

HOTSPUR

Nor shall it, Harry, for the hour is come
To end[28] the one of us, and would[29] to God
Thy name in arms were now as great as mine!

PRINCE

I 'll make it greater ere I part from thee, 70
And all[30] the budding honours on thy crest.
I 'll crop to make a garland for my head.

HOTSPUR

I can no longer brook thy vanities.[31]

[*They fight*

Enter FALSTAFF

FALSTAFF

Well[32] said, Hal! To it, Hal! Nay, you shall find no[33] boy's
play here, I can tell you. 75

Re-enter DOUGLAS; *he fights with* FALSTAFF, *who falls
down as if he were dead. Exit* DOUGLAS. *The* PRINCE
mortally wounds HOTSPUR

HOTSPUR

O Harry, thou hast robbed me of my youth![34]
I better[35] brook the loss of brittle life
Than those proud titles thou hast won of me;
They[36] wound my thoughts worse than thy sword my flesh:
But thoughts,[37] the slaves of life, and life, time's fool, 80
And time, that takes survey of all the world,
Must have a stop. O,[38] I could prophesy,
But that the earthy and cold hand of death
Lies on my tongue: no, Percy, thou art dust,
And food[39] for – 85

[*Dies*

40 *Ill-weaved . . . shrunk*. Hotspur's ambition is compared to a piece of cloth that has been badly woven and therefore shrinks.

41 *too small a bound* – "too small an area in which to be confined".

42 *two paces*, the length of the dead body lying flat on the earth or in its grave.

43 *sensible of* – "alive to experience".

44 *dear* – "great".

45 *favours*, coloured scarves or feathers worn by knights in their helmets. The Prince places his scarf over the dead Hotspur's wounded face.

46 *I'll thank myself*. This phrase might be thought to show an unattractive form of self-satisfaction in Prince Hal, but it is dramatically fitting for Hal to speak the thanks of the man who cannot say them himself because he is dead.

47 *Adieu . . . thy epitaph* (line 100) – "Farewell and let all that can be said in your praise rise into heaven with you; may your public disgrace (*ignominy*) lie forgotten and not be recalled in your epitaph".

48 *I could have . . . better man* – "The death of a better (more moral) man would have been a smaller loss to me", i.e. although Falstaff was not a worthy man, Hal felt his loss deeply.

49 *heavy miss* – "serious loss". Although he regrets Falstaff's death, Hal also jokes about his heavy weight and in the following line describes him as a fat deer killed in the hunt.

50 *vanity* – "worthlessness". Thus Hal judges his former pleasure-seeking life as Falstaff's companion.

51 *deer*, in two senses: (i) "so fat an animal"; (ii) "dear one".

52 *Embowelled*. The word is used to continue the comparisons made between battle and hunting the deer. It means to remove the bowels: (i) of the deer before preserving the body; (ii) of a dead man as a preparation for burial.

53 *by and by* – "in a short time".

54 *in blood*, in two senses: (i) "in the bloodshed of battle"; (ii) "in fat well-fed condition"; *in blood* was used in hunting to refer to an animal in first class condition.

55 *powder*, preserve with salt.

56 *'t was time . . . lot too* – "it was time to pretend (*counterfeit*), or that fierce, furious (*termagant*) Scot would have killed me altogether". *Paid* has the two senses: (i) "killed"; (ii) "paid a debt"; *scot and lot*, "payment in full", has a play on the word Scot, referring to Douglas.

so fat a deer [51]

252

PRINCE

For worms, brave Percy. Fare thee well, great heart!
Ill-weaved[40] ambition, how much art thou shrunk!
When that this body did contain a spirit,
A kingdom for it was too[41] small a bound;
But now two paces[42] of the vilest earth   90
Is room enough. This earth that bears thee dead
Bears not alive so stout a gentleman.
If thou wert sensible[43] of courtesy
I should not make so dear[44] a show of zeal;
But let my favours[45] hide thy mangled face,   95
And even in thy behalf I 'll thank[46] myself
For doing these fair rites of tenderness.
Adieu,[47] and take thy praise with thee to heaven!
Thy ignominy sleep with thee in the grave,
But not remembered in thy epitaph!   100

[*He sees* FALSTAFF *on the ground*

What, old acquaintance, could not all this flesh
Keep in a little life? Poor Jack, farewell!
I[48] could have better spared a better man:
O, I should have a heavy[49] miss of thee
If I were much in love with vanity:[50]   105
Death hath not struck so fat a deer[51] today,
Though many dearer, in this bloody fray.
Embowelled[52] will I see thee by[53] and by,
Till then in blood[54] by noble Percy lie.

[*Exit*

FALSTAFF *rises up*

FALSTAFF

Embowelled? If thou embowel me today, I 'll give you leave to   110
powder[55] me and eat me too tomorrow. 'Sblood, 't was time[56]
to counterfeit, or that hot termagant Scot had paid me, scot and
lot too. Counterfeit? I lie, I am no counterfeit: to die is to be a
counterfeit, for he is but the counterfeit of a man, who hath

57 *The better . . . discretion* – "The larger part of bravery is wisdom; common sense should form a large part of bravery".

58 *in the which better part,* in being wisely cautious.

59 *gunpowder* – "fiery".

60 *how if* – "what if (he should be only pretending to be dead)".

61 *better counterfeit* – "the better soldier of the two pretending to be dead".

62 *make him sure,* in two senses: (i) "put him to death"; (ii) "make certain he is dead".

63 *full . . . maiden sword* – "you have very *(full)* bravely stained your sword with blood for the first time".

64 *But soft* – "But wait a moment".

65 *fantasy . . . our eyesight* – "imagination that plays tricks with our sight".

66 *Without our ears* – "until we have heard with our ears (what you have to say)".

67 *double man,* in two senses: (i) "imaginary creature", from *double* meaning "deceiving"; (ii) "two men in one". Falstaff, carrying Hotspur, would appear to have twice the usual number of heads and limbs.

68 *Jack* – "a deceiver".

69 *so* – "good".

70 *look* – "expect".

not the life of a man: but to counterfeit dying, when a man 115
thereby liveth, is to be no counterfeit, but the true and perfect
image of life indeed. The[57] better part of valour is discretion,
in[58] the which better part I have saved my life. 'Zounds, I am
afraid of this gunpowder[59] Percy, though he be dead; how[60] if
he should counterfeit too and rise? By my faith, I am afraid he 120
would prove the better[61] counterfeit; therefore I 'll make[62] him
sure, yea, and I 'll swear I killed him. Why may not he rise as
well as I? Nothing confutes me but eyes, and nobody sees me:
therefore, sirrah [*stabbing him*] with a new wound in your thigh,
come you along with me.   125

[*He takes up* HOTSPUR *on his back*

Re-enter PRINCE *and* LORD JOHN OF LANCASTER

PRINCE

Come, brother John, full[63] bravely hast thou fleshed
Thy maiden sword.

LANCASTER

But[64] soft, whom have we here?
Did you not tell me this fat man was dead?

PRINCE

I did; I saw him dead,
Breathless and bleeding on the ground. Art thou alive?   130
Or is it fantasy[65] that plays upon our eyesight?
I prithee speak, we will not trust our eyes
Without[66] our ears: thou art not what thou seemst.

FALSTAFF

No, that 's certain, I am not a double man:[67] but if I be not Jack
Falstaff, then am I a Jack:[68] there is Percy [*throwing the body* 135
down]! If your father will do me any honour, so:[69] if not, let
him kill the next Percy himself. I look[70] to be either earl or
duke, I can assure you.

71 *Lord, Lord.* Here Falstaff pretends to disapprove of wickedness in other people to avoid being accused of deceit.

72 *grant you* – "admit to you".

73 *a long hour* – "at least an hour".

74 *bear . . . own heads* – "be held personally responsible (for neglecting to reward suitably)".

75 *I 'll take . . . death* – "If I am lying I will willingly die".

76 *luggage*, the dead body of Hotspur.

77 *if a lie . . . I have* – "if a false account will bring credit to you, I 'll give it a show of truth *(gild it)* with the most carefully chosen words *(happiest terms)* at my command".

78 *highest of the field* – "highest ground of the battle-field".

79 *If I do . . . purge* – "If I become an important man in the state, I 'll become thinner, for I 'll give up my vices *(purge)*".

PRINCE

Why, Percy I killed myself, and saw thee dead.

FALSTAFF

Didst thou? Lord,[71] Lord, how this world is given to lying! I 140
grant[72] you I was down and out of breath, and so was he, but
we rose both at an instant, and fought a long[73] hour by Shrewsbury clock. If I may be believed, so: if not, let them that should
reward valour bear[74] the sin upon their own heads. I 'll[75] take
it upon my death, I gave him this wound in the thigh; if the 145
man were alive, and would deny it, 'zounds, I would make him
eat a piece of my sword.

LANCASTER

This is the strangest tale that ever I heard.

PRINCE

This is the strangest fellow, brother John.
Come, bring your luggage[76] nobly on your back. 150
[Aside to FALSTAFF] For my part, if a lie[77] may do thee grace,
I 'll gild it with the happiest terms I have.
[A trumpet sounds for the enemy to retreat
The trumpet sounds retreat, the day is ours.
Come, brother, let us to the highest[78] of the field,
To see what friends are living, who are dead. 155
[Exeunt PRINCE and LANCASTER

FALSTAFF

I 'll follow, as they say, for reward. He that rewards me, God
reward him! If[79] I do grow great, I 'll grow less, for I 'll purge,
and leave sack, and live cleanly as a nobleman should do.
[Exit, carrying off the body

(v.v) The royal army is victorious. Worcester and Vernon are sentenced to death because they caused the battle through their false report, but the Prince orders the release of Douglas. The King divides the army to march against the remaining rebels and bring peace to the whole land.

1 *Thus ever . . . rebuke* – "Rebellion always found a chetk *(rebuke)* in this way *(Thus)*".

2 *Ill-spirited* – "Evilly disposed".

3 *grace . . . love* – "mercy, pardon, and kind words".

4 *Misuse the tenor . . . trust* – "Put to wrong use the nature of the trust (placed in you as a relation of Henry Percy)".

5 *Three knights . . . this hour* (line 8) – "Three knights on our side *(party)*, a noble earl (the Earl of Stafford) and many other people slain today, would have been alive now". Two of the three dead knights were Blunt and Shirley.

6 *truly borne . . . intelligence* – "carried without deception the right message between our armies".

7 *embrace* – "receive".

8 *Since not . . . on me* – "since it falls on me and cannot be avoided".

9 *to the death* – "to receive his punishment, death".

10 *pause upon,* wait and consider what punishment they should receive.

11 *How goes the field?* "What is happening on the battlefield?"

12 *The fortune . . . from him* – "that fortune had turned against him (in the battle)".

13 *Upon the foot of fear* – "running away from fear".

Scene V. The Same.

The trumpets sound. Enter the KING, PRINCE OF WALES, LORD JOHN OF LANCASTER, EARL OF WESTMORE-LAND, *with* WORCESTER *and* VERNON *as prisoners.*

KING

Thus ever did rebellion find rebuke.[1]
Ill-spirited[2] Worcester, did not we send grace,[3]
Pardon, and terms of love to all of you?
And wouldst thou turn our offers contrary?
Misuse[4] the tenor of thy kinsman's trust?   5
Three knights[5] upon our party slain today,
A noble earl and many a creature else,
Had been alive this hour,
If like a Christian thou hadst truly[6] borne
Betwixt our armies true intelligence.   10

WORCESTER

What I have done my safety urged me to;
And I embrace[7] this fortune patiently,
Since[8] not to be avoided it falls on me.

KING

Bear Worcester to[9] the death, and Vernon too:
Other offenders we will pause[10] upon.   15
                    [*Exeunt* WORCESTER *and* VERNON, *guarded*
How[11] goes the field?

PRINCE

The noble Scot, Lord Douglas, when he saw
The fortune[12] of the day quite turned from him,
The noble Percy slain, and all his men
Upon[13] the foot of fear, fled with the rest,   20
And falling from a hill, he was so bruised
That the pursuers took him. At my tent

259

14 *dispose of him* – "decide what is to be done with him".

15 *bounty* – "generous act".

16 *deliver him . . . pleasure* – "set him free to do what he pleases".

17 *His valours . . . today* – "his courage, the effects of which have been felt on (our soldiers') helmets *(crests)* today". A knight respected and honoured the courage shown by his enemies in battle.

18 *high* – "noble".

19 *give away*. Having received this great kindness (the honour of freeing Douglas), he will pass it on as a kindness to Douglas himself.

20 *power* – "army".

21 *bend you ... . speed* – "turn with your utmost *(dearest)* speed".

22 *To meet . . . in arms*. The Archbishop of York *(prelate Scroop)* has spoken of preparing to face the King's army in an earlier scene, IV.iv.36–39.

23 *his sway* – "its power".

24 *such another day,* another day of defeat in battle such as the rebels have received today.

The Douglas is; and I beseech your Grace
I may dispose[14] of him.

KING

With all my heart.

PRINCE

Then, brother John of Lancaster, to you   25
This honourable bounty[15] shall belong;
Go to the Douglas and deliver[16] him
Up to his pleasure, ransomless and free:
His[17] valours shown upon our crests today
Have taught us how to cherish such high deeds,   30
Even in the bosom of our adversaries.

LANCASTER

I thank your Grace for this high[18] courtesy,
Which I shall give[19] away immediately.

KING

Then this remains, that we divide our power:[20]
You, son John, and my cousin Westmoreland,   35
Towards York shall bend[21] you with your dearest speed
To[22] meet Northumberland and the prelate Scroop,
Who, as we hear, are busily in arms:
Myself and you, son Harry, will towards Wales,
To fight with Glendower and the Earl of March.   40
Rebellion in this land shall lose his sway,[23]
Meeting the check of such[24] another day;
And since this business so fair is done,
Let us not leave till all our own be won.

                                        [*Exeunt*

GLOSSARY

This glossary explains all those words in the play which are used in Modern English as they were in Shakespeare's day, but are not among the 3,000 most-used words in the language.

The notes opposite the text explain words which are *not* used in Modern English. In these notes it has been necessary to use a few words which are also outside the 3,000-word list; these are included in the glossary.

Explanations in the glossary are given entirely within the chosen list of words, except in a few cases where a word is followed by *q.v.*, meaning "see this (word)"; this shows that the word used will itself be found explained elsewhere in the glossary.

Only the meaning of the word as used in the text or notes is normally given.

n. = "noun"; v. = "verb"; adj. = "adjective".

A

abhor, hate.
abominable, hateful.
abrupt, sudden, short, rude.
abuse (n.), wrong use; insulting language.
accompany, go or be in company with.
acre, area of 4,840 square yards; *acres*, land.
adieu, farewell, good-bye.
ado, trouble, disturbance.
adversary, enemy.
advisedly, with due consideration.
afar, far away.
affable, friendly and talkative.

afoot, on foot, walking; in progress.
agate, stone often worn in a ring in Shakespeare's time.
alderman, one of the older councillors who govern a city.
ale, a form of drink.
alien (n.), foreigner.
allegiance, duty owed by subject to the sovereign.
ally, man or country that helps another to fight a battle.
aloof, at a distance.
amble, move slowly without dignity.
amen, so be it (Hebrew). The word used to end a prayer.

amend, improve, correct.

anchovy, small salted fish.

angle (v.), catch fish, use cunning means to catch someone or something.

anoint, make holy by touching with oil.

answerable, responsible, made to give an account of one's conduct.

antic, foolish trick.

ape, large monkey.

apprentice, a boy or young man who agrees to work for one master for a number of years while learning his trade.

Archbishop, one who holds high office in the church.

articulate, speak clearly.

artillery, weapons of war, formerly large engines for throwing stones; now big guns.

ashamed, feeling shame or guilt.

aside, to one side, out of the way; also words spoken by an actor which the other actors on the stage are not supposed to hear.

aspect, position of one planet in relation to another.

assign, make over, give.

athwart, slanting across.

audacious, bold.

auditor, man who examines accounts of money.

B

bachelor, an unmarried man.

back (v.), assist, support.

background, the part of a design or picture which is seen around and behind the principal object.

bagpipes, musical instrument, a bag from which air is forced out through pipes.

baker, one who makes and sells bread.

balcony, a platform extending out from the upper walls of a building, usually supported by strong posts. Inside theatres there are often several ,balconies, one above the other, containing rows of seats from which the audience looks down on the stage.

bald, having no hair on the top of the head; (of speech) without details or not closely connected.

ballad, story in verse form sung to music. In Shakespeare's time ballads were often made up about actual events and living people.

balladmonger, one who sells or writes ballads (q.v.).

banns, a proclamation of intended marriage.

barn, large shed for storing grain.

barren, bare; not able to support life.

base-string, string which gives the lowest sound on a musical instrument.

bawd, agent of vice, one who procures women for men.

bawdy, rude, immoral.

behold, look upon, see.

belie, tell lies about.

belly, stomach.

bench, a long seat made of wood.

beseech, ask, pray, request.

bespeak, order in advance; (past, *bespoke,* have *bespoken*).

bestir, stir to action.

bewitch, influence by magic.

bitter, severe (pain or sorrow).

blackberry, common fruit which grows wild in England.

bladder, empty skin which can be filled with air to become a ball.

blessed also *blest*, shown favour by God.

blunt (v.), dull.

blush, become red in the face from shame or modesty.

blustering, windy, stormy.

boar, male pig. A picture of a boar's head hanging outside a tavern shows that the tavern is called "The Boar's Head".

bombast, boasting.

bonfire, a large fire in the open air.

boot, strong heavy shoe covering part of the leg as well as the foot.

booty, goods gained by robbing or fighting.

borough, a town granted special privileges by the king.

bosom, breast considered as the seat of the feelings, particularly of love.

bower, shady place for sitting in a garden.

brawl, quarrel noisily.

brazen, of brass.

brewer, a maker of strong drink, especially of beer.

bridegroom, a man about to be married.

brief, official letter.

bristle (v.), stand up stiffly like bristles; (n.), short stiff hair.

brittle, easily broken, frail.

brook, allow, permit.

buckler, a small round shield.

buckram, coarse cloth.

budding, growing newly, shooting up.

budge, move from position.

buff, stout leather of yellow-white colour, made from skin of an ox.

buffet, a blow with the fist.

burgomaster, head man of a town.

by and by, after a short time.

C

camomile, a plant with daisy–like flowers. It is hardy enough to grow where it is frequently walked on.

cancel, cross out.

cannon, heavy gun.

caper, leap, dance.

capon, fat chicken.

carrier, man whose trade is to transport goods from one place to another.

catechism, an examination by means of question and answer, specially of the main principles of Christianity.

caterpillar, worm-like creature which feeds on leaves and later changes into a butterfly.

cavil (v.), argue over the smallest detail.

censure, express disapproval, find fault with, scold.

challenge, call on another person to fight, or to take part in a contest of any kind.

chamber, bedroom.

chamber-pot, pot in which to urinate (q.v.) in a bedroom.

chance (v.), happen.

chandler, one who sells candles, oil and other articles.

charge (with), accuse of.

chase, cause others to run away and follow them.

chaste, pure.

chat, conversation.

cherish, protect and treat with loving care, value.

chew, grind with the teeth.

chide, scold.

choler, anger.

chops, cheeks. The word is used with scorn.

Christendom, the part of the world where people believe in Christ.

chronicle, history of events in order of time.

clink (v.), cause a ringing sound by striking metal or glass objects.

cloak, loose outer garment without sleeves.

coffer, strong box in which money is locked.

colic, stomach-ache.

combatant, one who fights.

comet, a heavenly body like a star with a bright tail. Numbers of years pass between the appearances of a comet.

comic, funny, humorous, amusing.

commonwealth, the state considered as the shared possession of all the inhabitants.

compass, limit.

compound, mixture.

compulsion, state of being compelled; act of compelling.

confederacy, a joining together of men or parties for the purpose of mutual support.

conference, discussion.

confute, prove false.

conquest, victory.

constant, firm of purpose.

contagious, carrying disease.

contention, strife.

corporal, uncommissioned officer next below a sergeant.

corpse (Elizabethan spelling: *corse*), dead body.

corpulent, fat.

counterfeit (v.), imitate, pretend; (n.), an imitation.

counterpoise, balance, an object which weighs the same as another and so gives even balance if set in the opposite scale.

courteous, behaving according to the rules of good conduct.

courtesy (n.), gentle and well-mannered behaviour and speech.

cradle, small bed for a baby.

craft (n.), (i) skilled trade; (ii) cunning; *crafty*, cunning, deceitful.

crop (v.), cut short.

cross (v.), pass by.

cuckoo, a bird that cries "cuckoo" and puts its eggs in the nests of other birds.

cudgel, beat with a stick.

curb (n.), part of harness used to restrain a horse which is pulling too hard.

curtsy, woman's bending of the knee as a sign of respect.

D

dagger, short sword or sharp pointed knife used as a weapon.

dally, spend time in playful idleness.

damn, condemn to hell; *damnable*, fit to be condemned; *damnably*, in a manner deserving eternal punishment or severe condemnation.

daub, paint.

decree (v.), ordain; (n.), an official order.

deep (n.), sea.

defile (v), make dirty, corrupt.

degenerate, become base.

depose, to put a king down from his throne.

deprive, take away something (from somebody).

desperate, in a state of despair.

despise, view with contempt.

detest, hate.

detraction, the act of taking away honour from someone.

dexterity, skill.

dial, clock-face.

dice (v.), play a game of chance for money; (n.), small objects with numbered faces, thrown from a box, and used for playing games, usually for money.

diet, food.

direction, instruction.

discard, cast off, dismiss.

discomfit, put to shame.

discretion, quality of being wisely cautious.

disdain, contempt.

dissolute, morally weak.

ditty, song.

divers, several.

dog (v.), follow like a dog.

dote, show too great love.

doublet, close-fitting garment for the upper part of the body.

drench (n.), drink given to an animal.

drone (n.), continuing dull noise.

dropsy, diseased condition in which parts of the body fill with fluid.

drowse, be heavy with sleep.

drunk, affected by strong drink such as wine; affected by strong feeling.

drunkard, one who drinks too much strong liquor.

durance, captivity.

dwindle, become smaller or fewer.

E

eagle, a large bird of prey.

ease, make easy.

ebb, flow away like the tide; become less.

edict, order made by a sovereign which his subjects must obey.

eel, a long thin fish, shaped like a snake.

e.g., for example.

eloquence, power of speaking easily and well.

elsewhere, in another place, in other places.

enamoured, in love.

encamp, make or set up camp.

encounter, meet, fight.

enrich, make rich.

enterprise, bold or dangerous action.

entrap, catch in a trap.

entreat, ask earnestly.

epitaph, form of words specially suited to being placed on a tombstone at a grave.

equity, justice.

eruption, a breaking out.

everlasting, without end.

exceedingly, extremely.

exchequer, store of money; money belonging to the state.

execute, put into effect, carry out, do.

exeunt, they go out.

exhalation, out-going breath; gas, steam, or mist rising from a solid or liquid. *Meteors* (q.v.) were formerly thought to be exhalations from the sun.

exit (v.), he goes out; (n.), way out.

exploit (n.), adventure, act, deed.

extant, existing.

extempore, now, without preparation, readily.

extenuation, act of representing something as less wrong than it seems.

extremity, extreme suffering or danger.

eyelid, cover of the eye.

F

faction, group of people; a party within the state, usually opposed to the government.

falsify, make false.

favourite, one specially honoured by the king.

fellowship, partnership

fetch, go and get, *fetch breath*, breathe heavily or with difficulty.

fickle, changeable.

fiddle, violin; *fiddle-stick*, stick or bow used in playing the violin.

fiend, a devil.

fife, small flute, often used to provide music for soldiers marching.

filthy, very dirty. The word is also used by some speakers to mean bad or unpleasant.

fin, limb used by fish for swimming.

flea, blood-sucking insect which can live on the bodies of men and other animals.

fleece (v.), rob, strip.

flock, a company of animals or birds.

flocks, wool used as a soft filling.

floodgates, gates which can be opened or closed to control the flow of water through a channel.

foil (n.), anything that serves by contrast of colour or quality to show the greater brilliance of another thing.

foresee, see ahead.

forester, one who looks after a forest.

forfeit, give up, or pay as the result of a crime.

forswear, *(forswore*, have *forsworn)* give up; declare that one will use or enjoy (something) no longer.

forthwith, immediately.

fortnight, two weeks.

forward (v.), send forward, cause to be done quickly.

fourscore, eighty.

fowl, bird.

fox, a small dog-like wild animal of red-brown colour; the word is often used to describe a cunning, deceitful man.

fray, disorderly fight.

fret, worry; *fretful*, upset, worried.

frosty, cold, as cold as frozen dew (*frost*).

G

gait, way of walking.

gall, annoy.

gallows, high frame of wood from which a condemned man hangs by the neck until he is dead.

gammon, part of the leg of a pig.

garlic, plant with a strong onion flavour.

garter, a band worn round the leg to hold a stocking in position.

gash, long deep cut.

gaunt, thin.

gelding, horse.

gibbet, gallows (q.v.).

giddy, unsteady, foolish.

ginger, a hot-tasting spice; *ginger-bread*, cake flavoured with ginger.

glut, feed to the point when no more food is wanted; *glutton*, one who is too fond of food and eats to excess.

gorge, eat too much.

268

graft, cause a twig of one plant to grow on another plant.

grapple, contend in close fight.

grate, make a harsh noise by rubbing a rough surface.

gravity (n.), state of being grave, seriousness.

grievance, cause for complaint.

grossly, shamefully.

grove, group of trees.

gum (n.), substance used to make two surfaces stick together; also to stiffen fine cloth; (v.), stick, stiffen.

gurnet, small tasty fish.

guts, bowels.

gyves, chains worn by prisoners.

H

hack, roughly cut or chop.

halter, rope put round the neck of an animal in order to control it; rope used in hanging a man.

handsome, pleasant to look at.

hangman, officer who hangs those guilty of serious crimes.

hare-brained, not in the habit of giving serious thought to the consequences of acts.

harness (v.), put reins on a horse.

havoc, general destruction.

hazard, chance.

heinously, very wickedly.

heir-apparent, person recognised by law as heir to the reigning monarch.

hem, the sound of a quiet cough.

henceforth, from now on.

herald, officer who made public proclamations.

herd, group of animals.

hereafter, after this.

herring, a fish.

highway, main road.

hilt, handle of a sword or dagger.

hitherto, up to this time.

hitherwards, towards this place.

hobnail, strong nail used for heavy work.

horsemanship, skill in riding a horse.

hostess, a female innkeeper.

hostile, acting like an enemy; *hostility*, opposition shown by an enemy.

hourly, once every hour.

hue, colour; *purple-hued*, purple-coloured.

huge, very large.

husk, dry outside covering of fruits and seeds.

I

i.e., that is.

ignominy, loss of good name.

impawn, give as a pledge.

impeach, accuse of disloyalty.

impediment, something that hinders.

import (v.), convey meaning.

impudent, shamelessly bold.

inclination, a man's nature or character.

incomprehensible, impossible to understand.

indenture, contract, especially a written agreement to serve a master for a number of years while learning a trade.

indignity, disgrace.

infect, affect with disease.

infidel, one who does not believe in the Christian faith.

iniquity, wickedness.

inordinate, unrestrained.

instinct, natural urge, desire or fear; in-born knowledge of how to act.

insurrection, a revolt.

269

intemperance, lack of restraint, excess.

intercept, stop in passage.

interchangeable, able to be exchanged for a similar object.

interpret, explain the meaning of words, acts, or expressions.

intestine (n.), bowel; (adj.), of the interior.

intolerable, impossible to endure; very great.

irony, figure of speech in which the words are not intended to have their ordinary meaning but to be understood in a second, special sense.

issue, result.

J

jeer, mock, treat with contempt.

jerkin, short close-fitting garment worn outside shirt.

K

kidney, one of two organs in the body, usually surrounded by fat.

kinsman, relative by blood.

kitten (n.), young cat; *kitten* (v.), give birth to kittens.

knight, man of high rank, formerly one trained to fight on horseback. He is given the title of honour, *Sir,* before his first name. *knighthood,* rank of knight.

L

lackey, servant.

lad, boy.

lately, recently.

lath, thin flat strip of wood.

laud, praise.

lavish, giving very generously.

league, three miles.

lease, agreed period of time for which a house is rented.

leisure, convenience.

lest, for fear that.

lever, strong rod used for raising a heavy object.

levy, collect (an army or a tax).

liege, great lord or king whose men have promised to obey and serve him.

lieutenant, officer in the army next below a captain.

light (v.), come by chance.

likeness, state of being like, similar appearance.

loach, a fish.

loath, unwilling.

loathe, hate.

lock, curl of hair.

lop, cut off (usually branches of a tree).

lug (v.), pull something which resists or is heavy; (n.), animal's ear.

luggage, bags carried by a traveller.

lustre, shining light.

lute, a stringed musical instrument.

M

mackerel, a type of fish.

madcap (n.), man who acts in a gay but wild manner; (adj.), wild, foolish.

madeira, rich sweet wine from the island of Madeira.

magician, one with skill in magic.

maidenhead, state of being a virgin.

mail, armour made from metal rings or plate.

maintain, keep in existence.

malevolent, desiring evil to happen.

270

malt, substance prepared from barley and used in making the strong drinks, ale and beer.

mangle, cut to pieces.

manifold, various in kind, many in number.

mark, give close attention.

mass, a church ceremony.

massacre, the large-scale killing of people, especially with cruelty and violence.

melancholy, sadness as a habit of mind.

memorandum, note to remind one of something.

meteor, shooting star, solid matter moving rapidly through the sky and shining like a star.

metre, regular beat of sound-pattern in poetry.

mettle, spirit, strength, bravery.

Michaelmas, 20th September, the date when servants could change masters if free to do so.

milliner, one who sells hats and ribbons.

misbegotten, ill-born, monstrous.

mischance, ill-luck.

misconstrue, misunderstand, interpret (q.v.) wrongly.

mislead, deceive; *misleader*, one who leads another into trouble or danger.

misquote, quote wrongly.

misuse (n.), ill-treatment.

mole, small animal that lives under the ground and casts up little heaps of earth.

molten, melted.

monsieur, French word for Mr.

monstrous, enormous.

morrow, morning.

mossgrown, covered with moss.

move, persuade.

murmur, speak very softly.

musician, one skilled in music.

muster, summon up.

N

nag, horse of poor quality.

napkin, small square of linen or other material.

nativity, time of birth.

nether, lower.

nettle, a plant which stings.

nimble, quick and light in movement.

nobility, people of noble rank; quality of being noble.

noted, well-known.

nourish, provide for the growth of something.

O

oath, a solemn vow calling on the name of God, or one of the saints or some sacred object to witness the truth of the vow; sometimes words of little meaning added either to make a speech more coarse or to swear that it is true.

obscene, foul.

offence, fault.

omnipotent, having power over all things.

opponent, one who opposes another.

opposition, combat.

orb, sphere.

ostler, man who looks after horses at an inn.

ostrich, largest living bird, valued specially for its beautiful feathers.

otter, fish-eating animal that lives near water.

outlaw, one who is no longer protected by the law or one who is cast out by society.

outlive, live longer than someone; remain alive after an event.

P

pace, stride, rate of moving.

pacify, bring peace.

packet, bundle, parcel.

packing, to send (someone) packing, to send (someone) away.

pagan, heathen (used loosely to mean anyone who is not a Christian).

palpable, easily felt or seen.

parapet, a low wall to protect soldiers from the fire of the enemy.

parrot, a brightly coloured bird which can be taught to speak.

participation, sharing.

particulars, details.

paunch, fat stomach.

pennyworth, quantity sold for one penny.

peppercorn, a berry from the pepper plant; something of little value.

perpendicular, upright.

pester, annoy.

pewter, a metal of mixed tin and lead, used for making drinking cups.

pistol, small gun held in one hand.

pitch, thick black tar.

pitiful, deserving pity.

play (v.), act; player, actor.

pluck, pick, snatch.

plump, fat.

pontifical, belonging to a bishop or pope.

portend, indicate, especially indicate in the future; portent, something that tells of things to come.

potent, powerful.

potion, quantity of liquid, taken as a medicine or a poison.

pouch, purse.

poulterer, one who sells poultry, rabbits etc. (formerly poulter).

predicament, position of danger.

prelate, one who holds very high office in the church.

proceedings, acts, plans.

prodigal, waster, one who spends all he has.

prodigy, person or thing that causes great wonder.

profess, claim to be skilled in.

proffer, give, offer.

proficient, expert.

profitable, with profit.

prologue, introduction to a performance or play.

prophet, one who speaks for God, or who can say what will happen in the future; prophecy, statement of what will happen in the future; prophesy, to make a prophecy or prophecies.

prose, usual form of written or spoken language, not poetry.

proverb, short wise sentence in common use.

proviso, condition.

prune, dried plum.

pry, examine something that is closed or secret.

psalm, sacred song in the Bible.

pun, play on different meanings of words which sound the same.

puny, small.

purge, make pure.

puritan, one who wished to reform the Church of England by making its forms of worship simpler;

a person of very strict moral conduct.

Q

quail, give way, yield.

quilt, bed-cover of two thicknesses with padding stuffed between.

quip, sharp or witty (q.v.) remark.

quote, use the exact words of another speaker or writer.

q.v., which see, i.e. look in the Glossary at this last word.

R

rack, an instrument of torture on which the victim was tied or stretched.

radish, cheap root vegetable of red colour, eaten raw.

ragamuffin, person dressed in rags.

ragged, wearing clothes in rags.

ransom (v.), obtain the freedom of a prisoner by paying a sum of money; (n.), sum of money to be paid for the release of a prisoner.

rascal (n.), one who acts in a mischievous or bad manner.

rate, scold severely.

raven, large shiny black bird.

realm, state; an area ruled by one man.

rebuke (v.), scold; (n.), expression of disapproval.

reckoning, calculation; agreement about paying a debt; settlement of accounts.

recreation, amusement.

redbreast, small bird with a red breast.

redouble, double a second time; increase.

remorse, feeling of regret for past acts.

render, give back.

renown, fame.

repent, be sorry for what one has done and wish to reform.

resolute, brave, firm.

restore, bring back into original state.

retire, retreat.

reverend, worthy of being revered; a title used before the name of an officer of the church.

rite, ceremony.

roan, horse of mixed colour, usually a mixture of red and white.

rogue, man of evil habits.

rotten, corrupt.

rouse, wake from sleep, stir up.

rude, rough.

ruffian, rough violent man.

ruminate, turn over in the mind.

S

sack, 1. large bag made of coarse material. 2. Spanish wine.

saltpetre, substance used in gunpowder for firing guns.

salutation, words of welcome.

salvation, state of being saved (in religion) from hell by Jesus Christ.

sanguine, hopeful.

scarecrow, person clad in rags.

school (v.), teach.

Scot, native of Scotland, the country north of England, which was ruled by a separate king until 1603.

273

scour, wash clean.

secure, safe.

sedge, coarse green grasses which grow near water.

sepulchre, tomb.

sheath, cover to hold a knife or sword when not in use.

shed, cause liquid to flow.

sheriff, king's officer for a large district.

shortly, in a little time, soon.

short-winded, panting.

shower (v.), pour down like rain.

shrink, become smaller; move away in fear.

shuffle, move without lifting the feet or hoofs off the ground.

sigh, a long deep breath that expresses feeling.

simile, the comparing of one thing with another that is similar in one respect.

sin, an act of wickedness, especially any act forbidden by religion.

sixpence, coin worth six pennies.

skull, bones that enclose (usually: once enclosed) the brain.

slander (v.), tell lies about someone; (n.), false report.

slovenly, dirtily dressed.

smarting, feeling sharp pain.

smother, cover up completely; prevent air from reaching an object by covering it.

sneak, go secretly.

sneeze, make a noise with the nose by breathing out very suddenly.

snuff, perfumed powder placed in the nostrils to make one sneeze (q.v.).

soliloquy, speech by a character who is alone on the stage.

son-in-law, daughter's husband.

sound (v.), make a noise.

sparrow, small brown bird.

spoil, something or somebody seized by force from the enemy in time of war.

sprightly, active.

stab, wound by giving a short thrust with a pointed weapon

stable, shelter for horses.

stark, stiff.

starling, bird able to imitate sounds.

steadfast, firm.

steal away, go quietly or secretly.

steed, horse.

stew, boil slowly.

stink, smell foul.

strangle, kill by stopping the breath, usually by means of a tight grip or cord on the neck.

stubble-land, field where corn has been cut leaving stalks behind.

subornation, act of persuading someone to do wrong.

succour, relief, help.

sue, apply for something by law.

sugar-candy, sugar in large pieces.

sully, become dirty.

sumptuous, costly.

sup (v.), eat supper.

superfluous, more than sufficient.

supposition, act of supposing; guess.

surety, bond given as a promise that one will carry out a definite action.

surfeit (v.), have food or drink in excess.

survey, a wide view.

swift, fast.

swine, pig.

T

taffeta, stiff silk material.

tale, story.

tallow, grease used to make candles.

talon, strong hook-shaped nail of a large bird.

tapster, man who draws drink at an inn.

tarry, wait, delay.

team, small group of animals used together for such work as drawing a cart.

tedious, boring; causing one to become tired through lack of variety.

tenant, one who lives on land owned by another.

tenor, general meaning.

termagant, noisy, loud-spoken person who loves argument (usually applied to a woman).

theft, act of robbing.

theme, subject to be discussed.

thereabouts, about or near that place.

therewith, with that.

threefold, in three parts.

threescore, sixty; a *score* is twenty.

thrice, three times.

thunderbolt, lightning, thought of as an arrow of fire thrown by the gods to destroy things on earth.

tickle, touch or rub lightly, usually with the purpose of causing laughter.

tidings, news.

tilt, fight on horseback by thrusting with a spear (q.v.).

tinker, poor man who travels from place to place, mending pots and pans.

tithe, a tenth part.

topple, cause to fall down.

torch, flaming brand.

tractable, easily managed.

tranquillity, peace, calm.

transformation, change of shape or appearance.

treacherous, ready to betray; not to be trusted.

trench (v.), dig a channel; (n.), a channel dug in the earth in wartime to prevent the enemy from advancing rapidly across the land.

trickle (v.), flow in drops or as a small stream.

trifle, thing of no importance; small amount; *trifler*, one who wastes time on unimportant matters.

trim (v.), adorn; *trimly*, elegantly.

tripartite, relating to three parties; having three parts.

truant, child who stays away from school without reason; one who absents himself from work or duty.

true-bred, born and educated as a member of a pure race or breed.

truncheon, thick wooden staff.

tut, impatient exclamation.

'twixt, between (short form of *betwixt*).

U

unapt, not inclined.

undergo, suffer (past, *underwent*, have *undergone*).

undertake, plan to do; agree to organise.

underwent, see *undergo*.

unruly, undisciplined.

unsavoury, not pleasing the speaker's taste; foul-smelling.

unto, to.

uphold, support.

urine, fluid released from the body; *urinate*, release such fluid.

utter, speak.

utterly, completely.

V

valour, courage.

vanity, matters of no value or importance.

vapour, mist; steam.

variation, change.

vaunt, boast.

vein, 1. channel through which the blood flows; 2. manner of speaking.

vex, disturb.

vigilant, watchful.

villain (n.), wicked man; *villainous*, vile; *villainy*, vile deeds.

vocation, a way of life to which one is called by God.

vouchsafe, allow.

W

wag, mischievous young man.

wage, engage in.

wan, pale.

wardrobe, supply of clothes; cupboard for hanging clothes.

warrior, man skilled in the art of war.

waylay, wait in the path of someone and address (or rob or fight with) him when he appears.

weasel, small fierce animal.

weather-beaten, distressed by the weather.

weep, (past tense *wept*) allow tears to fall from the eyes.

wench, girl (a coarse word, seldom used).

whelp, young of a dog or lion.

whereabouts, about where; in what place.

whereby, by which; for which reason.

wherefore, for what reason; why.

wherein, in which; in what respect.

whereof, of which.

whit, smallest part imaginable.

wilfully, with intent.

windmill, a mill in which the power comes from the wind.

wit, intelligence; *witty*, able to amuse by clever use of words.

withers, the ridge between the shoulder-bones of a horse.

womanhood, qualities of a woman.

womb, part of a woman's body where babies grow.

wring, (past tense *wrung*) twist; (used of a horse), rub sore.

Y

yeoman, man belonging to the class of small farmers who owned their own land, the next class below a gentleman.

Z

zeal, strong feeling.

SOME ADVICE FOR EXAMINATION CANDIDATES

Begin by reading the examination paper through slowly and carefully. Then decide on the questions you are going to answer, making sure you have chosen the right number and that they come from the right sections of the paper.

Make sure you answer the question on the paper; do not write on something else; *do exactly what the question asks you to do*.

Examiners use a number of *types* of question on Shakespeare's plays. Here are examples of five different types, with some suggestions on how each of them should be answered. Your teacher will tell you which types of question are likely to come up in the examination you are taking.

1. You are given a number of *short passages* taken from the play, and are asked to write answers to questions on one or more of them. The questions generally refer only to the given passage and its immediate surroundings in the play. Choose the passage(s) you know best and be sure you answer every question you are asked about it/them.

For example:

> . . . . and so my *state*,
> *Seldom,* but sumptuous, showed like a feast,
> And *won by rareness such solemnity*.
> The skipping King, he ambled up and down
> With shallow jesters and *rash bavin wits*,
> Soon kindled and soon burnt. . . .

(i) Who is speaking, and to whom? Where are they?
(ii) What is the immediate occasion of the speech? What is its purpose?
(iii) Who is the 'skipping King', and how is he contrasted with the speaker of these lines?
(iv) Explain the meaning of the words and phrases printed in italics.

277

SUGGESTED ANSWERS

(The passage quoted is at III.ii.57–62.)

(i)   The King, Henry IV, to the Prince of Wales, Prince Hal. At the King's palace in London.

(ii) The Prince has been summoned to the court by his father because of the imminent danger of a new rebellion breaking out. The King wants to persuade the Prince to give up his low life and doubtful companions in the London taverns.

(iii) The 'skipping King' is Richard II, who all the time mixed freely with his subjects and joked carelessly with silly companions. The speaker, King Henry IV, contrasts himself with King Richard; he, Henry, does not often appear in public, and that way earns people's respect and admiration.

(iv) *state*: dignity, dignified appearances.

Seldom: rare.

won by rareness such solemnity: won such dignity by being seen only rarely.

rash bavin wits: thoughtless, flashy young men.

2. You are given *a longer passage* and have to answer questions on it. The passage may be printed on the examination paper, or you may be given a copy of the play to use at the examination. If you are given a plain text of the play, you will be asked to find the required passage in it. Make absolutely sure you find the right passage, where it begins and where it ends.

For example, the passage set is V.iv. lines 75–133 (pp. 251–255 in *New Swan*), i.e. from the stage direction:

Re-enter DOUGLAS; *he fights with* FALSTAFF ....

to: . . . . . thou art not what thou seemst.

Some of the questions which follow the passage are likely to refer to its setting in the play as a whole, not just to details of the passage itself and its immediate surroundings.

(i)   What has Prince Hal in mind when he refers to
  (a) Hotspur's 'Ill-weaved ambition';
  (b) his spirit — 'A kingdom for it was too small a bound';
  (c) his 'ignominy'?

(ii) What is the word-play which Falstaff makes on the word 'counterfeit' in lines 110–122?

(iii) Explain the significance of Hotspur's lines:
> I better brook the loss of brittle life
> Than those proud titles thou hast won of me (77–8).

(iv) Explain what Falstaff means when he says 'The better part of valour is discretion'. How far does this proverb of his apply to what he has just done and what he is going to do?

(v) What happens to Prince Hal and Falstaff after this passage in the play?

SUGGESTED ANSWERS

(i) (a) Hotspur was ambitious in wishing to win more and more state power for himself and his own people, by maintaining his private army, and by defying the King. But his ambition was 'ill-weaved', misguided, badly woven like a shrinking cloth, because he was rash and hot-tempered, and failed to realise his small chance of success.

(b) His ambition was so great that a whole kingdom was not big enough to hold it. At Bangor he was dissatisfied with the share of the kingdom which was to be his due if the rebels defeated the King.

(c) The public disgrace of his rebellion against the King, even though he had earlier fought against the Scots in the King's cause.

(ii) In pretending to be dead, he is 'counterfeiting' in the sense that he is pretending to be what he is not. So long as he stays alive, though, he is not really 'counterfeiting'; quite the opposite, he is remaining what he is, a true, living man. So it is really the dead man, not he, who is the 'counterfeit', because the dead man looks as if he is alive, but is not.

(iii) 'I can more patiently endure the loss of my life, which is easily destroyed, than the loss of my reputation for victories, which you have (now) taken from me.'

(iv) 'The larger part of bravery is common sense.' It was certainly common sense for him to pretend to be dead, but there was nothing 'brave' about it. Stabbing Hotspur's dead body in the

279

thigh has nothing brave about it either, but it also lacks common sense, since Falstaff can never hope to convince anyone, least of all the Prince himself, that he had any hand in Hotspur's death.

(v) Prince Hal justly claims it was he, not Falstaff, who killed Hotspur, but he allows Falstaff to take the body away. The King tells the Prince to join him in the army group which he is going to lead against Glendower.

3. You are asked to write an essay on certain *aspects of a character* in the play. You are *not* to tell this character's story; you are to write about the character from a particular point of view.

For example: How far do you agree that Prince Hal is getting to know himself better in *Henry IV Part 1?* You should use specific incidents and attitudes to support your views.

(from Associated Examining Board GCE, June 1984)

In planning your answer to this question, you should first think quickly through the play and note down some *incidents* which might be used to support the given idea, i.e. that the play shows Hal getting to know himself better. As for his *attitudes*, you will learn most about these by recalling what he says about himself and his way of life; but you should try to remember some places too where other characters' attitudes throw light on Hal's. About six 'incidents and attitudes', noted down by you in brief reminders, should form a good basis for your answer.

Now look again at what you have noted down, and decide whether or not you agree with the suggestion in the question. You are not compelled to agree with it at all; your aim is to determine your own view, and then use your reminders (on incidents and attitudes) to support the view you have taken. In this sort of question, make absolutely sure that

(i) you keep to your view once you have decided on it; and

(ii) you refer to incidents and attitudes which really do support your view.

In the plan for an answer suggested below, we shall take the view that Hal's knowledge of himself increases to some extent as the play progresses; but that nevertheless he knows at least enough about himself from the start to have a clear vision of the course he will follow as the Prince who will inherit his father's throne. On this course he will reveal talents in himself which were not apparent before. What he learns about himself, we feel, he learns for the most part on the way already set towards his fulfilment in the character of a noble prince of the blood.

Here are some 'incidents' and 'attitudes':

(i) His attitude to the planned robbery at Gad's Hill (I.ii.115–159); he is shrewd in his judgement of how far his involvement should go.

(ii) What he says about his motives for mixing with low company; his lines at I.ii.161–183 make up a key speech, one which you could usefully learn by heart.

(iii) Joining in the fun with Falstaff in mimicking scenes between himself and his father (II.iv.323–417) — but ending with a serious hint (415):

FALSTAFF (as Hal) ... banish plump Jack, and banish all the world (i.e. 'but do not banish fat Jack Falstaff; if you banish him, you banish all the world').

PRINCE HAL (as the King) I do, I will.

(iv) His declaration of active loyalty to his father against the rebellion (III.ii.92–3): 'I shall hereafter. . . . Be more myself'.

(v) His generous treatment of Hotspur, in confronting him and also praising him (V.iv.58–100). In this he shows a mature balance of mind which compares well with Hotspur's hot temper.

(vi) His intervention in saving Douglas (V.v.23–31). Outwardly, this is on the grounds of Douglas's bravery at the battle. But below the surface Hal here shows full political astuteness: Douglas is a powerful leader of men, and the King and Prince Hal will need his support and loyalty when they deal with the remaining rebels.

You will of course not need to remember any of the line references; they are given here to help you pin-point the places in the play we refer to.

Having brought together these incidents and revelations of attitude, you should find that a view of Hal and his self-knowledge will slip easily into place. The points, linked together with some expansion and explanation, could form the basis of a planned answer which would support the view set out above: Hal from the beginning of the play seems not to be lacking in self-knowledge; what increases in him is his skill in putting his intelligence, experience and clear idea of purpose to worthy ends, with the right amount of firmness, as in his treatment of Falstaff at the end of *Henry IV Part I*.

4. Questions sometimes ask about a *major theme* in the play, often by quoting something a critic has written about it and then asking you to comment on this quotation.

For example: How far do you agree that 'selfishness is a major theme in *Henry IV Part 1*'?

(from Associated Examining Board GCE, June 1984)

As with the previous question and answer (No. 3 above), you will need to support your view by means of careful reference to relevant points in the text of the play. However, as with other types of question, you will *not* be expected to retell the plot of the play or give a full account of what any of the characters says or does. As before, think through the play with the concept of selfishness in the forefront of your mind, and, to start with, make a note of places you remember where this explanation of a character's behaviour seems to you to be the right one. After you have noted down these points, consider what they suggest your attitude should be to the quotation given in the question. When you have made up your mind on this matter you can begin to write your answer.

Our own view will be that the selfishness of individual characters in the play is not generally a significant influence on their behaviour or on the course of events they are involved in. The only exception to this general view is Falstaff himself.

The King, Henry IV, is certainly not a warm, generous man noted for unselfish deeds, but nevertheless he is a ruler who genuinely has the good of his country, not himself, at heart. When he reproves his son (III.ii.29–91), his account of his behaviour towards his people shows that it is all for their good, not his own. His quick, decisive mind is forever on the welfare and safety of his subjects.

Prince Hal clearly has a taste for enjoying himself, and, unlike his father the King, he is warm and generous as well. But his early self-indulgence is not selfishness, and when we learn of his transformation into a brave, noble warrior (through Vernon, IV.i.97–110), we can be quite sure that he is motivated by a wish to gain honour for his side in the field, and with it the power and dignity which befits a prince.

Hotspur has a hot temper, rashness and impatience for action at any price. Yet the way he brushes aside grave set-backs in his determination to fight the King at Shrewsbury (IV.i.16-end) is not due to selfishness. He does what he does because he believes it is right for his country, even though the process threatens his loyalty to the King and the safety of the state.

Mortimer, perhaps, has a selfish interest in winning the throne as Richard II's heir, but this comes to nothing: he takes only a minor part in the planning of the rebellion, and does not fight in it.

Glendower is fiery and high-spirited, but not really on his own behalf. Like any good romantic, he sees the wider vision. He claims territory (III.i.102) but seems more concerned with what he sees as his people's rights than with the acquisition of personal power or property.

Only *Falstaff* among the major characters in the play never loses sight of his own pleasure, comfort and convenience. We laugh at him mostly because he is a sham: everything he does is motivated by selfishness, yet he goes to great lengths (usually unsuccessfully) to give the impression that it is not. Unselfishness would be to him more or less equivalent to honour, and honour plays a large part in what he says, as well it might, since the nobles he mixes with are very concerned with it. His speech at V.i.127–139 sums up his common-sense view of honour, which is entirely self-centred. He is always prepared to run away when the odds against him are too great (e.g. at the end of II.ii). When he is hopelessly trapped over claiming to have seen 'Kendal green' cloth in the dark (II.iv.193–209), not even he can think of an excuse, and so he turns the affair into a principle to suit himself: 'I would not tell you on compulsion'. Totally in character here, he has no thought for anyone but himself, least of all the fellow thieves who were with him.

Treating major characters in order on these lines, and filling out accounts of relevant aspects of what they say and do, make up one practical way of presenting your own views on the statement in the given quotation.

5. Your teacher may have been working with you mainly on *producing the play for the stage*. If so, he or she will be giving you a good idea of what you are likely to be asked. However, you may find the following hints useful.

Questions will probably be on the same lines as this one:
  Imagine you are working on a production of *Henry IV Part 1*. How would you direct . . . . ? What especially would you want to convey to your audience in this part of the play?

In planning your answer, your first job is to try to visualise what has to happen on the stage, i.e. the essentials laid down in the text of the play. Write some rough notes about these essentials so that you keep them in your mind while you are setting down in detail what you would do as a director. Do *not* write out the story of the play or of the part of it referred to in the question; your examiners will know the plot already, and if you just retell it you will not be answering their question.

We have chosen II.ii, the robbery scene, to illustrate the approach we recommend, and for this scene we set out below a number of aspects of the production which you will need to consider. Under each heading you will find some questions to think about, and your decisions on such questions will make up the body of your answer.

The scene chosen here is particularly difficult to direct successfully, because a lot of action in it has to take place in a very short space of time and yet be clearly understood by the audience; and because you have to create the illusion that it is all happening in the dark.

Lighting

How are you going to give the illusion of darkness? Perhaps the whole set could be lit in medium grey, and the immediate focus of attention in pure white, or white tinged with yellow, to simulate a patch of moonlight showing through the trees. What would you suggest if the movement of spot focus has to be extremely rapid? For instance, when focus has to be on the Prince and Poins, then Falstaff, joined almost immediately by the Prince again, who then goes straight off into hiding (lines 1–7); Falstaff, joined by the Travellers, who are very quickly bound and taken off stage (64–77); Falstaff and the other thieves set on by the Prince and Poins and then frightened away almost at once (78–87). If you find the quick switching of focus too distracting, are there places where the action might be drawn out without anything at all being said — 'dramatic silence' — or by adding the occasional cry from one or other of the men?

The stage set

Draw a sketch plan to show how you would arrange the set. The setting is the highway up the hill, evidently where it narrows into a lane (49), and there must be suitable places where the Prince and Poins can hide, and yet be seen by the audience. (These two whistle to one another — line 23 — so as to add to the general confusion.)

But narrow as it must be, there has to be enough space for the Travellers to be rounded up in, and bound up by the thieves. So, assuming you are using trees in the scenery as hiding places, they must not crowd in on the stage centre. Would you agree that if the Travellers come in on the *right* of the stage, the Prince and Poins will hide on the *left*, pretending to go down the lane on the side of Falstaff and his companions opposite to the side which the Travellers come in from (50–51). You will notice how Shakespeare makes sure that horses are not needed on the stage: Poins has taken Falstaff's away, and the Travellers have left theirs with a boy who will lead them down the hill.

Costumes and make-up
Bearing in mind that it is meant to be night, and the action is very rapid, how should the characters appear so as to easily identified and distinguished from one another?

Falstaff is no problem here: he will be obvious to everyone by reason of his paunch. You will make his face old and lined so as to stress the comedy of his reference to 'us youth' (71), said as if he were of an age with his young companions.

The Travellers can be richly dressed because they are important men on royal business (II.i.44–49).

How would you feel about the others being divided into two groups, i.e. the Prince and Poins in contrast to the rest? The Prince and Poins are the two who should show up as the so-called thieves who are going to trick the rest and have the last laugh. One way of bringing out the distinction between these two groups is as follows. You could put the 'real' thieves in simple robber's masks, covering the top parts of their faces like big spectacles with small eye-holes; these could be the *vizards* (44). The Prince and Poins could be given more elaborate disguises (62; 78 stage direction), involving masks covering the whole of their faces, and clothes which would completely obscure what they were wearing earlier in the scene. Of course, the Prince will not be identified *as a prince*, either in or out of disguise.

Movement on the stage ('Blocking')

This is complex, and you must control it very carefully. Shakespeare manages it with faultless skill, but it passes quickly. Here are just a few of the many points you will have to consider under this head: How is Falstaff to react to the loss of his horse at the beginning of the scene (4)? Should it be taken as one more thing for Falstaff to be angry about, leading to more and more anger and confusion? Or should he treat it fairly lightly, especially since he is, it seems, genuinely fond of Poins (13–15)?

Should he even attempt to get his ear to the ground in the hope of hearing the tread of the Travellers' horses (26–7)?

Would you like to turn Gadshill's word 'Stand!' (40) into a further joke at Falstaff's expense, so as to make him react as if he is himself going to be the victim of a robbery? Joke or not, it misfires in that Falstaff straightaway makes a pun on it: he *stands* against his will and would prefer to *sit*.

As it is printed in the First Folio (1623), the stage direction near the end (87) makes no mention of Falstaff's giving a blow or two in the fray before he too runs away. But this action is worth retaining from other early editions of the play (as *New Swan* does) because it extends the time taken to perform the scene.

Speech

Again harking back to the point about the rush of events in this scene, you will probably think that there is good reason to make every word clear and well articulated, especially so when a speaker has very little to say, such as Gadshill's 'Stand!', mentioned above. However, speed must be kept up in Falstaff's long speech (8–25) if it is not to become flat and boring.

There are a number of places in this scene where the word-play is easily lost: Paunch/Gaunt (55–6); 'youth' (71); 'that Poins' (84), where Falstaff carefully avoids implicating the Prince because of his royal blood. You will need to decide how many such words you would like pointed up. On the other hand, dramatic silence (see under *Lighting* above) can be very effective, e.g. in heightening the tension as the thieves wait for the Travellers (64–5).

For the rest, the Prince's verse at the end flows along beautifully as speech, and plays its part in distinguishing him as socially superior to the rest, who have to be satisfied with prose.

Sound effects

Would you like night sounds now and then (an owl hooting? rustling of trees in the night breeze?), or do you think the noise of the action and calling is enough? Would you like the Travellers' horses to make thudding sounds on the trodden-in soil as the boy leads them away, or would you prefer them to be imagined as out of earshot?

The list of possible questions for you to think about could go on indefinitely. However, when you come to write your answer you will need to limit it by arranging it under a set of headings, as suggested above, and take up points under each heading as you work out a plan for your production. The answers to your questions, written out clearly and briefly, could be the account which the examiners are looking for.